Pauline

Pauline

KENNETH BURCHETT

Amity America, Publishers
Branson, Missouri

Library of Congress Control Number: 2020906097

ISBN: 978-1-733006-8-1 (hard cover)
ISBN: 978-1-7333006-6-7 (paper)
ISBN: 978-1-7350442-0-0 (paper)

On the cover: Vincent van Gogh, *Oleanders.*
1888. Oil on canvas, 23 ¾" x 29".
Metropolitan Museum of Art.

Amity America, Publishers
One Seventeen Westwood Drive
Branson, Missouri 65616

For Zula

Contents

Acknowledgements

A debt of gratitude goes to Miss Zula, the Amity teacher who steered my education through the first five formative years in a little white, one-room schoolhouse. She instilled a love of learning that fills the pages of this book. My loving appreciation extends as well to Mrs. Fisher who drove the dirt roads of Cedar County in all seasons, her car packed with art and music supplies to teach us the joys of creativity. In addition, a fond remembrance to the bookmobile that each month brought eagerly awaited new books and Little Orly recordings to stretch the imagination of young minds.

I wish to thank the many teachers both past and present whose work inspired my own. This book will undoubtedly fall short in many respects in capturing every nuance of the teaching experience. Although every effort went into rendering a true account of the life of Pauline Jeidy and an accurate description of events that shaped her life, I take full responsibility for any errors of fact or omission.

A very special thank you goes to Dee Willauer who opened her collection of family memorabilia and records to make this book possible. Unless otherwise noted, all the illustrations in the book are from the Willauer collection. Thank you, also, to David

Gay for access to family archives that provided many of the illustrations. A heartfelt thank you goes as well to Rene Wehler and the late Mark Brandemuehl for their invaluable support.

With apologies to anyone I may have missed, I wish to acknowledge the special assistance of the staffs of the institutions and organizations that contributed to the research: Brooklyn Public Library; California State Library; Dwight Parker Public Library; Green County Archives and Records Center; Greene County Library Center; Library of Congress; Missouri State Archives; National Archives and Records Administration; National Diet Library, Tokyo; NYC Municipal Archives; University of Central Arkansas; University of Iowa; University of Wisconsin Libraries; University of Wisconsin-Plattville; Ventura County Historical Museum; Ventura County Library; and Wisconsin Historical Society.

Finally, I greatly appreciate the patience and encouragement of family who stood by a seemingly endless project.

Preface

The main character portrayed in this book was an inspirational figure. Her early life first as a student and then as a teacher in small country schools was of a different time in rural America. The era of the one room school ended before many of us completed grammar school. Yet, we remember reciting homework before the teacher. Listening and learning from older kids reciting their homework. It made an indelible imprint that captured our imaginations and moved us to do our best. To readers who remember those days, this is a book to rekindle a few memories. Above all, it is a book about one person making a difference.

The American sociologist C. Wright Mills defined the sociological imagination as the vivid awareness of the relationship between personal experience and the wider society. It enables us to grasp history and biography and the relations between the two within society. This book does not attempt to expand the sociological imagination as Dr. Mills defined it. Nevertheless, this is a biography of the personal experience of someone deeply committed to community work and the singular importance of teachers within society. The story unfolds in the context of the history of education in the 20th century.

Pauline Jeidy never sought fame or notoriety. Few history books remember her. Her father died in 1912 when she was a teenager and a student in high school. Soon after her father's death, she, her sister Verda, and their mother left Missouri and moved to Wisconsin. The year was 1917. After a few years of itenerate teaching on provisional teaching certificates, Pauline entered college at the age of 32 to study for her degree. Taking courses off and on when she could, she received her master's degree in 1936.

Pauline became a collector of American folktale stories and a master at telling these tales. She wrote articles and produced important studies on reading and reading behavior. She developed a special interest in minority education well before the passage of civil rights legislation. A soft-spoken individual who championed women's causes, she approached life with a disarming sense of humor.

She spent most of her life in Ventura, California, except for two years in Japan when Gen. Douglas MacArthur asked her to join the Allied Occupation of Japan to help oversee the rebuilding of the education system of postwar Japan. Some of her most valuable work came out of the Occupation working with the Japanese Ministry of Education in planning and organizing curriculum for the Japanese elementary schools.

Chapters include extraordinary accomplishments as a trailblazing teacher, from her unique workshop methods for preparing teachers to her theory of individuality in teaching reading to first graders.

1

Introduction

Education in America has a long and storied history. Well before the founding of the United States, the colonists started the first Latin grammar school in Boston in 1635, followed the next year by the creation of Harvard College. In 1642, Massachusetts passed the first education law in the New World requiring the teaching of children to read and write. In 1690, John Locke published his *Essay Concerning Human Understanding*. Locke's work appeared coincidentally with the *New England Primer*, which became the most popular schoolbook in New England. Virginia established the College of William and Mary in 1693, and the first public library went up in Charles Town in 1698. Benjamin Franklin formed the American Philosophical Society for European enlightenment in 1734, followed in 1751 by his establishment of the first English Academy in Philadelphia.

In 1779, Thomas Jefferson proposed a two-track education system, one for the laborer and the other for the learned. As the governor of Virginia, Jefferson tried to create his public school system funded by taxes, but the Virginia courts composed of the wealthy members of the respective counties thought it a plan to educate the poor at the expense of the rich and promptly defeated it.[1] Jefferson's comprehensive plan for a national education system elementary through college never materialized because the ruling elite in the southern colonies were hesitant to foot the bill for such general education.[2]

Noah Webster introduced a spelling book, reader, and grammar book in 1783, and in 1787, the Young Ladies Academy opened in Philadelphia as the first academy for girls. Meanwhile, the Pennsylvania state constitution provided in 1790 for a free public education for poor children; rich people paid for their own children's education. Thus, Pennsylvania preempted the Bill of Rights, in which the Tenth Amendment recognized education as a function of the states rather than the federal government.

The invention of the blackboard occurred in 1802, the same year Johann Pestalozzi published, *How Gertrude Teaches Her Children*, a psychology of elementary education. Other teaching models appeared that included rote lessons to older students who passed them down to younger students.

Public education in the United States for many years covered only the first eight grades. Not until 1821 did the first public high school open in Boston. Later on, in 1837, Mount Holyoke Female Seminary became the first college for women. Two years after that, a state funded school for teacher education (the Normal School) opened in Lexington, Massachusetts. Part of the Normal School curriculum was an education psychology course called Mental Philosophy. Massachusetts followed its Normal School model with the first compulsory education law to require children of poor immigrants to learn obedience and restraint to become good citizens.

Through the period of the 1850s into the period of the Civil War, schools and philanthropic organizations established priorities in different public educational models, including the first public school kindergarten, which originated in St. Louis, Missouri. During the Reconstruction era following the Civil War, states created the first school systems supported by general taxes, a financing model confirmed by the courts as a legal remedy for the support of public schools.

Going into the 20th century, the national goal in the United States expected children to attend school until the age of sixteen; in practice, however, most kids never finished the eighth grade. They went to work on farms, in factories, and in some places in coal mines to add to family incomes. Some kids went to high school and a few went to college, but in those days, hardly any women went to college.

Pauline Kastendieck grew up on the family farm outside Billings, Missouri, a small town in the southern part of Polk Township, in the rural panhandle of Christian County.[3] She spent her childhood surrounded by a large extended family for which being one of the youngest kids had its privileges. She did not receive special treatment different from any other kid in the Kastendieck clan except that there was always an uncle, aunt, or cousin to look out for her when she needed help, as she sometimes did.

The Kastendieck family was part of a sizeable German immigrant presence in Christian County that held education to be a worthy objective in the lives of everyone, which encouraged Pauline to pursue a path toward excellence.

Public education came relatively late to the Midwest compared to other communities in the eastern parts of the United States. Nevertheless, Billings owned a worthy history of steady improvement. The first Billings school started in 1859 in Dayman's blacksmith shop. The German population at that time was so heavy in the region that an all-German school was established. Upon the arrival of the Kastendiecks in 1877, a public education school district organized to build the first school building in the community. Later, the first brick schoolhouse went up in 1884 to house a grade school, which was the highest level of education for Billings' youth until 1912 when teaching high school began.[4] In 1912, a new high school marked a substantial improvement and became a symbol of the local citizenry's pride in its schools.[5] Steady advancement in the schools over a half century of time stood as proof of the community's dedicated interest in learning.

Education was an essential quality of all the Kastendieck family. Pauline's parents were both literate at a time when that was not always the case among early Christian County residents. They saw to it that their children studied. There were three elementary schools in the Kastendieck neighborhood, one about three-quarters of a mile east of the Kastendieck farm; the other a mile and a quarter northwest. A couple of miles up the road stood the Billings Brick School.

Pauline attended grade school through grade eight. Fortuitously, near the completion of her elementary years, the new high school went up in Billings. She grew up attending school regularly, got the best education available in rural southwest Missouri, and stepped from grammar school to Billings High and then to college. She overcame seemingly unsurmountable hardships to become a teacher.

The passion of Pauline's life for more than forty years was education. She taught eleven years in elementary schools, prelude to a long and distinguished career as an educator, a career built on life's lessons first learned in the small rural community of Billings, Missouri. Pauline rose to new heights in her life to infuse the art of teaching with the aim and purpose of humanity that she first knew on her father's farm in rural

Christian County. She became an education leader, selected at the close of World War II to oversee the rebuilding of the elementary schools of Japan.[6] Along the way, all that went into who she became reaffirmed the lessons of her youth.

Ahnentafel

2

Immigrant Roots

Down a narrow dirt road off the beaten path lived Andrew and Mollie Kastendieck. Their small house stood on forty acres of hardscrabble farmland two miles southwest of Billings, Missouri, at the far end of the panhandle of Christian County.[1]

Mollie and Andrew had a daughter named Pauline, born on the family farm March 7, 1898, the last of the Kastendieck name to be born in the 19th century, making of her a kind of bookmark in Kastendieck family history.

Pauline Kastendieck was a second-generation German American of British heritage with a discernable strain of Irish from her grandmother. Like her immigrant grandmother who came from a tiny village in Ireland, her Kastendieck ancestors were likewise immigrants, originally from the little farming town of Morsum, Germany, a very old village located on the fertile soil of the marshlands along the Weser River, in the Kingdom of Hanover.[2]

Pauline's German roots stemmed from the patriarch Johann Friedrich Wilhelm Kastendieck and his wife, Anna Maria Bremer, both of Lower Saxony.[3] They had a son named Johann Dietrich Kastendieck who was born in 1792.[4] He married

Catherina Trina Maria Gömann, daughter of Christian Gömann and Anna Dorothea Thies.[5] Johann Dietrich and Trina had six children: Anna Dorothea, John Friedrich Wilhelm, John Heinrich, John Herman, Mary Catherina, and John Dietrich.[6]

The elder Johann Dietrich died in 1842 leaving Trina his wife of twenty-five years a widow with six children in a country facing political turmoil. Germany stood on the brink of revolution.

Four years passed following Johann Dietrich's death before the first of the Kastendieck family made the long voyage to begin a new life in the United States. From the Kastendieck home at Morsum, it was a short boat ride down the Weser River to ships that regularly departed from the Port of Bremerhaven, once an important harbor of immigration to America.

Trina and her children immigrated to America at different times over a period of the next seven years, beginning with Pauline's grandfather, John Herman, in 1846. In time, all left the quiet farming community of Morsum to settle in the booming city of Brooklyn, New York. John Herman led the emigration out of Germany, guiding the generation that made up the circle of the paternal lineage of the Kastendieck family, and anchoring it in the cultural diversity of New York.

In due time, he decided to leave Brooklyn.

He had his eye on leaving for some time, perhaps as long as a decade, dating back to the death of Bridget, his wife, in 1869. Her death and many other personal tragedies that befell him ended his close attachment to the environs of the Red Hook community where he lived and kept his grocery business. Red Hook was in an insalubrious state amid a steady decline in the environs of New York. One observer wrote, "New York is a study of contrasts. It has no virtue without its corresponding sin; no light without its shadow; no beauty without deformity; for it is a little world in itself."[7] What once stood as a poetic ode to America's largest city took on an ominous tone for those trapped within the sinking fortunes of the city in the decade of the 1870s. Things were changing in Brooklyn in ways John Herman found hard to accept.

Construction of the new Brooklyn Bridge was changing the entire shoreline around the old familiar Fulton Ferry near John Herman's grocery business. *The Brooklyn Daily Eagle* regularly protested the disposal of dead cats, dogs, horses, goats, and cows in Brooklyn waters, especially around Coney Island. Large animals shared the premises with many households, stabled on vacant lots or in lean-tos attached to the houses and adding to the health risks. At the same time, the city was becoming too metropolitan. East New York voted by a ratio of three to one in 1872 for annexation with Brooklyn.[8] The old Brooklyn of John Herman's early days was changing into a crowded bustling metropolis.

By 1872, John Herman's part of Brooklyn was not a good place to raise a family. One writer said, "Red Hook Point stands out in bold relief as being the grand central and amalgamated cesspool and sink of low life in Brooklyn."[9] Brooklyn, the writer went on, could boast of having within her boundaries localities where every crime that mind could conceive had been perpetrated. Red Hook fell prey to a denizen of river thieves who worked at night relieving schooners of whatever cargo they deemed of value usually without interference from the local constabulary. One writer said, "There is such a state of barbarism and filth, that the entire aspect of the place is a spectacle revolting in the extreme."

John Herman made up his mind to leave the squalor of Brooklyn, a place he called home for almost thirty years, On September 17, 1875, he sold his store and home on Van Brunt

Street.[10] He stayed on in Brooklyn for a while after selling out; however, a string of events in 1876 convinced him for the last time to leave. Noisy steam trains were increasingly replacing the old horse drawn carts. Things became so insufferable that citizens staged a protest against the changes and conditions coming over the city. The Brooklyn Board of Education decided not to teach German and French in any schools because, it said, "schools should not serve interests of any class of people."[11] With four school-age children still at home, such an announcement to a man of proud German heritage could not have set well. John Herman worried, too, about the future condition of the neighborhood. Work began in May 1876 on the East New York end of the Brooklyn Elevated Railway promising to bring even larger streams of people of unknown character into the city.[12]

In 1877, with Brooklyn in a steady state of decline, after years of unspeakable family tragedies that included the deaths in quick succession of three wives and five of his ten children, John Herman moved Andrew and the rest of his family out of the environs of Brooklyn to the rural countryside of southwest Missouri.

Andrew Kastendieck was the youngest son of John Herman and Bridget Ford. He was born in Brooklyn in 1863 at a time when the American Civil War raged across the country.[13] When he was six years old, his mother died. Bridget Ford Kastendieck was thirty-three. Andrew was a boy of thirteen when he came to Missouri, a young man with the pre-teen experiences of an eighth-grade Brooklyn education. There were no high schools at that time in his new location in Billings, Missouri. He spent his teenage years on the Kastendieck farm in Polk Township learning to farm. The move away from city life in Brooklyn and his job as a grocery clerk in his father's store thrust him abruptly into the agricultural prospects of Christian County.

For several years, Andrew remained one of Christian County's most eligible bachelors. He was a handsome lad of German Irish heritage who enjoyed attention in the social circles of the mostly German community of Billings. Tall and lean in physique, he sported a full mustache that made him look older than his years. It was a manly characteristic shared by his friends in the frontier fashion of 19th century Middle America.

Andrew's single status ended when he met Mary Ann Dewey, a young woman ten years his junior destined to be Pauline Kastendieck's mother.[14] Her name was Mary Ann, but everyone called her Mollie. Missouri-born in Greene County, her family came to Missouri from Wisconsin. She was the youngest daughter of Austin Dewey and Samantha Richmond; Austin of upstate New York and Samantha descended from the Richmonds of Massachusetts and New York.

3

The Legacy of Austin Dewey

Pauline never knew her grandparents. It is possible that she did not even know the tragic circumstances of her mother's life. Nevertheless, behind every life, a history helps to shape a person, and so it was in the life of Pauline Kastendieck and the family heritage that formed the background of who she was.

The story of the Dewey family is such a history.

Austin Ransom Dewey grew up in New York, the son of James and Mary Ann Dewey. He moved to Indiana to live with his uncle Austin Ransom who raised him as a teenager. He then settled near Mt. Ida, Wisconsin, where he married Ohio-born Samantha Elizabeth Richmond in December 1860 at Fennimore, Wisconsin.[1] At age 21, Samantha was a homebody, never away from home until she married. She bought a wedding dress from a married cousin for the occasion.

Samantha temporarily gave up her teaching career to give birth to a son, James. The Civil War put family plans in a hiatus when in the summer of 1862, at the age of twenty-five, Austin enlisted for three years as a Union private in Company C, 20th Infantry Regiment of Wisconsin Volunteers.[2] Upon arriving in

Madison, the army rejected his enlistment for unspecified reasons. He returned to Fennimore and successfully re-enlisted in Company K of the same regiment.

The 20th Wisconsin Regiment saw duty at Yazoo City and the Siege of Vicksburg, to name two crucial engagements, and in campaigns in Missouri and Arkansas, including the Battle of Prairie Grove, Arkansas, in 1862.[3]

After Vicksburg, the 20th Wisconsin embarked on a mission down the Mississippi River by boat that took them to the vicinity of New Orleans and along the southern coast. Starting in July 1864, after weeks aboard ship, illness began to take a toll on Austin. He continued with his regiment to Texas where they disembarked at Brownsville and went into camp at Fort Brown, in November 1864.[4]

Austin became too ill to perform his duties at Fort Brown. In December 1864, he took furlough from the 20th Wisconsin, and in January 1865 entered Harvey US General Hospital, at Madison, Wisconsin. Harvey Hospital, once the home of the governor of Wisconsin, had converted to a Union hospital at the direction of President Abraham Lincoln, open to Wisconsin soldiers convalescing in the South.

Suffering from black scurvy and its complications, Austin's health did not significantly improve at Harvey Hospital. On May 5, 1865, the army honorably discharged him four days before the Civil War officially ended, and he mustered out on May 25, having served for the duration of the war.[5] He received a military pension of $8 a month, the amount allotted by the service to a fully disabled soldier whose incapacitation occurred during the war and left him physically unable to do manual labor.

Following the war, Austin returned to Grant County, Wisconsin, where he and Samantha recommenced building their family. Two more children were born, Nellie Hattie and Willard.

The couple divided their time living first at Boscobel, and then Woodman, Wisconsin, where they lived with Samantha's family because Austin was never able to do much work. A friend who worked with him at the limekiln in Woodman remembered Austin's health was always bad after he returned from the war.

For reasons lost in the passage of time, the Deweys decided to leave Grant County, Wisconsin, for the better farming prospects of southwest Missouri, a place well known to Austin, having spent the better part of two years in Missouri during his Civil War service.

They moved to Missouri from Wisconsin in 1870 and settled on a rented farm in Center Township of Greene County, near Bois D'Arc, a small Missouri town near Springfield, north of Billings, and not far from Ash Grove, the small town where they got their mail.[6] Three more children were born in Greene County: Lillie Jane, Mary Ann—Pauline's future mother—and Austin. Mary Ann, nicknamed Mollie, was born on the Dewey farm in the summer of 1873, named for her Grandmother Mary Ann Dewey. She was the fifth of six children, second youngest before Austin namesake son of his father. A seventh child named Samantha Elizabeth did not survive infancy.[7]

Suddenly, in the spring of 1877 Samantha Dewey died, probably from complications of childbirth because six months after her death, baby Samantha Elizabeth died, also. Samantha's death made Austin a widower, unable to work, in poor health, and left to care for six children ranging from two to fifteen years of age.

Austin soon remarried. He met the redoubtable Sophronia J. Burfield in January 1878, a 34-year-old divorced widow. She had four small children of her own, but for unknown reasons, they were never a part of the Dewey home.

Austin's poor health continued to decline. Suffering from protracted bouts of scurvy, stomach trouble, and recurrent swelling of his lower body, the outcome was inevitable.[8] His oldest daughter, Nellie who was age four when the family moved to Missouri, remembered his last days. "I remember him calling us all to his bedside and kissing us all good bye."[9] The children did not give it much thought at the time, she said, because everyone thought Austin would get better.

Less than a year and a half after the death of his wife Samantha and barely ten months after he married Sophronia, Austin Dewey died in mid-October 1878.

When Austin Dewey died, Widow Sophronia immediately filed an application to claim his Civil War pension. However, her interest in it was short lived. A year later in October 1879, she married again, at least her third marriage. In remarrying, she relinquished her claim to a widow's pension and subsequently disappeared from Greene County and from the lives of the Dewey children. She appears also to have indulged in one or two other matrimonial adventures later on. According to the Pension Office, "The evidence clearly points to the fact, that at no time, after the death of the soldier, did the stepmother, Sophronia have the care and custody of any of the [Dewey] children." The last anyone knew of her, she was in Kansas on her fourth or fifth husband. Nellie said, "I never tried to find her. She took all the household goods and everything belonging to the family including the family Bible."[10] The Bible contained the birthdates of the Dewey children.

4

Civil War Orphans

The Dewey heritage of Pauline Kastendieck was a regrettable part of her family background, a sad legacy owed to the premature deaths of her maternal grandparents. Her childhood education came without the guiding hands of her mother's family, of aunts and uncles she barely knew. Nevertheless, her story interweaves with theirs.

The orphaned children of Austin and Samantha Dewey, left alone with only the kinship of neighbors to survive, disintegrated as a family; each child departed to live in a different home. Nellie recalled, "After father's death we all scattered. None of us stayed with our stepmother two weeks after father's death."[1]

Almost all the kinfolks lived in Wisconsin and not Missouri. There was Austin's sister Hattie and Grandfather Richmond who lived at Mt. Hope, in Grant County. Samantha's brother, Henry Richmond, also lived in Wisconsin and a sister lived at Little Rock, Arkansas. There were other aunts and uncles, too, whose names the children did not even know. None came forward to help the orphaned Dewey children, perhaps unaware of events unfolding in Missouri. If someone had known that Harvey Hospital where their father saw the end of the Civil War had closed and reopened its doors to orphans of Wisconsin soldiers, the Dewey children could well have ended up in Madison. However, Madison was never an option.

"My father gave us all away before he died," remembered Lillie Jane Dewey. Subsequent investigation revealed that Austin Dewey in fact did arrange for the welfare of his children in the event of his death. A Pension Office investigator wrote, "It appears that this soldier, shortly after the death of the first wife, gave away all of his children, with possibly the exception of the youngest. There is some little evidence to the effect that he kept his children with him during the period covered by his second marriage, and parted with them only just before he died; but the weight of evidence seems to be that he made provision for them, by giving them into the care and custody of other parties, considerably before the date of his death."[2] Austin must have known that the end was near. The care of his children he did not entrust to his then wife Sophronia. Instead, he gave them to his neighbors.

James Austin who was the oldest Dewey child at age sixteen took a job as a laborer with Henry Jones, in Brookline Township. Willard, age seven at the time of his father's death, also went to Brookline to live on the A.F. Brown farm, located near the Jones place. Willard later left the Browns to become the legal ward of Mr. Jones. Meanwhile, Nellie, thirteen, went to live with the Harrison family before moving in with the James Bray family. The fourth child Lillie, age six, found a home with the wealthy young farmer J.W. Frame and his wife, at Ash Grove. Mrs. Frame was the daughter of Mr. Jones. Lillie later became the ward of B.G.W. Jones. Jeremiah (aka Jere) Kiblinger, a farmer newly arrived in the area in 1894 and living near Ash Grove, raised Austin who was only two years old at the time. Meanwhile, Mollie, orphaned at age four, went with Nellie to the Harrisons, and then became the ward of Ranson Dudley Blades and his wife Gillie. The Blades were farmers who lived in Pond Township, in Greene County.[3] The 1880 census listed the Dewey children in the various households as laborer, servant, or orphan.

Dudley and Gillie Blades welcomed Mollie into their home. She grew up on the Blades farm about four miles north of Billings, toward the town of Republic. She was safe but separated from her orphaned brothers and sisters who went to other homes.

The details of how Ranson Blades came to bring Mollie into his home have faded into obscurity. It was common for families of the 19th century to offer acts of charity to those less fortunate within their community.

Ranson's younger brother, Isaac Tillman Blades, may have played a role. Like Ranson, he was a native of Tennessee who came to Greene County about 1836, part of a large family of farmers that settled in Pond Township when it was an untamed wilderness.[4] It is likely that Tillman Blades knew Austin Dewey from the Civil War. Although Dewey hailed from Wisconsin, his 20th Wisconsin Volunteers saw service in Missouri. The Blades and Dewey units encamped at Cassville, Missouri, together at the same time and saw joint action in skirmishes and battles in Missouri and Arkansas.[5] Blades fought on the Union side at the Battle of Elkhorn Tavern, also known as the Battle of Pea Ridge, Arkansas.[6] Austin Dewey was at various places in Missouri and Arkansas, including the Battle of Prairie Grove, before following the 20th Wisconsin to the Siege of Vicksburg. After the war, Dewey came to Missouri possibly at the invitation of Blades and took up farming not far from the Blades homestead.

The extension of friendship to Mollie by the Blades family was not their only act of generosity. According to family history, "Around the beginning of the Civil War, Ranson and his younger brother Isaac Tillman, were instrumental in constructing the first school in Pond Creek Township." Isaac donated the land, which was located near the site of the present Blades Chapel Cemetery. This 14 x 15-foot log building aptly named Blades School later burned. Nevertheless, it was a testimony to the value the Blades' family placed on education in the same spirit of learning attributed to the Kastendieck family, the other line of Pauline's ancestral heritage. Similarly, in 1889, Ranson donated the land and $400 toward the construction of Blades Chapel, a small denominational house of worship located in Pond Township. The Blades families were Methodists, and Ranson brought the opportunity to practice that faith into his home township.[7]

Ranson Blades was a successful farmer in Greene County who had already reared a large family of seven children by his first wife, Francis Garoutte, before taking Mollie into his home. Francis died in 1863, and it was Ranson Dudley and his second wife, Gillie, who opened their home to Mollie in 1877.

More sadness came into Mollie's life at age eleven when Gillie Blades died in the fall of 1884 leaving Mollie once again without a mother.[8] Mr. Blades soon married a third time to Mary Swift who raised Mollie through her teenage years into adulthood.

5

Mollie's Estate

Sometime around 1888, it occurred to the different foster parents of the Dewey children that under military pension rules, the children as minors at the time of Austin Dewey's death might successfully apply for his pension should the cause of his death relate to his military service. Thus began a decades-long effort to gain minor pension approval. Mr. Blades and other overseers of the Dewey orphans appeared in probate court to establish their legal guardianship of the children as curators of their estates, a step required under pension law for minors under the age of 16.

The families hired a Springfield lawyer name E.D. Ott to manage their pension claim and agreed to pay him $25 for a successful application. Immediately upon receiving the application, the Pension Office in Washington, D.C., questioned the birthdates of the children because they had no records to prove their births as children of Austin Dewey or even if they were his children. When Sophronia Dewey left the Dewey household upon Austin's death, she took everything with her, including the family Bible. Thus, began a lengthy string of depositions from neighbors and acquaintances of the Deweys in both Missouri and Wisconsin to verify the legitimacy of the children. In the end, the word of the children had merit. A Pension Office official observed, "All these children...insist that they have, from their earliest remembrances celebrated certain dates as their birthdays, each of them fixing the date that they were accustomed to consider the correct one from memory, as far back as they can remember anything. It may be remarked that inasmuch as preciseness is not an absolute necessity this mode and manner of fixing a birthday commends itself to the average mind."[1]

Nevertheless, in 1901, a special examiner of the Pension Office summed up the status of the minors' application. "It seems impossible for the Bureau to form any definite idea as to the exact dates of birth...What there is is contradictory...this may also be said of the soldier's death...The widow Sophronia J. Dewey formerly of Ash Grove has remarried [and] gone to parts unknown...she has disappeared with the family Bible containing dates of births as well as with other of the soldier's effects. The widow has disappeared and the minors seem to have done about all that can be expected under the circumstance, the whole case has come to a standstill."[2]

Primarily upon the insistence of Nellie Dewey who by 1903 was married and living in Kansas City, the case gained new attention. Impressed by Nellie's presentation, the Pension Office recommended further examination of the claim. Nevertheless, notwithstanding Nellie's perseverance, the Office rejected the claim in the spring of 1903 in part because Sophronia's whereabouts could not be determined pending her original claim to benefits that remained open in the Pension Office.

The Pension Office appeared to grow weary of its own bureaucracy

In September 1904, the Assistant Secretary of the Interior that maintained oversight of the Pension Office wrote a scathing report of the Bureau's efforts. "The evidence is sufficient to establish the dates of birth of the minors," he wrote, "the date of death of their father and to determine the pensionable status of the widow." He rebutted each point of the Office's rejection concerning the ages of the children and the previous claim of the widow Sophronia, "By reason of the foregoing," he ended his report, "none of the several terms of rejection can be sustained, and the case is remanded with instructions that it be readjudicated in conformity with this opinion." Upon legal review, the Pension Office accepted the claim and signed off on the pension.

However, one must assume that politics intervened because moving in a parallel approval process, the medical examiner's office determined that the cause of Austin Dewey's death did not appear connected to his military service. The attending physician had died who originally reported Austin's cause of death due to scurvy of the left leg and chronic stomach problems, which clearly related to the illness that forced his discharge from the military and for which he received a pension. Nevertheless, without corroborating evidence, the medical examiner found insufficient proof of death and rejected the claim as cause of death unknown. The claim ended.

Meanwhile, although the Dewey children grew up separated as siblings, they kept in touch and looked out for the well-being of each other. In due time, all went their separate ways. James Dewey disappeared from contact soon after Austin Dewey's death. By 1902, no one in the family had seen or heard from him for 18 to 20 years. They were sure he was dead, maybe killed in a railroad accident, rumors said.[3] However, there is reason to believe that he went to Nebraska, first to Omaha, and then

Lincoln, Nebraska, where he died in 1914 at the age of 52, apparently never having reconnected with his Dewey siblings.[4]

Nellie Hattie Dewey went to Golden City, Missouri, and then to Kansas City where she married Harry Johnson, a telephone operator. Unfortunately, Harry was an alcoholic and the marriage lasted hardly two years. The couple separated but Nellie remained Nellie Johnson. Her siblings lost track of her and no one heard from her after the Great Kansas City Flood of 1903.[5]

Willard Dewey eventually returned home to Wisconsin, married Martha Borah, and went into farming west of Fennimore. They had two sons, Clarence and Herbert. Willard died in 1943 at the age of 76, after a long illness.

Lillie Jane Dewey went back to Wisconsin, too, but only briefly. She married George Andrew, a man thirty years her senior. The couple spent time in Pearson, Iowa, before settling in Randolph, Nebraska. They had two children, Paul and Clyde. Lillie died in 1937, having outlived her husband a quarter century, and perhaps without knowing that her estranged brother James was also a resident of Nebraska.[6]

Austin Ransom Dewey also returned to the family seat in Grant County, Wisconsin, where he married Geneva Gingrich and became a farmer. Austin had the regrettable misfortune to lose his left arm in the fall of 1901 in a corn shredder accident.[7] The Deweys had a daughter, Nieves, an only child. She died at the age of thirteen. Geneva died in 1927, and Austin married again to Jennie Hoffman. He died in Lancaster, Wisconsin, in 1963 at age 87.[8]

Of all the Dewey orphans, Mollie Dewey alone stayed in Missouri, close to the farm in Pond Creek Township where she grew up, and where she married Andrew Kastendieck.[9]

JOHN HERMAN KASTENDIECK **immigrated from Morsum, Germany, to the United States in 1846. Pictured about 1863 when he was about thirty-seven years old, he operated a successful grocery business in South Brooklyn, New York. He moved his family from New York to southwest Missouri in 1877.**

BRIDGET FORD **married John Herman Kastendieck in 1855 at the age of nineteen. This studio portrait pictured her about 1863 when she was a wife and mother in her late twenties. She died in 1869 at the age of thirty-three, in Brooklyn.**

Augusta Kastendieck Family Album

RANSOM DUDLEY BLADES and **Mary Swift Blades were the adopted parents of Mollie Dewey. Mr. Blades was a successful farmer in Christian County, Missouri. He died in 1901, dating this photograph between 1901 and 1886, the year in which he married Mary Swift his third wife.**

HARVEST TIME IN CHRISTIAN COUNTY. **Shocks of grain stand stacked and capped to dry. Cut and tied by the horse-drawn binder machine in the background, harvest and thrashing time meant long days in the field. Pictured are unidentified members of the Kastendieck family.** ***Augusta Kastendieck Family Album.***

MOLLIE DEWEY. **Orphaned at age four, Mollie Dewey faced an uncertain future with her brothers and sisters when her biological parents died unexpectedly. Different neighbors welcomed the orphaned children into their homes. Mollie became the ward of the Ransom Blades family who raised her to adulthood.**

The Billings Years

6

Family Circle

Andrew and Mollie Kastendieck bought a small farm in the south part of Polk Township, in the panhandle of Christian County.[1] The newlywed couple owned forty acres about two miles southwest of Billings, and approximately a mile from the Lawrence County line.[2] Their house stood about two hundred yards off the road. The familiar sound of the Frisco train regularly passing a half mile to the north gave a reassuring rhythm to the daily routine of farm life. Their surrounding neighbors represented the solid German farming community that Billings was known to be. By the time Andrew married, he had acquired enough personal property to pay taxes, but he was not a wealthy man.[3]

Into this modest but idyllic setting, Pauline Kastendieck was born in the spring of 1898, exactly a year and six months to the day behind her older sister Verda. She was born into the Kastendieck family circle, a relatively large clan by the standards of small-town Billings, Missouri.[4]

Pauline's German-born grandfather was a New Yorker, who had lived and worked most of his adult life in the grocery business in Brooklyn. He—John Herman Kastendieck—watched Brooklyn grow from a swamp-laced dock town into a cosmopolitan city. He saw the great East River Bridge rise up to connect Manhattan to the teeming city of Brooklyn. When overdevelopment threatened the education and life he wanted for his children, he sold his grocery business and apartment houses for a good profit and moved to Missouri. Although Pauline unfortunately never knew him, she inherited his vision and expectations. His strong belief in a good education he passed on to her.

When the patriarch John Herman died in January 1897, it severed the anchor that had long held the Kastendieck family together through many personal tragedies. He had seen three of his wives die and lost five of his ten children who died in infancy. Pauline was born the year after he died and never knew the elder John Herman. The memories of her grandfather could only be those related to her second hand.

Pauline's family history was at once tragic and inspirational. She never knew her grandparents on either side. Bridget Ford Kastendieck, her grandmother, died in 1869 at the age of thirty-three when Pauline's father Andrew was not yet six years old, and long before Pauline's birth. Meanwhile, both of her blood-related grandparents on her mother's side—Austin and Samantha Richmond Dewey—likewise died long before Pauline was born. Of her foster grandparents, Ranson Dudley Blades died in 1901 and Mary Swift Blades passed in 1920.[5] Mr. Blades died before Pauline turned three; so, the only grandparent figure remembered from her childhood was Mary Swift Blades, guardian of Pauline's mother Mollie.[6]

Few children experience what it is like to grow up without grandparents; few people understand how it may shape ones view of life. Because Pauline had no memory of her ancestors, it helped to drive her toward excellence, to claim for herself, and the grandparents she never knew, a life of good accomplishments, to fulfill a dream that seemed always just beyond their reach but never far removed from their vision and expectations of the next generation.

In addition to Uncles John Herman, Jr. and George Dietrich, and Aunts Amelia and Hermina, the Kastendieck family circle included the family of the immigrant John Dietrich Kastendieck.[7] He followed his brother John Herman—the Kastendieck brothers shared the same first name of John—from Morsum, Germany, to Brooklyn. He likewise moved his family to southwest Missouri to join his brother and take up farming after a successful business career in the grocery trade. Great Aunt Dora, the oldest of the immigrant Kastendieck siblings, moved to Missouri with him. Two other Kastendieck brothers remained in Brooklyn.

The Missouri Kastendieck families together occupied a sizeable piece of real estate in south Polk Township.[8] Altogether, they owned 280 acres in the same general location, most of it in the hands of Pauline's Great Uncle Dietrich and John Dietrich, Jr., his son. The two of them together owned 160 acres near to or adjoining Andrew's property on the west. Great Uncle Dietrich occupied eighty acres just north of Andrew's forty while John D., Jr. farmed another eighty to the east of him. Uncle George Kastendieck worked a forty-acre farm adjoining Andrew's land on the east. Meanwhile, Uncle John Herman, Jr. owned land in the same vicinity. Great Uncle Dietrich had another forty-acre farm directly across the road north—overall a large but relatively compact family settlement.[9] In addition to the land holdings of Great Uncle Dietrich and his son, the elder Dietrich also had a sizeable financial interest in the Kastendieck-Blades Milling Company.

They had a distinct nature, the Kastendieck family—a quality that valued good character and instilled in the Kastendieck children the merits of a good education. This was not the typical southern-rooted family clawing out a meager existence in which illiteracy passed from generation to generation. Education was an essential quality of all the Kastendieck families. Andrew and Mollie were both literate at a time when that was not always the case among early Christian County residents. They saw to it that their daughters studied from an early age.

As the 19th century rolled over to the 20th century, Billings, Missouri, was an up and coming community of 702 souls served by the Frisco rail line and a network of solid rock roads that were once Indian trails and dirt paths. Billings grew from a brush-covered plot of land to a good business town. The old businesses prospered and new ones came at a rapid pace. New businesses and well-built houses appeared on a regular basis; Billings had a reputation as a place of opportunity.

Life in the early part of the 20th century in Billings when Pauline was growing up was much the same as it was in many other parts of the country. A visit to the home of a relative or friend offered the prospect of playtime with cousins and classmates. In the tradition of neighborly friendship, it also meant the expectation of a return visit and more playtime. Any excuse for going into Billings conjured up visions of entertainment and a break from the daily routine of farm chores. A Billings destination might include the home of Uncle John Herman, Jr. and Aunt Mary. Uncle John had quit farming for the construction business and moved to Billings. His children were older than Pauline was, except for Mildred the youngest who was both Pauline's cousin and classmate. At the same time, Uncle George Dietrich had a carpentry shop on Pine Street. George Dietrich and Aunt Lizzy's kids were likewise somewhat older than Pauline, except for Hazel born in 1900 and a couple of years younger. Just as Pauline was the last Kastendieck born in the 19th century, Hazel was the first one born in the 20th century.

Many reasons existed for a trip from the family farm to Billings, among them, of course, a chance to visit Great Uncle Dietrich at the mill. Meantime, Aunt Amelia and Aunt Hermina both moved off to Oklahoma to follow the careers of their husbands working for the Frisco Railroad.

The Kastendieck sisters—Verda and Pauline—when not in school worked on the farm and at odd jobs around town. There was plenty of local entertainment, and if not in Billings, Springfield was a stone's throw up the road, or Marionville and Aurora were easy visits just across the Christian County line. Something was always going on.

7

Country Girl

There were three elementary schools in the Kastendieck neighborhood, one about three-quarters of a mile east of the Kastendieck home, the other a mile and a quarter northwest. A couple of miles up the road stood the Billings School. Pauline started school in the old Hale school district, in a one-room school not too far from the family homestead outside Billings.[1] That school closed—her dad later bought it for a barn—and she completed elementary school in the newly finished brick school at Billings.

Pauline always brought home good grades. Her grades were never quite as good as the grades of her sister but sufficient in most years to rank her at the top of Miss Neyer's class. Pauline's best subjects were reading and grammar; however, she did well in all her basic subjects except perhaps spelling, which did not always reach Miss Neyer's high expectations.[2]

Louise Neyer taught the basics. She was Catholic, which no doubt brought a discipline to the classroom that made her one of Pauline's best teachers. Miss Neyer never married; her devotion to education lasted a lifetime until her death in 1966. She was an early model for Pauline of the noble life of teaching.

The task of getting to school every day on time, as Miss Neyer expected, posed a challenge especially during bad weather because the two-mile distance from the farm to Billings made for a long trek for a young pupil. Pauline's parents kept her at home on the worst inclement days, but most of the time she was in her seat and ready for class promptly. Some students that came to school from other rural areas had ways of travel besides by foot. Some rode a horse to school and either tethered their horse nearby all day or turned it loose to return home. Other times, families took turns picking up neighborhood children by horse and carriage or other conveyance and delivering them to the school. Automobiles were not yet a common fixture in 1907 Christian County.

Farm life seemed to agree with the family as the girls grew up in the countryside of Christian County. Pauline's parents had a mortgage on their farm and house where they lived but they made payments regularly. Her father had a streak of obstinate independence. He took pride in the ownership of his own farm, which he worked on his own account. He kept a few head of livestock, raised crops, and milked a small herd of dairy cows that produced enough milk to sell the excess to the Billings Creamery for a few extra dollars.

Pauline's mother did the housework, helped with chores, and gathered the eggs that added to the family income. Eggs from her prized flock were in demand. A neighbor wrote, "Mollie, Will you please save all the eggs you get the rest of this week and bring them in for this Sunday morning. We want to set the incubator—we have about 100 already engaged. I wish you could get as many as that if possible. Do you think you could get any from Elmer?"[3] Farm families incubated their own chicks to produce not only future additions to a flock but also to stock a valued source of food. Mollie had her own incubator that she put into service whenever the need arose.

Pauline grew up with a sublime love of nature. She reveled in the seasons and the beauty that came with them. She wrote often and eloquently of her childhood. "A tiny, gaily dressed bird perched precariously near the end of a slender twig and, because the grass was green, the sky was blue, the sun was warm, the breeze was gentle, and worms were plentiful, he tuned his little beak toward heaven and poured out a riotous, joyous, beautiful song. I listened and my heart was glad."[4]

There were chores for a girl to do on the farm. There being no boys in the Andrew Kastendieck family, there was no distinction made between household and farm chores. Pauline helped with the farm work wherever she could; taking turns with her sister as the labor required. It was hard work sometimes, but it was a time also to delight in the solitudes of her country life, to enjoy the marvels of the natural world. She once said, "In my childhood days I never objected to herding the cows for a half day because in the patch where the cows were supposed to stay there was a pond, on the banks of which there were always a few green-backed, pop-eyed, smiling frogs." It is easy to picture her playing a childhood game with these little critters that were her easy companions and odd playmates. "I liked to creep up behind one and see just how near he would allow me to come before sounding a warning to his brothers and making a beautifully arched leap into the water." Pauline tried to dive like that, but her dives were always half leap and half fall with none of the grace of her little four-legged friends. "When his funny little face appeared far out in the water, blinking and smiling at me," She said, "I liked to throw a clod or a rock at it and see it disappear as if by magic; then I liked to guess at where it would appear again.[5]

Pauline loved cats. At one time, there were fifteen cats on the Kastendieck farm, all crowding into the milk barn at dinnertime. Ebony Tom was her favorite, a little kitten companion who wore a glossy black suit, immaculate white mittens, and a captivating little white bow tie. Of all fifteen cats, Ebony Tom was special because of his superior intellect, manners, and disposition. He was a spoiled kitten. He had a feeding dish of his own and politely waited until a pan of milk calmed the ravenous riot of the common cats, and saw his own dish filled. The other cats slept any place they could find protection and a degree of comfort, but Ebony Tom had a soft comfortable bed provided for him. Pauline carried him to it every night and deposited him with tender care, never the slightest doubt that he would remain there in innocent sleep all through the night.

One afternoon after school when Pauline went as usual to the barn to feed the cats, Ebony Tom was not there. She fed the other cats, and then sat down with patient unconcern to wait for him. She mused that he must be near by watching to see the effect of his absence on her. When the other cats finished their milk and began to wash their faces still Tom had not appeared. Pauline became anxious. She began to search, then to call, then to weep, all to no avail. Ebony Tom was gone. When she gave up the search and expressed her fears to her parents, they explained that Old Mr. Jackson had come and asked if he might have a cat. He lived all alone and wanted a pet for company. They had told him to go right out and take his choice, and he chose Ebony Tom.

"Of course! Who wouldn't?" she thought. They tried to check her tears by reminding her that she still had fourteen other cats.

Mr. Jackson came back the next day for another cat and told of his experience with Ebony Tom. He had fed him the night before, but he would not eat, and, thinking that he probably was afraid of him, he went away and left him alone for a time. When he went back to see if he had eaten, the food was untouched and Ebony Tom was gone.

It may have been just animal instinct that made him run away, but Pauline always thought he was looking for her while she was looking for him. That night when she fed the others, she became aware of one of life's hard lessons— "that which we love is hardest to keep and those we care little about are with us always."[6]

Andrew Kastendieck's farm operation was hardscrabble by comparison with most of his neighbors. He kept a few head of livestock and raised the crops needed to sustain a basic farming life. Mollie hatched a sizeable brood of chicks each year in a good incubator that was one of the prized items of the household.[7] Eggs provided income and a nice source of barter in the Billings community. Andrew owned a few head of dairy cattle, not a large herd, but enough to qualify his participation in the Billings Creamery Cooperative, a joint concern that came to life in 1899 and unknowingly started a historic tradition of fine dairy herds populating the ample pastureland in the highland region around Billings. The Creamery enabled farmers like Andrew to pool their extra milk production, turn it into butter and other dairy products for sale, and return income to the cooperative participants. Andrew's annual check totaled about $50, hardly anything compared to the $725 Tom Garoutte made, for example, off his large dairy operation in Greene County. Or even the $200 produced by Andrew's cousin John D. Kastendieck, Jr.[8] A half dozen dairy cows, however, supplied ample work for the two Kastendieck girls who had to help milk them twice a day by hand and prepare the milk for transport to the Creamery. A workable milking machine had been around for a decade or more but did not gain widespread use until well into the 20th century.

As small as Andrew's herd was, it was nevertheless twice the size of that of his brother George. Uncle George owned the forty acres adjoining on the east. He enjoyed the title of gentleman farmer and used his small cooperative income of $25 a year to augment his job in town as secretary of the Kastendieck-Blades Milling Company. He became a stationary engineer and sometime carpenter building houses with Uncle John Herman, Jr.[9]

8

Andrew's Sword

Pauline Kastendieck grew up in the verdant countryside of Christian County. She watched the Ozarks seasons come and go, knew the burdens of hard work on a farm, and basked in the love and guidance of her extended Kastendieck clan. Her dreams were those of any schoolchild learning from the studious model of her older sister and hoping someday to make her parents proud.

The older generation of the Kastendieck family passed into history. By the time that Pauline entered elementary school, only Great Uncle Dietrich remained as a living reminder of the original immigrants who had so many years ago left Germany for the promise of a better life in America.

The 20th century brought new challenges and opportunities to Billings and to the nation. The average worker in the United States made $12.98 a week for fifty-nine hours of work. The automobile made its entrance but not for a while in Billings, Missouri. The industrial age was in full swing. Mass production meant lower prices that ushered in the decade of materialism and consumerism. People read the catalogs of Sears Roebuck and Montgomery Ward more than any book except the Bible.

The catalogs were a fixture in most rural outhouses. The *Billings Times* followed the great events that swept the nation—good and bad. The assassination of President McKinley happened in 1901; the first flight of the Wright Brothers at Kitty Hawk occurred in 1903; and the devastating San Francisco earthquake that killed more than 700 people was in 1906.

On the political side, the United States Supreme Court ruled in 1904 that African Americans had no right to vote, accenting some of the worst of the Jim Crow years. The number of blacks lynched across the country rose to 115 during the decade, including several in the Ozarks.[1]

On the lighter side, sheet music to the most popular songs was on sale at the dime store, especially *Sweet Adeline*, the most popular song of the decade. The hand-cranked Victrola went on the market in 1903. Moreover, the era of silent films did not bypass Billings, Missouri.

Andrew Kastendieck was a dedicated fraternal man, basking in the social status that a club brought, and engaged in the opportunities that membership afforded to serve the Billings community. He was a member of the order of Select Knights of America, a quasi-masonic order that originated as part of the Ancient Order of United Workmen

Founded in Pennsylvania in 1868, the Ancient Order of United Workmen was a fraternal organization in the United States and Canada that provided mutual social and financial support after the Civil War, a time of economic stress and uncertainty for many families. It was the first of many fraternal benefit societies that offered insurance for sickness, accident, death, and burial policies.

Life insurance became a prime focus of the Ancient Order. Upon the death of a member, the Order paid $500 to his legal heirs. In 1869, an amended charter required each new member to pay a $1 initiation fee to the insurance fund, and then granted a more generous $2,000 death benefit. When a participant died, members replenished the fund by a new levy, usually a $1 on each member. Those refusing to pay the assessment, and lodges that failed to forward the money to an insurance fund within a month underwent ejection from the Order.

The organization prospered. By 1885, the Ancient Order of United Workmen was the largest fraternal benefit group in the United States, boasting several branches. A number of offshoot fraternal benefit societies sprung up, each with its own ritual and ceremonial accouterments, and each one popular as a means of providing financial help to working class people. A member paid his fee of $1 to $3 into the organization and the money went to aid dependents when a member died or suffered a serious injury.

Andrew's fraternity, the Select Knights of America, was the first of many of these post-Civil War fraternal benefit societies to offer life insurance under the umbrella of the Ancient Order. As self-help groups, the Knights operated as fraternal insurance societies to provide members with financial protection and at the same time with the security of a fraternal brotherhood. Like its parent organization, the Select Knights took care of widows and children when the head of the house died unexpectedly.[2] Andrew's reason for being a Select Knight was therefore practical a well as social.[3]

In its heyday, the Select Knights of America had more than 3,000 lodges across the country. They had a ritual, secret grip, password, and a burial service, plus all the paraphernalia of a secret society similar to the Freemasons and other fraternal organizations.[4]

Part of the ritual paraphernalia was a ceremonial sword, ornately appointed with symbols of an eagle, full-figure shielded knight, and the member's name engraved on the blade.

Andrew's sword was unique because of its image of a Holy Bible instead of the usual skeleton hand common to other chapters of the Select Knights society.

Usually about 36-38 inches long, swords representing the Select Knights appeared at the end of the 19th century. Andrew likely purchased his toward the end of the century about the time of his marriage in 1894. Several manufacturers in the United States and abroad offered them for sale, including a company in St. Louis.

Other Kastendiecks in Christian County besides Andrew belonged to Masonic fraternal organizations. Andrew's brother George Dietrich, for example, was a Freemason in two lodges. He had a son who followed him as a Freemason. George Dietrich and Andrew's half-sister, Hermina belonged to the Order of the Eastern Star, the women's female companion organization to Freemasonry. How she gained entry into the Eastern Star is speculative and points to other unknown family members in the secretive Freemason society. A woman received an invitation to join the Eastern Star only if she had a qualifying relationship to a man who was an affiliated Master Mason. She could not join on her own merit. It is possible but unproven that Freemasonry in the Kastendieck family extended to the immigrant generation of John Herman. Andrew likely continued a long family tradition of secret society membership.

Fraternal organizations, by proximity if nothing else, were a part of growing up for Verda and Pauline. The Ancient Order of United Workmen Hall in Billings was a large building, popular as a meeting place for the community. High school commencements occurred there, and various entertainments kept the calendar busy. The Kastendieck girls found themselves occasionally part of the program. Fundraisers were a popular event. The audience paid 15 cents apiece, 25 cents for a reserved seat, to hear the youth of the community practice their oration skills, usually seven or eight pieces styled as a competition among the contestants. Pauline and Verda participated in fundraisers on a regular basis beginning in grade school, as did other Kastendieck children.[5] At one event of eight presentations, half of them were the Kastendieck girls. Proceeds went to the insurance fund of the Silver Knights and to the Woman's Christian Temperance Union, one of Mollie's favored societies. W.C.T.U. was a national movement organized in 1873 by women to fight the destructive power of alcohol and the problems it caused families and society. One of the largest and most influential women's groups of the 19th century, it expanded its platform to crusade for labor laws, prison reform, and women's suffrage.

Fraternal organizations served their communities and often provided for the future of a member's family. Nevertheless, some orders had a political side, too. The Silver Knights of America, for instance, an organization whose initials closely resembled those of the Select Knights, came into being in 1895 at the behest of the Democrats advocating for the free coinage of silver. The Silver Knights enjoyed a strong presence in western Missouri but a short-lived one. The movement underwent political defeat in 1896, and the organization dropped out of sight. Although this was about the time Andrew bought his sword, it is doubtful that he had a connection to the Silver Knights of the Democrat Party. The Kastendiecks were steadfast Republicans.

9

Remember Well and Bear in Mind

Most Sunday mornings found Andrew, Mollie, and the girls at the Methodist Episcopal Church at Hamilton and Oak streets, in Billings. Sunday for Pauline meant dressing up and spending time with friends outside of school and away from the chores of home. It would not be correct to say that Pauline grew up as a deeply religious person, as some of her kinfolks did. It would be naïve, too, to think that her Sunday school lessons were all for naught. A child absorbs far more than we think, some of it never far from ones adult memory.

Try to picture Pauline at Sunday school on an overcast day, posing for a family photograph with her Sunday school class. Twenty-three members of the class, men, women, and children—most of them of the Kastendieck clan—face the camera, looking altogether too serious even for church. Pauline's gaze at the camera is penetrating, inquisitive, a little glib perhaps, and slightly impatient, but she is taking in the experience. Auburn hair parted down the middle, pulled back on the sides, and fastened in the back with a large ribbon that accents the fullness of her face showing the slight plumpness of a normal pre-teen kid.[1] A faint summer breeze catches the skirt of her ivory-colored dress with white lace collar as if to add a spark of play to the apparent seriousness of the occasion. Dark stockings and a pair of good service shoes complete her Sunday wardrobe. The photo session is over. It is time to go back inside the church, and then home.

The Kastendiecks took time to socialize. Sundays usually found them at Sunday school and church dressed in the fashion of the day. Then, there were the occasional pie suppers and community events to attend not the least of which was the annual Billings Fair when people from miles around converged on Billings in the fall of the year to sample the best produce, home brew, and confectionary concoctions that the year had to offer.

Reading was a favorite pastime in the Kastendieck household usually in the evenings by the light of a coal oil lamp after chores. Pauline's father loved to read and often read aloud to Mollie and the girls. A highlight of the week was delivery to the mailbox on Thursday of the latest copy of the *Billings Times* newspaper.[2]

Andrew had a talent for music and knew many songs. He never had a lesson but could play drums.[3] He always had some rib bones trying to shake along with his singing. On a winter evening, he would come in out of the cold, put his feet on the oven door, sing, and clatter his bones. Anyone who knew him liked him. He was a friend to everybody. Witty and upbeat, he liked a good practical joke, which seemed at first out of character with his serious German heritage until he made the point that he was as much Irish as he was German.

Andrew and Mollie's fifteenth wedding anniversary rolled around in 1910. They had two teenage girls in school, and farming provided the needed livelihood. There was still a mortgage on the farm, but that was common because in 1910 there were mortgages on most of the farms in Polk Township. The extended Kastendieck family circle grew ever wider with the births of more nieces and nephews. John Herman, Jr. built a summerhouse next door to Andrew in a growing Kastendieck neighborhood. The census taker visited Andrew and John Herman, Jr. consecutively in 1910, going first to the home of John Herman at dwelling 107 and then to Andrew's at 108.[4] Otherwise, the neighborhood stayed essentially the same, as it had been a decade earlier with relatives making up the Kastendieck community of Polk Township.

Uncle John Herman, Jr. embodied the same veneration for education as the other Kastendiecks did. He turned fifty-four in 1910, still living on Oak Street, in Billings. His kids were all teenagers at various stages of their educations and intent on completing high school and beyond at a time in America when only one-third of children enrolled in elementary school and less than 10 percent graduated from high school. Education was always a point of pride for the Kastendieck family going back at least to the years in Brooklyn. Uncle John Herman, Jr. took out a mortgage on his home, in part to fund college.[5]

Meanwhile, Andrew Kastendieck took care of his own family. There was food on the table; Mollie saw to it that the girls were always well dressed. Entertainment was plentiful. Aside from Andrew's self-made entertainment offerings, school and church functions were regular events, spiced up by a few community dances here and there, to which the Kastendiecks were always welcome guests. Once a year, the Billings Fair renewed itself as the social event of the year. Meanwhile, nature provided its own diversions. "When the robin sings we know that spring is coming," Pauline wrote, "but when the frog sings we know spring is here!"[6] Late in the evening at home, the sounds that came out of the darkness were steady companions at bedtime—

"What is more delightful than the singing of frogs after sunset?" Pauline would lie awake on a quiet night listening to a chorus of sounds, the Frisco train passing in the distance, and wondering if ever it would take her out of Christian County to some place new and fantastic. It was a happy childhood; and then tragedy struck.

Andrew died.

The spring season was at its peak, flowers were in full bloom, and the trees awakened all green with life from their winter's rest. Andrew Kastendieck died on May Day, 1912. He became ill on April 23 with what progressed to Lobar Pneumonia; he never recovered.[7]

He got progressively sicker as the week of April 23 wore on. It had come on suddenly with chills and fever, the usual indicators of the flu. It had been a colder than usual spring and it was flu season. When he did not get better in the first few days, he rode into Billings to see Doc Shafer—Dr. W.W. Shafer. Whether Dr. Shafer misdiagnosed the problem or the disease had advanced too far to stop, Andrew's condition rapidly deteriorated. Dr. Shafer visited him at the Kastendieck home on May Day, the last time that he saw him alive. Andrew died that evening. His family was there—Mollie, Pauline, and Verda. Friends and neighbors had come and gone during the day. John Herman, Jr. informed authorities of Andrew's death and took control of arrangements for the funeral.

R.E. Thunney, the undertaker, came out from Republic to prepare Andrew's body for burial. Notification of his death went out. The funeral announcement gave exactly the right touch of dignity to the occasion. Laid out in Roman serif type centered on an eight by five inch card and surrounded by a black border of mourning, it said simply, "Died at his home near Billings, Wednesday, May 1, 1912."[8]

Thus, it was. Pauline's father, the first of the second-generation of Missouri Kastendieck siblings to die, went quietly to rest beside his father in Rose Hill Cemetery, on a gentle slope of rural Christian County far from the bustling streets of his birthplace in Brooklyn, New York.

ANDREW KASTENDIECK FAMILY. **The Kastendiecks sat for this portrait about 1903. Clockwise, Mollie, Pauline in back, Andrew, and Verda seated in front. This photograph pictured Pauline at about age five.**

BILLINGS STREET FAIR IN 1910. **Held each September, the festivities included competitive shows in such categories as horses, mules and jacks; cattle; swine and sheep; poultry; agriculture; and textile and household.** ***State Historical Society of Missouri.***

THRASHING SEASON. **Machinery and thrashing crews were a common sight at harvest time in the farming community of Billings, Missouri. Pauline Kastendieck grew up on a farm accustomed to the annual ritual of harvest time. The thrasher and steam engine stayed in use well into the 20th century. Neyer Hardware did a booming business for many years.**

SUNDAY SCHOOL. **The Andrew Kastendieck family posed for this photograph with a church group of relatives about 1908. Pauline Kastendieck stands at the far left of the photograph in the white dress and dark stockings. Her sister Verda (in glasses) is in the middle row in the jumper dress in front of their father Andrew who stands framed in the window; Mollie is on the right with the high collar. The elderly bearded man (back left) is Dietrich Kastendieck, the lone surviving immigrant Kastendieck brother.**

SELECT KNIGHTS OF AMERICA FRATERNAL SWORD. **The SKA organization was a fraternity that specialized in life insurance for members. Ceremonial swords of this style appeared in the late 1800s. Andrew Kastendieck purchased this one about the time he married in 1894.** ***Rene (Brandemuehl) Wehler***

Into Grant County

10

Carrying On

The Kastendieck family gathered at the bedside of Andrew Kastendieck in his last days, but his disease took him in a matter of a week. On the evening of May 1, 1912, at 8:50 p.m., he passed away—about the time he would ordinarily be reading or singing and clattering accompaniment on his bones.[1] The house went deathly silent, never again to revive the gaiety it had once known.

Andrew Kastendieck died at the age of forty-eight, much too young everyone said. There was a nice funeral at the Methodist Episcopal Church where he had happily lent his voice in song, where he and Mollie had diligently raised their daughters to value the teachings of Christianity.

They buried Andrew in Rose Hill Cemetery, in the Kastendieck plot next to his father. Upon his grave they placed a small gray tombstone of granite plainly inscribed, "In Loving Memory—Andrew Kastendieck, 1863-1912, Father."[2]

Verda and Pauline Kastendieck were in their teens when Andrew died; Verda was sixteen, Pauline age fourteen, both old enough to understand fully their loss and to miss their father very much. A parent's loss of a child probes the depths of grief, but a child's loss of a parent leaves an indelible mark of sorrow.

Memories were insufficient to fill the great depth of loss that Mollie, Verda, and Pauline felt. Daunting was the prospect of facing the future without the steady guidance of Andrew. However, they did not retreat into the past, but inwardly dedicated themselves to rise above the provincial life of Polk Township, to go steadily forward, and to steer a new course into the 20th century.

There were only three in the family now left to survive on forty acres of poor land in a place that challenged the best of men, let alone a widow in her thirties and two teenage daughters. It is fearful to think what might have happened to Mollie and her girls had it not been for the extended Kastendieck clan and the help of her orphaned brothers, brothers who came together to help her despite having grown up apart in time and distance. The Billings community came together as it always did in a time of need to help one of its own.

When Andrew Kastendieck died in 1912, Billings was on the verge of becoming a boomtown. More than a convenient stop on the Frisco railroad as it once was, it had a population of 860 and all the services of a modern town. The new Bank of Billings stood at the corner of Elm and Washington streets; businesses ranged up and down Elm Street, from Sanders Mercantile, Neyer Hardware, grocery, and dry goods stores, to a drug store and Watkinson Jewelry, plus various other sundry and convenience shops. Local residents liked to brag about the peaceful nature of Billings by pointing out that in the whole town there were only two lawyers.

Good jobs were plentiful at either the Canning Factory or a host of other manufacturing concerns around town. The canning factory had gone up in 1891 "equipped with the best labor saving machinery." Processing of large quantities of tomatoes every season added to farm incomes and jobs. The

Billings Creamery cooperative was in full swing, and local farmers marketed their products through the Creamery Station.[3]

Local agents represented several insurance establishments, including the large Farmers' Mutual Fire Insurance Company that covered four counties. The Kastendieck-Blades Mill was a going business on the northeast corner of Billings, near the railroad tracks. The mill was a partnership between Dietrich Kastendieck and the Blades family, part of the same Blades family that raised Mollie when her parents died.

Billings boasted something for everyone. Built next to the railroad tracks, it rapidly became a shipping hub, which greatly benefited the outlying farming communities. It was common to read in the newspaper, for instance, "Hodges shipped two cars of hogs from here last week; Mr. John Stine shipped out a carload of tomatoes Saturday."[4]

The Indian trails and dirt roads of the early days changed to gravel-paved thoroughfares, greatly increasing the value of both city and farm property. Meanwhile, the city had a good start on sewer and water works; a telephone system connected the town with rural districts, as well as Springfield, St. Louis, and all neighboring towns. Almost within a decade, Billings grew from a brush-covered wayside to a full-fledged town.

The people of Billings constructed the new Billings high school in 1912. "This large, modern structure is well lighted, ventilated, and steam heated," the local press reported, "supplied with the best apparatus, and located on high and beautiful ground in the south part of the city." The reporter also took the opportunity to say, "The school board of Billings has always done all in its power to employ the best teachers and principals available and bring educational work to its present standard."[5]

The new high school was a substantial improvement over the first Billings school started back in 1859 in Dayman's blacksmith shop (where the Canning Factory now stood). Steady improvement in the schools over a half century of time stood as proof of the community's dedicated interest in education.

The Kastendieck sisters—Pauline and Verda, or Andrew and Mollie's girls as folks around Billings affectionately knew them—were sisters in every way except looks. To see them together, one would not suspect they were siblings unless they knew before.[6] Exactly one year and six months separated them in age and a noticeable difference in their height confounded the situation; Pauline stood a good two inches taller than her older sister did.

The petite Verda was for sure one of the prettiest girls in the county. Her wire-rimmed glasses, which she wore from an early age, did not disguise her attractive features. The spectacles, however, and a slight squint did punctuate a scholarly appearance that caused one to think Verda was a teacher long before she entered that honorable field. Pauline later wore eyeglasses, too; however, in the Billings years, glasses helped set the sisters apart as two individuals with very distinct looks and personalities.

The Kastendieck girls went on to graduate from Billings High School, Verda first and then Pauline. Verda finished high school, went to college, and became a teacher. She commenced teaching school at the Brick School at Billings, had charge of room three, and after two years at Billings became a teacher at Oak Hill School north of Billings not far from the Greene County line and the farm where Mollie, her mother, grew up.[7]

Pauline, meanwhile, was one of twelve in her 1914 high school class comprised of three boys and nine girls. The class picture showed all twelve graduates with Principal Phillips seated front and center.[8] Looking at the graduation picture, one could easily mistake it for a funeral instead of graduation day.

No one smiled. Smiling in front of a photographer was apparently a talent that few in Billings possessed. Pauline looked intently into the camera with that same arresting gaze she had showed the Sunday school photographer a few years before. The three young men in the picture wore the obligatory suits and ties, looking like fashion models but fooling no one. The young women, each in a long white graduation dress, made new for the occasion, plainly overshadowed their male counterparts in the photograph.

Two of the twelve graduates were Pauline's cousins making of the class 25 percent Kastendieck. In addition to Pauline, there was Katherine, Uncle George Kastendieck's daughter; and Cousin Mildred, daughter of Uncle John Herman, Jr.

Pauline graduated at the top of the class, captured valedictorian honors, and opened eyes to what was to come when she addressed a capacity crowd during commencement exercises at the AOUW Hall. The local newspaper reported, "Miss Pauline Kastendieck, valedictorian, had a very fine Irish piece, which we intended to publish in full, but as we are crowded with ads, and the length of the article, we did not have room."

Unfortunately, the speech was lost and with it, one of the early indications of the gifted ability of Pauline to capture an audience. Nevertheless, she was proof to the Billings community that good education produced good results. "All seem to think that Billings is coming to the front along educational lines, and we hope it will continue to push ahead each year," wrote the *Billings Times* reporter.[9]

Members of Pauline's graduating class went their separate ways after graduation. Mildred Kastendieck married, divorced, and went to St. Louis. Classmate Edgar Turner went into the Army and served as a sergeant in World War I, until his discharge in 1918. Helen Watkinson went to Kansas City with Elizabeth Griesemer and both became bookkeepers there. Helen later returned to southwest Missouri and lived in Aurora, Missouri, until age ninety-seven.

About half the class became teachers, yet another nod to the high value put on education by the Billings community.[10] Laura Conrad taught at a Springfield business college. Katherine Kastendieck taught in the public schools. She later married a veterinarian and moved to Iowa. Ruth Ely likewise became a public school teacher, and so did Celestine Leitensdorfer who was the youngest daughter of Dr. J.N. Leitensdorfer, the town physician. Dr. Leitensdorfer died in 1908, giving Celestine, Pauline, and Verda the unfortunate common circumstance of graduating from high school without their fathers.

Miss Celestine never married and spent her entire life teaching in the Billings community.[11] A common practice in those days expected the youngest daughter in a family to remain single in order to care for an elderly parent. This tradition produced many an unmarried woman like Miss Celestine. Tradition also expected daughters to marry in order of age. Woe was it to a younger daughter who married before her older sister.

Following her graduation from Billings High School, Pauline entered Springfield Normal School, in Springfield, Missouri, with the intent of following her older sister Verda into teaching. The primary purpose of Springfield Normal at the time was the preparation of teachers for the public school system.[12]

Pauline approached college with the same enthusiasm for learning that she had demonstrated in high school. She attended summer sessions for teacher training, volunteered for extra work, and participated in meetings. In her first year at Normal, she delivered a paper at the District Educational Meeting that had the elements of appeal that would guide her future work.

She spoke on "The Reading Circle Work and Its Value to the Community," emblematic of the three pillars of her future career: organizational involvement, reading, and community service.[13] She attended Springfield Normal for two years, finding time when she could to spend a weekend at Billings to visit friends and home folks, another pillar of her values: the importance of family.[14]

Pauline got a job in Springfield and tried her wings at teaching for a brief time but quickly gave it up because she did not think she liked it.[15]

11

Out of Billings

For a long time, Austin and Willard Dewey, Mollie's brothers, tried to get Mollie to move to Wisconsin. The brothers had left Missouri several years before to resettle in the Dewey family homeland in Wisconsin. Austin and Samantha Dewey were from Wisconsin, and three of the Dewey children were born in Wisconsin before they moved to Missouri. Wisconsin was home. Austin and Willard returned to the old homestead in Grant County as soon as they were old enough to leave their adopted families in Missouri, to resettle near Fennimore.

Despite the fruitful promise of Billings and southwest Missouri, Wisconsin was the new land of opportunity at the beginning of the 20th century. Grant County, Wisconsin, and Iowa County next to it grew rapidly around the turn of the century because of the rich lead and zinc deposits in that region of the country. Opportunities were abundant. Lancaster, the county seat of Grant County, grew to be an important hub of mining activity. Towns like Fennimore offered opportunities for merchants and farmers to provide the necessary goods and services that mining required.

Prospects of a new beginning for the Kastendieck women—Mollie, Verda, and Pauline—in Wisconsin were increasingly attractive. Austin finally convinced Mollie that a future in Fennimore for a widow and two young daughters looked brighter than life on a broken forty-acre farm in southwest Missouri. Mollie began to think about leaving Billings.

The exodus of Mollie, Verda, and Pauline from Billings did not occur all at once. Although Austin Dewey had tried to get Mollie to join him in Wisconsin starting soon after Andrew's death, Pauline was still in high school at the time, and Mollie did not want to leave until she graduated.

Mollie moved the family and their household goods from the farm into a house in Billings at Hamilton and Oak streets, nearer to the high school, and two blocks northwest of the Methodist Episcopal Church where Andrew used to take the family on Sunday. The house stood a few houses southwest of where Andrew's brother George Dietrich kept his carpenter shop on Pine Street.

Mollie did not try to keep the farm going. She sold it for $1,800.[1] Andrew's insurance settlement from his membership in the Select Knights of America helped the financial situation. However, Andrew was not a rich man. Mollie faced an uncertain future with two teenage daughters, alone.

The extended Kastendieck family did not have the same close-knit relationship that it once had only a few years before. Of the original immigrants, only Great Uncle Dietrich remained now in his eighty-fourth year, frail and in failing health. Aunts Amelia and Hermina had not lived in Billings for many years, not since they married and followed the fortunes of their railroad-career husbands working for the Frisco Railroad in Oklahoma. Only uncles John Herman, Jr. and George Dietrich lived nearby in Billings as the lone Kastendieck presence of

Andrew's family. Many of the Kastendieck cousins had left Billings for better work prospects elsewhere. All of the Kastendieck cousins went to college, qualifying them to look for career opportunities beyond Christian County. Raymond Kastendieck, John Herman Jr.'s son, studied to be an architect. Roy, his brother, followed the example of his father in the construction business in Oklahoma. Pauline's classmate, Cousin Mildred, married and set up housekeeping in a log cabin near Marionville. She divorced within two years and pursued a teaching career in St. Louis. Meanwhile, Cousin Minnie moved to Joplin, Missouri, where her husband was in the lumber business.

The children of Uncle George Dietrich likewise left Billings, dispersed to new locations to either follow husbands or partake of prospects for better careers. Cousin Katherine moved to Springfield. She later married and settled in Iowa. Cousin Hazel was in and out of Billings, seen occasionally in Billings at her parent's home. She married an oilman and moved to Oklahoma. Cousin George went into engineering and eventually rose to the position of Greene County Surveyor with an office in Springfield.

The only one of Uncle George Dietrich's children to stay close to Billings was Cousin Frank Kastendieck. He went into farming north of Billings on a gift of land from his father-in-law in 1913. He remained there until his death in 1969. Coincidentally, his farm adjoined the property of Dudley Blades, the farm where Mollie Dewey Kastendieck grew up.

Billings changed and the Kastendieck family with it. In the end, Mollie chose to be closer to her original family roots. She signaled her intent to leave Billings in the spring of 1916 when she sold her only means of conveyance, a nice gentle mare, good buggy, and new single harness.[2] There would be no further need for it. A year later, she put the house up for sale—house, barn, and two lots in a good location. However, it did not sell right away.[3] Nevertheless, in October of 1917, Mollie left Billings for good.[4] Five years after Andrew's death, she returned to the Dewey family seat, in Grant County, Wisconsin.

She moved to Wisconsin by herself, leaving Verda and Pauline behind in Billings.[5] Verda remained in Billings for the time being to take up a new teaching job at Oak Hill.[6] Pauline finished teacher preparation at State Normal and joined her mother in Wisconsin in 1917.[7] Living alone in Billings, Verda advertised their five-room house for sale or rent and sold the family goods at auction in 1918[8]. "Having decided to change our location," Verda wrote on the public bill of sale, "I will sell at our home in the town of Billings, corner of Pine Street and Hamilton Avenue Saturday April 20, 1918, our household belongings."[9]

Estate sales were a common occurrence in the early 20th century, usually upon the death of the head of a household whose property required court-ordered distribution to heirs. The Kastendieck sale had remnants of such a sale, but a court did not order it, and compared with other sales, it was small. The sale bill listed about twenty-five items, including Andrew's 50-gallon coal oil barrel and some of his farm tools. Mollie's clothes wringer, boiler, and washboard sold, along with furniture and various utensils. One of the items hardest to part with was Mollie's chick incubator that for many years helped to sustain the Kastendieck farmstead.

Friends and acquaintances stepped up to make the sale a success. The auctioneer was John W. Washam who had a farm in Pond Creek Township north of Billings, in Greene County. Pond Creek was where Mollie grew up with the Blades family. She counted Washam in her circle of friends. He worked off and on as a department store sales clerk in Billings and took on the occasional auctioneering job

A week after the sale, the teaching term at Oak Hill ended and Verda joined Mollie and Pauline in Grant County, Wisconsin. The *Billings Times* took note of her departure. "Miss Verda Kastendieck left on No. 4 this morning for Fennimore, Wisconsin to join her mother and sister, and they will make that place their future home."[10]

There was one poignant note to add. In the course of moving from Billings to Grant County, Mollie and the girls sold most of their personal belongings. They chose to keep Andrew's Select Knights of America sword.[11]

12

Prairie Land

Grant County, Wisconsin, lies in the far southwestern corner of the state of Wisconsin, an irregular shaped county wedged between the Wisconsin and Mississippi Rivers, touching on Illinois on the south and bordering the state of Iowa across the Mississippi on the west.

In 1836, Wisconsin Territory split off from Michigan Territory, and organizers created Grant County in 1837 from part of Wisconsin Territory, once Indian land that gave Wisconsin its name.

Grant County took its name from a colorful local fur trader who in the 1820s gained a reputation as an eccentric loner who plied his wares as a traveling salesman going door-to-door, happy to live off the land. He traveled light, carrying his trading stock with him, and wearing a cooking pot on his head. He died a mysterious death, according to one account, at the hands of some of his Indian customers. Nevertheless, his pioneering reputation lived on as one of the frontier names in Wisconsin history embedded in the folklore of Grant County.[1]

Meanwhile, Fennimore, Wisconsin, lies midway between Prairie du Chien and Dodgeville, Wisconsin, in the north central quadrant of Grant County, situated on the Western Highland, a high divide between the Mississippi River drainage on the south and the Wisconsin River basin on the north. The old Military Road, built in 1835 to connect the forts of Wisconsin Territory, ran along this high ridge, carving out a way along the easiest contours of the crest. The high ground between the two drainage systems provided a road over the low hills without the need for bridges or fords. The road passed through Fennimore.

An anonymous historian wrote, "Long before Fennimore was a town of any kind, it was part of a waving prairie of grass with a patchwork of trees that grew along the streams. Over these prairies and hills roamed great herds of bison and the red men came to hunt them."[2]

The name Fennimore shared the same kind of mysterious origin as its parent Grant County. The Fennimore name appeared in the 1830 US census in the person of John Fennimore, an early settler who had a cabin next to a large spring on the north side of the trail, the trail that became the Military Road. Reputed to be a congenial person, travelers often stopped to rest at the spring and partake of John Fennimore's hospitality. A common destination of visitors was a stop at the spring in a place they called Fennimore Grove. According to his descendants, John Gerard Fennimore came from Philadelphia and settled on a farm in Wisconsin Territory in 1826, shortly after his marriage to Elizabeth Mary Wadsworth, a Virginia girl who divided her time growing up between Washington, D.C., and Philadelphia. The adventurous young couple still in their twenties settled at the unlikely place of Fennimore Grove and started a family.[3] John fought in the Black Hawk War in 1832 when the Sauk and Fox Indian tribes revolted against white settlement threatening the lives of anyone living in the region. The penultimate engagement of this brief war took place at Wisconsin Heights on the Wisconsin River in Dane County, not far to the east of Grant County and the John Fennimore home.

John Fennimore, according to family tradition, was a young captain and owner of a steamboat that ran the lower Mississippi River. After the war, he and his wife resumed steam boating on the Mississippi and Ohio Rivers, ostensibly returning to Fennimore Grove from time to time. About 1837, on his last trip to New Orleans, he contracted Yellow Fever and died. His wife returned to Philadelphia, and John Fennimore's name disappeared from Wisconsin records, except for the legacy of Fennimore Grove and the village and township that bear his name.[4]

In the spring of 1847, Silas McGhan left his home in Erie County, Pennsylvania, and moved his family to 160 acres on the Fennimore Prairie, passing along the way the John Fennimore cabin and Fennimore Grove. Sophronia McGhan, the young daughter of the McGhan family, said she remembered John Fennimore as an old fur trapper who later died and whose burial was near his cabin in the woods. However, John Fennimore died in 1837 and not 1847, and his name did not appear again in the 1840 US census. Sophronia's memory likely depended on second-hand lore. Nonetheless, it confirmed that more than a decade after Fennimore's death, the name Fennimore continued to identify a particular area along the Military Road.

Around the year 1849, there was an inflow of people coming into Grant County, attracted by the promised riches of mining. Families wanted for their children some semblance of a formal education. The first footprint of education in Fennimore Township occurred when Silas McGhan gave an acre of land on which to build the first school. A creative enterprise, it consisted of a wood frame, roofed with the canvas covering removed from the wagons used by the McGhans when they moved west, an odd but serviceable tent schoolhouse equipped with board seats. The following spring, a small frame schoolhouse went up out of need for both a better school, and at the same time a place to accommodate the patrons of the local Baptist church.[5]

In the beginning, only the lush wild grass of the prairie covered the trackless stretch of ground that became the town of Fennimore. About the time of the Civil War, a post office went in at Michael Bowers log house. Settlers came from miles around to get their mail. Seeing a trading opportunity, Mark Finnicum built a store nearby stocked with the necessary goods of pioneer life. Soon, Batten's blacksmith shop stood a short distance northwest of the Finnicum store. About the same time, Gilman's tavern went up as a wayside inn for travelers.[6] By 1856, there were enough inhabitants to warrant a survey of the site and to lay out the town of Fennimore. At the outbreak of the Civil War, several buildings made up the little village.

A Civil War drill camp operated on the Military Road on a flat piece of land about a quarter mile from Fennimore. Soldiers from across Grant County drilled there for a week or two before going to Camp Randall, in Madison, Wisconsin. Captain John McDermott organized Company C., 20th Regiment of Wisconsin Volunteers, at Fennimore. Austin Dewey, future father of Mollie Kastendieck, enlisted in McDermott's company in the summer of 1862 only to have his enlistment rejected at Madison. Austin returned to Fennimore and enrolled in Company K of the same regiment. A few months later in December 1862, Captain McDermott died in the battle of Prairie Grove, Arkansas. Austin took part in the battle and saw his captain buried on the battlefield.

During the Civil War, county officials saw the need for a new north-south road to connect Boscobel, Wisconsin, to Lancaster. The new road bypassed Fennimore and crossed the Military Road about a mile to the east of town. When Mark Finnicum returned home from the war, he moved his store from Fennimore to the conflux of the two roads. The rest of Fennimore steadily followed him. There were now two Fennimores: Old Fennimore and Fennimore Center, the new town at the intersection of the Military and Lancaster roads. By 1869, Fennimore Center, or Center, as locals commonly called it, was ready to incorporate as a village.[7]

The railroad came to Fennimore Center in 1878, ushering in an era of development and manufacturing. The Chicago and North Western Rail Road followed roughly the same path across the region as the Military Road. Today, U.S. Highway 18 traces about the same route from the Wisconsin River through Fennimore, across the Fennimore Prairie to Dodgeville, and on to points east.

The C & NW Rail Road built a station at Fennimore Center. Wanting to distinguish the station from Old Fennimore and the township, also named Fennimore, the company retained only the name Center, the small village that grew up around the train station. In 1881, the town dropped the word Center, and it has ever since been Fennimore.[8]

By 1881, the village had a population of 295 inhabitants. Fennimore Township contained fifteen schoolhouses and three churches.[9] Within the limits of the town of Fennimore were three merchandise stores, two blacksmith and wagon shops, and a harness shop, all doing a good business. Two shoe stores, a hotel, and two saloons complemented the commercial sector to go with the offices of two physicians. Notwithstanding this progress, the dusty main street became a quagmire of mud in the spring rains; sidewalks did not exist; and no lighting or waterworks yet served the town. Residents carried water from a large spring at the foot of the hill until the town dug a city well where the two highways crossed. Life was difficult. Nevertheless, the future foreshadowed good things for the small town of Fennimore.

13

The Millinery Shop

By the 1890s, Fennimore was on its way to becoming a modern, thriving city. Population more than doubled. Four passenger trains a day arrived at the Fennimore station. Every hotel and rooming house had a special carriage that met the trains and ferried passengers to their destinations. New amenities brought the symbols of civilization to town. There were plank sidewalks, which the town marshal dutifully kept securely nailed down. Good grade, quarried limestone paved the streets.

In 1890, the village inhabitants petitioned the village trustees asking them to light Lincoln Avenue with street lamps of some sort. They installed a dozen coal oil lamps and hired a lamp lighter to maintain them at $7.50 per week. Soon kerosene street lamps on poles lined the length of the street. In 1896, the *Times Review* newspaper reported that city officials might cut the pay of the lamp lighter from $7.50 a month because, they said, someone else offered to do it for $1 less a month.[1]

The lamps provided very little light, prompting citizens to complain that they were doing about as much good unlighted as lighted. For a time, the embarrassed trustees suspended lighting the lamps until public opinion demanded something better than kerosene street lamps. Citizens began to ask for electric lights on the streets and in their homes. In 1904, electricity came to Fennimore coincidental with the opening of the new city well waterworks, all under the auspices of the Fennimore Electric Utility Company.

Meanwhile, the economy was good. Eggs sold for 75 cents a baker's dozen. The program booklet of Fennimore's First Annual Fair listed thirty-seven business organizations and professionals who supported the fair, many of them also mounting exhibits at the fairgrounds. The booklet included several saloons that invited patrons to partake of their sample rooms.[2]

A highlight of the year in Fennimore was the Fennimore Fair. Dubbed Big Days, the annual fairs drew large crowds from the surrounding communities of Lancaster, Mt. Hope, Boscobel, and Montford, all towns within twelve miles of Fennimore.

Big Days began in the summer of 1889 in Worden Stephen's Grove on the north edge of Fennimore when the town had less than a block of sidewalk. According to one old timer, "The cows munched peacefully along the streets at all hours of the day, and to hear the squeal of a pig was nothing at all uncommon, as nearly every citizen kept a porker or two either in his front or his back yard."

Ballgames were major features of Big Days each year until William Rogers built his kite-shaped racetrack and parlayed the event into the Fennimore Fair to feature horseracing instead of ballgames. A tornado swept away the compound of the racetrack in 1899, and Rogers never rebuilt it. Big Days ended in 1922, coincidental with the sheriff's raid that seized 40 pints of moonshine in the Franham Building.[3]

Mollie moved to Wisconsin first, coming to live initially with her brother Austin at Lancaster, Wisconsin. Pauline soon joined her. The two of them quickly resettled in Fennimore, Wisconsin. This was in the year 1917.[4] Verda joined them coming from Billings in 1918.

It was an inauspicious new beginning. The year 1918 was a year of great turmoil. The decision of the Kastendiecks to leave Billings for Wisconsin was by comparison hardly of much consequence. The world cowered in fear of the great Spanish Flu pandemic at its height in 1918 that eventually killed more than fifty million people worldwide. The flu calamity coincided with World War I, the Great War that raged in Europe and ultimately claimed the lives of nine million combatants. The lead mining region around Lancaster and Fennimore buzzed with activity producing the one commodity war needed most, the raw materials of ammunition.

In Fennimore, Pauline's thoughts went back to Billings where friends, classmates, and cousins left in a steady stream to fight in the war. The United States had abandoned its policy of non-intervention in the war in April 1917 when Congress declared war on Germany. Lawmakers enacted the draft a month later, and by the summer of 1918, the U.S. was sending ten thousand soldiers to France every day. Wisconsin became the first state to meet draft requirements. Almost 4,000 Wisconsin men died in the war. In Missouri, Pauline's Cousin George Kastendieck left Billings for Europe in June of 1918, followed in succession by cousins Roy in August and then Roy's brother Raymond Kastendieck in September, the first Kastendiecks to fight in an American war.[5] The German Spring Offensive of 1918 stalled, and the US Hundred Days Counter-Offensive started in August. It led to a cease-fire in November, and finally ended the war.

Mollie's brothers, Willard and Austin, did not serve in the war. Willard's age of 47 exempted him from the Selective Draft Act of 1917 that required all males ages 18 to 45 to register. However, Austin at age 43 was within the required age bracket. In the fall of 1918, he rode over from his farm in South Lancaster to enroll his name at the local draft board in Lancaster, knowing it unlikely that the board would select him for service. One-armed since 1901, an accident with a corn-shredder had cost him his left arm. The draft board noted the enrollment of the tall, slender man with gray eyes and black hair; and then added, "Left arm amputated at elbow," thus assuring his exemption from the draft. Fortuitously, the war ended two months after Austin registered.[6]

Meanwhile in Fennimore, Mollie, Verda, and Pauline started a new life, far from Billings, Missouri, without the familiar household goods of home, and with no jobs, and with little in the way of financial support. When Andrew Kastendieck died in the spring of 1912, all the property he had was a forty-acre farm of poor soil. Mollie sold it for $1,800 and shared the money evenly with Verda and Pauline, $600 apiece. With part of the money, Mollie and Pauline took out a mortgage and opened a millinery shop in Fennimore. They pooled their shares of the money—$1,200 between the two of them—and applied it to the Kastendieck Millinery of Fennimore, store and stock.

Neither of them knew how to run a millinery shop. Pauline said, "Neither of us knew how to run it, but I learned how to make hats." Pauline became the half of the partnership that made the merchandise.[7]

Nevertheless, admitted amateurs about hat making, Mollie knew something about shop keeping. About the time she met Andrew Kastendieck, his stepmother had a dress shop in Billings, Missouri. That experience became a celebrated multicounty court case when a Springfield company sued Caroline Kastendieck for not paying her bills. Mollie would have known about the case through Andrew who testified on Caroline's behalf. Mollie possibly worked in Caroline's dress shop.

There had been a millinery shop in Fennimore before, located in what locals called the Wright Block. That establishment burned in 1896. Nevertheless, the idea of a hat shop in Fennimore was not farfetched considering that a precedent existed for such a business.[8]

The Kastendieck Millinery of Fennimore was in Fennimore's second ward. It offered, in addition to Pauline's handmade hats, "all the later ideas in materials," including Hair Braid, Maline Lace, and Raffia in all the accepted colors. A broad selection of novelties in flowers rounded out the products offered for sale.

How much of popular fashion reached Fennimore, Wisconsin, we do not know. Nationwide, the popular and voluptuous but fragile Gibson-Girl-look of the 1890s had faded. Women of the new 20th century were thinking about comfort. Fabrics were lighter, colors brighter with more of them, and styles looser. Lower necklines became popular. Styles variously dubbed as the sack, the sheath, oriental costume, harem trouser and the Hellenic tunic all came into fashion. Hemlines inched up to show ankles. Furs were important additions to the well-dressed woman. World War I brought imported fashion design to a standstill. "Made in America" became a necessary slogan. Meanwhile, the well-dressed man sported a pressed white shirt, striped trousers, frock coat, and a top hat.

Mollie and the girls settled into a new life. Verda became a schoolteacher in the public schools of Grant County. She had the most teaching experience in the family. She passed up the millinery profession and kept her attention on teaching, as the steady breadwinner of the family.

Meanwhile, Fennimore was growing, concurrent with big changes in America. The Common Council of the City of Fennimore organized in 1919, complete with a mayor and council members.[9] Moreover, the political climate in the United States offered new possibilities for women in an ever-changing political landscape, especially in Wisconsin. In 1919, the Wisconsin legislature ratified the Nineteenth Amendment for women's suffrage, and Wisconsin became the first state of the Union to deliver ratification of the amendment to Congress. Women gained the right to vote with its full passage in the summer of 1920, after a protracted battle of more than sixty years to obtain equal voting rights going back at least to 1848.

The Nineteenth Amendment to the Constitution came on the heels of the Eighteenth Amendment passed in 1919. After decades of efforts by the temperance movement, in which Mollie had an invested interest, the adopted amendment prohibited intoxicating liquors in the US and remained in effect for more than a decade, until its repeal in 1933. Consequently, the "roaring twenties" oversaw a period of outlaw bootlegging of spirits and a spike in organized crime that spread across the country. Fortunately, organized crime as it existed in many places in the country did not reach Fennimore.

PAULINE KASTENDIECK. **This undated portrait taken in Missouri around 1915 dates to about the time of Pauline's graduation from high school. It shows her at approximately age seventeen.**

BILLINGS HIGH SCHOOL GRADUATION CLASS OF 1914. **Pauline Kastendieck stands at the right end of the back row. Shown in the same graduating class are her cousins, Katherine and Mildred Kastendieck. Front Row Seated (left to right): Mildred Kastendieck, Helen Watkinson, Principal Phillips, Ruth Ely, Callie Frank; Second Row (left to right): Edgar Turner, Luia Conrad, Katherine Kastendieck wearing a pendant, Harold Turner, and Celestine Leitensdorfer. Back Row (left to right): Lucille Andre, Herbert Berger, and Pauline Kastendieck in white hair band.**

VERDA AND PAULINE KASTENDIECK. **This studio portrait of the daughters of Andrew and Mollie Kastendieck, Verda (left) and Pauline (right), dates to about 1915. The photographer was Robert E. Hinchey who kept a photography studio in Aurora, Missouri. He traveled around southwest Missouri doing photography work. One of his most famous photos was a 1926 picture of "Uncle Ike and Son" made famous by Harold Bell Wright's novel, *Shepherd of the Hills.***

VERDA KASTENDIECK CLASS. **Verda, Pauline's sister, taught school at various schools in Missouri and Wisconsin. The above photograph (top) pictures her (left) in 1915 with her class at Center School, located about a mile and a half south of Billings on present South Pine Road, in Christian County, Missouri.**

ONE-ROOM SCHOOL. **Pauline Kastendieck attended one-room schools like this one (bottom) in rural Christian County, Missouri. Pictured is the all-girl class of her sister, Verda (seated center) in one of Verda's first teaching jobs.**

The Fennimore Years

14

Fennimore

FEnnimore, Wisconsin, was a town much like Billings, Missouri, a growing community in post-war Middle America on the brink of a new wave of prosperity. The three Kastendieck women arrived at Fennimore at a time of historic community growth and change. The "roaring twenties" brought a decade of new facilities and improvement of old ones.

Fennimore had a fire department from the date of its incorporation as a village in 1885. The old hook-and-ladder fire cart apparatus had room to carry 100 pails of water drawn from the city well at the center of town. When the Kastendieck women came in 1918, it was about the time the all-volunteer fire department added its first fire truck in 1922, complete with a pump and fire hose that could reach 800 feet. Unfortunately, it came too late to save the lumberyard and the feed store that burned in February 1922.

Fennimore was not an isolated prairie town. Telephone service came to Fennimore in 1897 when the Grant County Telephone Company installed lines from Lancaster to Boscobel via Fennimore. More than 100 farmers enjoyed the convenience not only of connecting to each other and to Fennimore but also to the villages of Mt. Hope, Millville, and Mt. Ida.

Mollie and the girls eventually enjoyed phone service that reached friends and relatives in Billings, although infrequently and sometimes unreliably. The switchboard-operated system depended on operators to ring patrons by hand, answer fire alarms, and call the police, the light company, and the doctor. Operators also tended the stove, carried out the ashes, and scrubbed the floor.[1]

Electricity was available to many homes and businesses in Fennimore as early as 1904. The town later discontinued its own power plant in favor of contracting for electricity service from the Interstate Power Company at Lancaster.[2] Electric lights lit most homes and lined Lincoln Avenue.

The daily routine in town included a trip to the post office. City mail delivery did not exist in the early days. However, a patron could call the post office and inquire about their mail much to the annoyance of the postmaster. Four times a day trains delivered and received mail at Fennimore, making communications by letter easier in many ways than by telephone. Although there was no mail delivery in town, carriers did deliver the mail to farmers via the rural free delivery service routes, an improvement over the early days when farmers picked up mail at the post office in Michael Bowers log cabin.

News came via the venerable *Fennimore Times*. Commenced in 1889 under the editorial guidance of the Roethe family, the paper published first as the *Times Review* and later the *Fennimore Times*. Progressive in both content and technology, the first linotype machine replaced the old handset, hand-press work in 1900, ushering in a new era of letterpress printing. In 1921, the paper took up permanent residence on Lincoln

Avenue. The *Fennimore Times* always made school news a central feature of its reporting.[3]

Many thriving shops comprised the business district. A favorite place to eat was Duster's Cafe. Hamburgers were a nickel each. Farmers coming into town were regular customers. The Cafe had a small banquet room outfitted with a phonograph (jukebox) and the proprietors allowed dancing at any time.

Dances were likewise a favorite pastime at the old Opera House. Alternatively, you could go down to Alber Weber's jewelry store and listen to the first player piano in Fennimore.[4] These were lightweight entertainments compared to Maso's Dance Hall, Movie Theater, and Roller-Skating Rink, which operated in competition with the Rainbow Dance Hall.[5] However, one had to be cautious about entertainments. The court cited Joe Harrington, for instance, for running a gambling house in the basement of Storrs Hotel. Shortly thereafter, Mr. Harrington entered the lawful business of raising Angora cats.[6]

Meanwhile, Charlie Lomas and his sister had a dress shop to complement Mollie's hat enterprise. Yep Tung opened a new Chinese hand laundry specializing in all kinds of laundry work.[7]

There was a bus garage on Lincoln Avenue that sold Oakland and Star cars. The first horseless carriage appeared in Fennimore in the summer of 1904. People still talked about how A.E. Summer traded 300 acres of land to buy his Stanley Steamer.[8]

There were six churches in Fennimore; the oldest was the Methodist Episcopal Church that became active in 1844. This was the Kastendieck church with a history similar to the Methodist Episcopal Church of Billings. The earliest congregations met in homes during the winter months and outdoors in the summer. Methodist circuit riders helped build membership in the church. The church erected its first building in Fennimore in 1867. It served the congregation for three decades until the dedication of a new structure in 1899.[9] This was the church Mollie and the girls regularly attended.

After Sunday church services, a Sunday stroll around Fennimore invariably included a visit to Marsden Park, a beautifully kept acreage of tree-studded ground given to the town courtesy of the estate of William Marsden. Mr. Marsden, who began his family in Fennimore in 1863, had great plans for his five children. He saw that they had the best educations in a community that prided itself in its schools. His children attended college in Iowa and studied to be leaders in their chosen professions. Then tragedy struck the Marsden family. By 1902, all five of the Marsden children were dead, victims of illness or natural disaster. When Mr. Marsden's wife died in 1910, all his dreams were gone. He died in 1916, having lived in Fennimore for sixty years. His will bequeathed his considerable fortune to benefit the town of Fennimore, including endowments to schools and the construction of a town park maintained in perpetuity.[10]

There was a nice library in Fennimore housed in the Old Fennimore House. The Kastendiecks arrived in Fennimore about the time a new library building was under construction to replace the venerable old structure. The library, a resource Pauline had not had in Billings, beckoned anyone with a curiosity in learning.

Local banker and philanthropist, Dwight T. Parker donated money to build and operate the Parker Public Library. The red brick two-story building boasted an Italianate theme with red clay tile roof and round arched windows. Small terra cotta columns flanked an entryway that opened inside to planed oak moldings and furnishings placed around a cozy tile fireplace. All and all, the Fennimore library was an elegant invitation to anyone seeking knowledge, and an enjoyable setting in which to improve an education.

Fennimore was a place long established as a community dedicated to learning and education. Almost from the time of its founding, educational needs stood high on the list of priorities. In 1849, when people met to organize Fennimore, they raised the sum of $50, half of which was to pay for books for the town library. The first regular school term started in 1868 in a classroom above the hardware store. By 1879, the School Board had established an elementary school, and in 1896, a new high school replaced the old White building that served the town for many years as both school and church. The new school was a fancy two-story masonry building complete with a tower and a place for a clock, which unfortunately no one ever installed. By 1910, the town library had grown to 200 books housed in an upper room of the Methodist Church. School attendance increased rapidly until a second high school went up in 1912. Education steadily grew across the region, and by 1913, there were some 50 schools in Fennimore Township, all needing teachers.[11]

When the Kastendieck women arrived in Fennimore, a teacher shortage opened the door to teaching opportunities. So acute was the scarcity of teachers that high school graduates received teaching certificates in the absence of qualified college-prepared teachers. Pauline and Verda were both qualified to teach.

Going into the year 1920, both Kastendieck daughters were still living with their mother in Fennimore. The census taker found them in January, living on Spring Street (present Twelfth Street), near Warner and Perkin streets, both girls living at home with Mollie, in their twenties and still single. Verda was age 24 and Pauline 21.[12]

The Kastendieck Millinery did not go as expected from the beginning. It kept going for a few years but without much success. The year 1922 came, and Pauline needed to work to help support the family. Although she had eschewed teaching back in Missouri because she did not think she liked it, teaching was a job she knew how to do. When they finally sold the millinery shop, it sold at a loss. Pauline said years later, "We sold it at a $600 loss, which I paid off teaching school. Those were the days," to which she parenthetically added, "(or daze)!"

Even before they sold the millinery business, Pauline was thinking of other options besides hat making for a career. Whether it was due to Verda's influence or another reason, Pauline's interest in teaching rekindled, and she quit making hats to study to become an educator. The passion of Pauline's life for the next forty years became education. She took teaching methods classes during the summer of 1922 at La Cross Normal School, La Cross, Wisconsin, and attended summer sessions at Platteville Normal School, Platteville, Wisconsin, to add to her teaching credentials.

She qualified to teach second grade in Iowa County, Wisconsin, next door to Grant County, obtaining her elementary teaching certificate for Iowa County on September 1, 1922. Her certificate qualified her to teach in Iowa County for a period of three years. She scored high marks on all subject areas, especially arithmetic, history, and library. She qualified to teach elementary grades in the public schools through third grade.[13] However, her certificate authorized her to teach only second grade perhaps because of her youth, although she was 23 at the time and single.

Across the nation, the budding field of education gained new emphasis. The first *Journal of Educational Psychology* was in its second decade of publication, and John Dewey had published his influential *Democracy and Education*. New on the scene of education was William S. Gray and colleagues at the University of Chicago who pioneered studies in reading behavior and achievement, areas of study destined to become Pauline Kastendieck's educational specialty.

15

Cokerville

Pauline's first regular teaching job was at the Cokerville School where she taught second grade.[1] The school was located in Iowa County, Wisconsin; about 12 miles north of Platteville, and about four miles southwest of Livingston, near the Iowa County-Grant County line, in the lead and zinc mining district that covered much of southwest Wisconsin. The school stood about 15 miles southeast of Fennimore. The village of Rewey occupied a place nearby on the line of the Chicago and Northwestern Rail Road, on the high prairie that divides the waters of the Pecatonica and Platte Rivers. The Cokerville School sat two and a quarter miles west of the village of Mifflin, at the end of Bollant Road where Bollant met the highway going to Rewey. Cokerville was one of several rural schools in the area that served miners' families in Grant and Iowa counties.

Southwest Wisconsin had a reputation for mining as well as for the products of its rich farmlands. There were numerous mines located throughout the region of Cokerville, many of them concentrated in the area bounded by the Pecatonica River on the east and the Chicago and Northwestern Railroad on the west. Cokerville was the site of some of Wisconsin's oldest diggings. At one time, more than four thousand miners worked the mines in this 40 square mile mining district, producing much of the nation's lead. Schools and teaching jobs were plentiful. Miners were careful not to neglect the educations of their children.

The History of mining in the region dated to the early 1800s. The little mining village of Mifflin was at one time a thriving municipality with an industrious population of mining families.[2] Mifflin gradually fell into decline, and for a period of forty years, farming and other livelihoods occupied the attention of the people of the region. At the dawn of the 20th century, the Coker diggings on the farm of John M. Ellsworth reopened new interests in mining. By 1880, the Coker-Ellsworth company employed 150 men turning out more than 400 tons of lead ore a month.[3] The rise in the price of ore in 1899 renewed interest in the area, and after 1903, mining developed rapidly. Many mining outfits began what became the second period of mining in the Cokerville mines west of Mifflin. During this period, mining in southwest Wisconsin reached the height of its glory days.[4] By 1922, when Pauline arrived there mining was at its peak; schools welcomed good teachers, even those of limited teaching experience.

The many mines clustered in a relatively small area posed significant dangers for the people working there. A few years before Pauline arrived, two men died in a train accident on the tracks that ran behind her school. The railroad company issued repeated warnings about the hazardous way of travel walking along the tracks. However, the men generally ignored the warnings because the route cut off a mile of distance on the trip to the mines.

The accident occurred the day after Christmas, 1916, around 6:00 a.m., about a mile south of Livingston when a party of five men walking south on the track was overtaken by a switch train. The weather was stormy. Sleet and snow covered the track in high wind, surrounded by darkness.

A local newspaper reporter described what happened, "An accommodation train was due out of Livingston at 6:10 a.m., and the party stepped off the track to let it pass. The extra train was running with a boxcar in front of the engine with no light. The weather was stormy and the track covered with sleet and snow and in the high wind surrounded by darkness, it was an easy matter to catch the party unawares." Unaware that the train was running with a boxcar in front of the engine with no lights, the men were unable to get off the tracks in time and two men died, their mangled bodies discovered at daybreak far down the track, the first the train crew knew of the accident. [5] People still talked about it years later when Pauline arrived there in 1922.

When Pauline came into the region, she came at the height of mining activity. From about 1900 to 1928, the Livingston-Mifflin-Cokerville mining area was one of the most active mining areas in Wisconsin, and the Cokerville group of mines included some of the largest zinc mines in Wisconsin. The lead deposits, particularly those near Mifflin, were among the largest and most extensively worked in the district. [6]

There were seven mines clustered around Cokerville operated by the Vinegar Hill Mining Company: Sunrise, Sunset, Big Tom, and Ellsworth, Coker #1 and #2, and Udell. Miners often gave other names to the mines in language never seen on a mining survey. The names of some of the reopened mines faded from memory. For example, miners had no idea that the old Peni Mine located at Mifflin was a contraction of its original name, the Penitentiary Mine.

To Pauline, Cokerville was a new experience and a dramatic change of scenery. The landscape was interesting and formidable. Weather could be a challenge, particularly in the wintertime. The terrain consisted of mounds or hills, flat divides, wide flood plains bounded by steep banks, and many small V-shaped valleys. The Pecatonica River wound snakelike around the east edge of Mifflin, flowing south to the Rock River in Illinois. Winters could be severe. Snowstorms blocked roads with heavy snow that left drifts still in evidence into March. [7]

In less than a decade from the start of its mining resurgence, Cokerville grew from a montage of farms, four houses, and a boarding house for miners to a village of fifty houses strung out along the main road. Known alternately as Stringtown or Stringtown-on-the-Pike, Cokerville by 1922 was a town that took pride in its Stringtown Band made up of miners that played at Fourth of July celebrations. To preserve its rural character, two farms continued to operate within the confines of Cokerville.

The people of Cokerville divided into two groups—those who spoke English and those who did not. Those who spoke English lived in the houses along the main road. The others lived in shacks clustered around the mines. Most of the English-speaking families came from the small towns and farms in the area or from places like Dodgeville whose Norwegian roots infused a class of educated men into the assorted mix of miners. Jobs at the mines attracted men of diverse backgrounds, including a sizeable number of immigrants from several different countries. The most colorful and most disdained by the English-speaking clique were the Hungarians.

Cokerville could be a bawdy place. Minors from foreign countries saved their money, sent it to friends and relatives for passage to America, and thus added to the immigrant group. It was common for a new arrival to have to wait for up to a couple of months before going to work, usually assigned to a job next to someone who spoke their language. This hiring policy produced a number of loafers hanging around the mines, among them were professional gamblers, some drunkards, and others just waiting for a job. The immigrant shacks were an undesirable section of town to avoid because it was the site of much drinking, gambling, and fighting. Poker games often lasted for days.

The Hungarians all owned guns and used them freely. The Colt Automatic was the firearm of choice. Poker games frequently ended in fights. Fists, furniture, knives, and guns were weapons of choice—anything that was handy. Living in such a wild community required most miners to sleep with a Colt Automatic under their pillow.

Although fighting was common, there was only one murder within Cokerville. The janitor for the mines wore a money belt that contained $1,000. Miners recovered his body from the burned ruins of his shack, dispatched by a massive head wound, and his money belt missing. No one ever did anything about it.

Cokerville possessed few of the amenities of a normal town. One former resident recalled what it was like as a child. "The road of Cokerville was very quiet—the horses and teams belonged to the mining company. The miner who owned a car or a horse was indeed rare. Walking was the established form of transportation. If one had to go somewhere out of walking distance, one called the livery stable at Livingston, and they would send out a team and wagon—or a team and buggy. To use the train, one went to Rewey. Mother said that for one whole year—she went nowhere—had absolutely no form of entertainment in that year—no wonder she hated the mines."[8]

The need of a new pair of shoes or other clothing meant a trip to Livingston. Cokerville had only one store owned and patronized only by the Hungarians. Vanwell's grocery store in Livingston delivered groceries by order each week to Cokerville miners. Larken and Jewel Tea men made regular visits to the village.

During the years when Cokerville flourished as a mining town, it had no churches. There was no doctor at Cokerville. The closest doctor lived at Livingston. If one needed the doctor, one went to the mine to use the telephone in the superintendent's office. The doctor at Livingston would come out sometimes by bobsled in winter months, a five-mile trip that could take two to three hours in bad weather. One doctor had a cantankerous streak. If he did not like the name given to a newly delivered baby, he refused to put it on the birth certificate, entering instead "baby—female."

Pauline was a keen observer of human nature. She often found purpose in simple stories that she relished in retelling. Cokerville was rich in such stories. One story was about a neglected old man whose loneliness made an imprint on her own encounters in life, often spent alone in unfamiliar places. She had a knack for writing in parables. Pauline might have been reflecting on her own situation when she wrote, "The old man looked tired, lonely, and discouraged, yet patient and resigned, as he trudged along the street with his lunch pail in his hand. A squirrel scurried across the street and came to a sudden halt in front of him. For a moment, the two stood and looked at each other. The squirrel stared at the old man in a bright, interested way with his head cocked saucily on one side and his paws held daintily before him. The old man looked at the squirrel in a kindly, friendly way and smiled. The squirrel scampered on about his business of moving nuts from one hiding place to another and the old man trudged on down the street, but the smile lingered on his face. Perhaps he was just smiling at the cunning antics of the squirrel, but it might have been because something had noticed him."[9]

The Cokerville School where Pauline taught was one of several rural schools in the area that served miners' families in Grant and Iowa counties. Carpenter's School was another.[10] The school at Linden situated north of Mifflin was another. All shared similar qualities. Donna Perkins, a student at Pauline's school at Cokerville remembered, "After the mines began to boom, the small wooden school at the cross-road a fourth of a mile south of town was found to be too small to accommodate all the children from the mines. The school, consisting of one room, had held all eight grades prior to the mining boom. A new brick school, also one room, was built alongside the old school. The Big-Tom Mine was located kitty-corner from the schools—it was an old mine and not in operation. We walked past the Coker Mine (which was operating at full capacity) on our way to school. The Ellsworth mine was directly behind our house. This house was located directly over one of the tunnels of the Ellsworth, when they blasted underground, everything in the house rattled."[11]

Pauline's second grade class was a cross section of the ethnic diversity of Cokerville. There were bullies who preyed on the few handicapped children, some of whom were epileptic and carried combs to stick in their mouths in case of a fit. Kids with unpronounceable names sat among the children of more recognizable local labels. Sometimes the names of immigrant children were not their real names, but rather names given to them by the mining paymaster who wanted a more pronounceable name for his records. The practice led to one comic situation. As the story goes, "Potato Pete was crazy about bananas. When he asked the miners for the American word for bananas, they said it was 'Potato.' He went to town and asked the storekeeper for some potatoes—when the grocer brought him potatoes instead of bananas, he was furious. He kept repeating that he wanted potatoes." Thus, he entered the paymaster's books as Potato Pete. Likewise, the Bulgarian John Maxwell owned a Maxwell car; his children were the Maxwell kids, although that was not their real names.

There was no playground at the Cokerville School other than the pilings left from the mines. One big piling near the school was especially dangerous. Kids could play only on its eastern slope. At the bottom of the western slope lay the 200-foot shaft of the mine. A miner narrowly escaped falling down the shaft one time when he fell through boards covering the shaft but managed to catch himself by his armpits. Parents warned children continually of the dangers even of the eastern side of the slope. A young boy of twelve lost his footing, reached out to catch himself, and grabbed an electric wire that electrocuted him. Regardless of warnings, kids disobeyed and played on the tailing piles and along the fascinating stream that flowed down from the mine between the piles.

There were few entertainments in Cokerville. In the winter months, the millpond froze over and made a skating rink, smooth and fine as one could find anywhere. Wrestling matches occupied an occasional respite from boredom. John Maxwell liked to challenge his adversaries. In the summer, there were baseball games among the miners. Fourth of July celebrations invited attendance at nearby towns.

Nevertheless, Pauline was not entirely isolated from civilization. The mail delivered newspapers, including the *Chicago Tribune*. Some read the *Dodgeville Chronicle* and the *Fennimore Times*. The state library at Madison provided reading material and kept the mails busy with books going back and forth to Cokerville.

The railroad connected Cokerville to Livingston on the northwest and Rewey to the south. Pauline likely lived in one of these nearby towns or with one of the several rural families around the mines. Boarding houses and miner's cottages lined the roads. Livingston and Mifflin were within walking distance of Cokerville; and an accommodation train ran multiple times daily out of Livingston. People who lived in Livingston found employment at the mines and worked at various other jobs, commuting from Livingston to Cokerville by foot along the tracks each day.

We may imagine Pauline taking a room at the boarding house, a once elegant structure that had been the Ellsworth home. The hallway was the most impressive part of the house, being of polished marble. Otherwise, the boarding house was barren—sparsely furnished, with no curtains at the windows. The boarding house operated for several years until it burned down. A miner first noticed the smoke from where he was working at the mine. He called the alarm, and the men rushed out of the mine to fight the fire. They could not save the building, but went in to save as much of the furniture as they could. Many of the things that they brought out were stacked against the burning building!

Then one day, the mines suddenly closed without warning. A resident at the time recalled, "The word went through the village like wildfire. People stood around in bewildered groups talking. They were stunned by the sudden news—what to do and where to go?"[12]

Most of the miners migrated to the mines at New Diggings. By 1926, Cokerville disappeared from the landscape. Only the foundations of houses moved to other mining towns marked the once thriving community. Pauline's school at Cokerville, once a substantial brick building put there primarily to serve the children of the miners, fell into disrepair. It burned several years later.[13]

16

Oscar and Casey

After a year at the Cokerville School, Pauline decided to move closer to home in Grant County. She received her Grant County teaching certificate on August 22, 1923, at Lancaster, Wisconsin. Again, as in Iowa County, the certificate reflected her high standards in several teaching areas and was good for a period of three years.[1]

She found work teaching second grade at the Brick School, a little country school at Bloomington, Wisconsin, about twenty miles southwest of Fennimore. It was not as close to home as Cokerville was; nevertheless, it was outside the mining district and more of a lifestyle to which she was accustomed.

Bloomington—once called Blake's Prairie—was a small town of about 600 population located on Blake Fork, or Blake Creek, surrounded by well-kept farms in a sparsely populated landscape similar to where she grew up on the Kastendieck farm outside Billings, Missouri, a small town about the size of Bloomington. The town stood eight miles from the Mississippi River on the west, and about the same distance to Fennimore as Cokerville was, except in the opposite direction, away from the mining district.

Other things were happening in the Kastendieck family. Verda turned 26 years old in 1923, in her fifth year of teaching in Grant County. No one of suitable companionship had yet caught her eye. She was fearfully on a path to becoming the proverbial "Old Maid" schoolteacher.

Oscar Brandemuehl was a tall, stoutly built young man of German descent and of definitive Aryan looks, including blue eyes and light brown hair.[2] Born April 14, 1899, the youngest of four children, Oscar was one of several of the Brandemuehl name whose extensive presence in Grant County, Wisconsin, accounted for a good segment of the population. By the fate of happenstance, Oscar shared much in common with his future mother-in-law, Mollie Kastendieck. Like Mollie, he lost his parents at an early age. His mother, Johanna (aka Hannah)—Wisconsin-born of immigrant German roots—died in 1907 when Oscar was eight years old. His father, Fredrick Brandemuehl, himself a German immigrant, died four years later in 1911, at Lancaster when Oscar was not yet a teenager.[3] Oscar went to live as the ward of Albert Brandemuehl, of rural Bloomington, a relative who raised him to adulthood as his guardian.[4] On this unlikely commonality, Oscar Brandemuehl and Mollie Dewey Kastendieck shared regrettable beginnings as orphans in a lifelong friendship.

When Verda Kastendieck met Oscar, he was working as a 20-year-old, Dutch-speaking hired hand for George Borah on the Borah farm in Mt. Ida Township.[5] The George Borah connection added another segment to the family circle. Willard Dewey, Mollie's brother, married Martha Borah of Mt. Ida, daughter of Albert Borah and part of a large extended family of the Borah name who with the Brandemuehls had a significant presence in Grant County.

Verda and Oscar married June 6, 1923. They married notwithstanding the two years seven months age difference Verda had over Oscar. She was nearing her 27th birthday; he was 24.

From time to time, Aunt Lizzie Kastendieck wrote to Mollie at Fennimore to catch her up on the news at Billings, to tell her who was ill and recovering, who had died and where the kids were, and the general circumstances around Billings. Cousin Frank Kastendieck was recovering from a bad electrical accident that nearly killed him. His eyesight was improving and Lizzie thought he would be better after his burns entirely healed. "I tell you, Mollie, that poor boy has had a time one way and another."

Lucy Ely had upset things at the school. "I guess you know some of her doings at the school. Since then I have not had much to do with her...I do not like that kind of a friend...some things you know do not get forgotten in a hurry."

Invariably, the conversation came around to Mollie's flower garden. "You wrote about your tulips. Mine are about all gone," Lizzie complained, "I had some beauties last [month] but moles have gotten them all but one and the gladiolas you sent me are preparing to bloom now. I am anxious to have them bloom for Kathryn [*sic*] said you had such beautiful colors. I have a number of dahlias in bloom nearly all in lavender color 'tho...hope I have a white and yellow. We are having plenty of garden such as potatoes, beans, onions, cucumbers, and the like."[6]

Lizzie Kastendieck sent her congratulations on Verda's recent marriage to Oscar the month before, and then added good-naturedly, "Tell her [Verda] do not think she made her name any easier to pronounce."

Meanwhile, Pauline finished her teaching job at Cokerville, and in the summer of 1923 prepared for her next teaching assignment at Bloomington. By the fall of 1923, she took up her new duties as Bloomington's second grade teacher. It soon became apparent that Pauline, too, had other interests at Bloomington, in addition to teaching.

Casey Jeidy lived on a farm near the small town of Little Grant, Wisconsin, a couple of miles from the school at Bloomington, and about 10 miles west of Fennimore.[7] Fennimore, Mt. Hope, and Little Grant lay at the corners of a 10-mile long triangle of farmland in central Grant County, tucked into southwestern Wisconsin between the Wisconsin River on the north and the Mississippi River on the west.

His name was Melvin Lavern Jeidy (pronounced Yi-dee), but his friends called him Casey. The eldest son of Charles and Ethel Belle Garthwaite Jeidy, he came from a relatively large family of second-generation Wisconsin farmers.[8] The Jeidy name was of German origin while his mother's Garthwaite family came to Wisconsin by way of Pennsylvania and Ohio.[9]

Those who knew Casey described him as a boy of pleasant nature, always with a cordial greeting for all who met him.[10] Somewhere along the way, his gregarious personality attracted the friendship of Pauline, the Missouri farm girl from Fennimore. Pauline and Casey married "officially" in June 1924. People suspected that Pauline and Casey carried on a secret romance for several months and probably married well before the 1924 "official" date. They apparently wanted to marry earlier. However, Mollie, according to family lore, refused to give her permission because it was customary for the oldest daughter to marry first. Verda was exactly a year and a half older than Pauline was and single at the time, although she had caught the eye of Oscar Brandemuehl and their marriage appeared imminent. Pauline and Casey waited, so the story went, while Oscar courted Verda. When Oscar and Verda married in the summer of 1923, Pauline and Casey took their vows a year later.[11]

No one seemed to care that the union of Pauline and Casey was a bit of an age mismatch. Born February 12, 1902, Casey was almost four years younger than Pauline was; he was 22, she was 26. They set up housekeeping on a small farm south of Mt. Hope and north of Bloomington, there to chase the dreams of a young couple starting out on their own. Summer went by quickly. The months passed with the usual signature of a Wisconsin winter giving way to the approaching spring.

In late March, 1925, as signs of spring began to appear, Casey came down with a fever. The fever would come and go but by April, it grew progressively worse, and by mid-April, the doctor had diagnosed it as typhoid fever. Casey made a brave fight against the disease. With Pauline's care and the strength of his youth, everyone thought he might recover from the deadly infection, but he did not. By May, high fever had brought on periods of delirium; telltale red spots covered his lower chest and abdomen; and the signs of organ failure began to show. In the last days, Casey kept to his bed. Pauline and Casey's parents stayed close by his side. He had been under a doctor's care for six weeks but to no avail. He contracted pneumonia; it and the complications of the fever took his life. Melvin Lavern Casey Jeidy died at home at 6:00 p.m. May 15, 1925.[12] He was 23 years, three months, and three days old. Pauline and Casey fell just days short of celebrating their first wedding anniversary.

The death of a young person causes a lot of guilt. Could anyone have prevented Casey's death? After all, a vaccine for typhoid fever had been available for at least a decade. However, antibiotics to combat the disease once it set in were not available, and the disease continued to claim many victims well into the 20th century, including those who had ample access to the best of care. For instance, Wilbur Wright of the famous Wright Brothers died of the disease in 1912, ironically in the month of May same as Casey.

No one was to blame for Casey's death, but that did not lessen Pauline's grief. For Pauline, Casey's death recalled the sadness of the loss of her father a dozen years before. Her thoughts must have flashed back to another day in May 1912, when she lost another love of her life when her father Andrew died on May Day at the age of 48. Pneumonia, which claimed Andrew's life, also added the final blow that took her husband, Casey.

Meanwhile, at Billings, Missouri, word came of Casey's death. The local newspaper remembered Pauline "who had been reared in Billings and who has a number or relatives and friends here who will be sorry to hear of her loss." The bonds of friendship and childhood memories stretched across the miles.[13]

R. M. Hoskins, the undertaker, came out from Bloomington for the sad task of removing Casey's body back to Bloomington for funeral services.[14] They buried Casey at Little Grant Union Cemetery east of County Road A, about where it intersects Bedrock Road, in Grant County, less than a mile from home. A large gray stone marks his gravesite, inscribed in large block letters, "Jeidy', and in smaller print simply "Melvin, 1902 – 1925".[15]

The entire Little Grant community from Mt. Hope to Fennimore and Bloomington mourned the premature death of Casey Jeidy. In his few years, he left many friends and acquaintances throughout Grant County, remembered by them and missed for his amiable and welcoming character.[16] None missed him more, however, than Pauline. He was her soul mate. We cannot know how deeply she felt the pain of his loss. Despite their brief union cut short by fate, her memory of him never faded. For reasons known only to her, she remained a widow for the remainder of her life and never remarried. She always gave her name as Mrs. Pauline Jeidy.

17

Finding Hope

Life went on.

The year 1926 came. Oscar and Verda's first child, Ruth Margaret, born April 14, 1924, was a year old. Verda was teaching, housekeeping, raising a family, and lending her considerable agrarian skills to helping with the farm.

Mollie lived and worked in Fennimore at her hat shop for a few years until sometime after 1924—after Verda married—when she went to live with Verda and Oscar at their home in Mount Hope, Wisconsin.[1] Mollie did not remarry choosing to live on as Mrs. Andrew Kastendieck.

Billings was never far from Mollie's memory. She sent a picture of herself and her new granddaughter to a friend in Billings. The friend wrote back a congratulatory note wanting to know more. "Write me a long letter. Tell me all about yourself and the girls." The writer added a quip that brought a smile to Mollie's day. "Tell Verda," the friend wrote, "I got a wedding present 20 years after I was married, and who knows but what she may get a belated one, one of these days."[2]

There were, of course, unpleasant memories of Billings. In 1927, for example, Mollie came across some old letters that recalled the unsuccessful attempts by the Dewey children to file a claim for their father's Civil War pension. The letters prompted Mollie to write to the Pension Office in a short but plaintive letter to ask if there was any chance the government might allow the claim. The Dewey children were no longer minors. Nevertheless, a successful claim would garner back-benefits for each child up to age 16 following Austin Dewey's death. Mollie received a prompt and curt reply from the Pension Office. "The best obtainable evidence failed to show the cause of the soldier's death, hence his death cannot be attributed...in any manner to his military service."[3] The letter bore the signature of Commissioner Winfield Scott, head of the Pension Bureau. Mollie put the letter away, and that was the end of it.

Mollie's letter contained a small fragment of the history of Fennimore. She wrote it with a return address of Werley, Wisconsin, a small town west of Fennimore that served for many years as the post office for Mt. Hope and Mt. Ida. The Werley facility closed in 1930, after which mail transferred to Woodman, Wisconsin.

These small Wisconsin towns also embraced a unique feature of the transportation services of Grant County. All the major railroads in Wisconsin operated small, narrow gauge trains that carried passengers and freight from small towns to larger centers for transfer to regular gauge trains. One such train anchored at Fennimore. The locals affectionately called it the Dinky because of its toy-like appearance scooting along a track three feet wide. The Dinky ran daily between Werley, Livingston, and Woodman to Fennimore and other points along its path, meandering 16 miles through the Green River Valley. The Dinky was famous for a horseshoe curve that lifted it out of the valley and up the steep slope onto the ridge west of Fennimore. In its heyday, the Dinky had a reputation for its versatility, carrying farmers, business people, schoolchildren, and teachers, as well as the US mail and other freight. Unfortunately, for economic reasons, the railroad stopped operating the Dinky in 1926 and abandoned the Dinky narrow gauge tracks. The automobile rendered the convenience of narrow-gauge trains obsolete.[4]

Pauline continued to live in Grant County, keeping close family ties with the Jeidy family. Holidays often found them in the company of each other; they exchanged letters and pictures for many years after the death of Casey. Although Pauline was part of the Jeidy family for only a brief time, Charles and Ethel Belle Jeidy continued to think of her as their daughter and included her as part of the family, remembering her at special times like Christmas.[5] The Jeidys always included Pauline as a member of the Jeidy family.

After teaching at the Brick School at Bloomington, other teaching assignments followed. Altogether, Pauline taught eleven years in elementary schools, prelude to a long and distinguished career as an educator, a career built on life's lessons first learned in the small rural communities of Billings, Missouri, and Fennimore, Wisconsin.

By 1926, Pauline was at Prairie du Chien, Wisconsin, and a widow at age 30, working as a supervising teacher in the public schools of Crawford County.[6] She rented a place to live near the village of Gays Mills, nestled among the steeply chiseled bluffs of the Ocooch Mountains located in the heart of the region known as the Driftless Area of Southwest Wisconsin.[7] She had close friends in La Crosse, Wisconsin, and frequently availed herself of the town's hospitality and professional opportunities.[8]

Each year La Crosse hosted the West Central group of supervising teachers at the La Crosse Teachers College in a conference that honed her skills as a teacher supervisor. It was here that she first developed her unique approach to demonstration teaching and used school fairs, especially in rural schools as a tool of teaching.[9]

Notwithstanding her fondness for La Crosse, she soon made Prairie du Chien her new home. She took lodging with the August Herpel family at 608 South Church Street (present South Beaumont Road) in the second ward of Prairie du Chien, a very old Wisconsin city of 4,000 inhabitants, located near the confluence of the Wisconsin and Mississippi rivers. Pauline's apartment was on the Mississippi about a block east of the river.[10]

Crawford County endeared itself to Pauline. She came to the county alone, not knowing what to expect and left with a fondness for its land and people that remained with her throughout her life. She wrote eloquently about the county, its beauty, and its sometimes-forlorn past.

"In the wedge made by the junction of the mighty Mississippi and the turbulent Wisconsin and cut into halves by the lazy meandering Kickapoo lies old Crawford County, the laughing stock of the state of Wisconsin. The finger of derision is pointed at her by her sister counties on account of her poverty, for counties are judged as people are.

"Some of her inhabitants are so humiliated by her reputation for backwardness that when they travel out in the world and are asked where they are from, they blush and hesitatingly say, 'Why, I'm form the—ah, southwestern part of Wisconsin.' But Crawford does not mind; she is old and wise; she knows that even though they deny her they love her and would not trade their homes in Crawford for palaces in any other county."[11]

Crawford County was a place of rugged, jagged ridges, clear noisy little streams, and narrow, fertile valleys of creek bottoms where corn grew unsurpassed in quality. Crawford produced a little tobacco, said to be the best of its kind anywhere, including Kentucky. The valleys of Crawford County were warm and cozy where winter winds seldom blew and where birds lived all the year round,

Wyalusing State Park, situated on the bluffs across the Wisconsin River in the northwest corner of Grant County overlooks the panorama of hills and valleys that is Crawford County. The view overlooking the junction of the Mississippi and Wisconsin rivers is one of the remarkable scenes in the United States. Grant County proudly hosts thousands of people who come each year to stand on Point Lookout uplifted and inspired by the landscape before them, imprinted on their memories without knowing that the scene upon which they gaze is Crawford County.

Pauline turned Crawford County into a model of integrated education. Ever looking for opportunities to make a difference, she took the lead in reshaping the Crawford County Annual Fair and turned its entertainment purpose into an educational experience. There had been a fair for several years conducted by a private association. In 1928, the people of Crawford County themselves undertook its organization with wide approval. Putting into action her theory of community involvement in the teaching process, Pauline took charge of the educational department and had a pivotal role in the fair's success. Always looking for the teaching moment, each division of the fair had a student director making decisions under the watchful eye of an adult supervisor.[12]

In the summer of 1931, Pauline again traveled to La Crosse to the State Teachers College. However, she went this time as teacher and not student. Her reputation as an educator and innovator of teaching methods landed her in charge of a summer session course devoted to practical problems arising in rural and state grade schools, a topic she understood better than perhaps anyone going back to her own experiences as a student in Christian County, Missouri. One of the early features of her workshops, of which there would be many to follow, was a time for members of the class to present problems to the group for discussion, a classic technique of involvement and ownership of the learning experience. Her workshop sessions stressed the correlation of social studies with language, reading, and history particularly in the primary grades, which was another feature in her theory of integrated, democratized leaning.[13]

Meanwhile, Verda quit teaching and never finished her college degree beyond her two years of college for teacher preparation.[14] She was content to be a homemaker and helpmate to Oscar Brandemuehl. In 1931, on December 7, she gave birth to their second child, a son who they named David Andrew, namesake of Andrew Kastendieck, the grandfather he never knew.[15]

Oscar and Verda eventually acquired a sizeable farm of 187 acres in Section 23 of Mt. Ida Township.[16] The farmhouse sat two miles west of Fennimore and south of present US Route 18, about a half mile off the main highway on present Pine Road. Here on the farm, the Brandemuehls and Mollie Kastendieck lived out the rest of their lives.

STATE OF WISCONSIN

Second GRADE

Teacher's Certificate

OFFICE OF County Superintendent.

COUNTY OF IOWA

This Certifies That Pauline Kastendieck has satisfactorily fulfilled the requirements of the law for a 2nd Grade Certificate and is legally qualified to teach in the Public Schools of Iowa County, Wisconsin, for 3 years from the date of this Certificate, unless annulled.

The holder of this Certificate has attained the following standings in the branches required for this Certificate and the same are on record in the office of the County Superintendent:

THIRD GRADE				Additional for Second Grade		Additional for First Grade
Arithmetic	92	Manual of the Course of Study	85	Domestic Science or Manual Training	81	Elementary Algebra
Civil Government of the U.S. & Wisconsin	85	Penmanship	84	General Science	80	English Literature
Composition and Grammar	85	Physiology and Hygiene	80	American Literature	80	Modern History
Cataloging and Use of School Libraries	90	Reading	87			Theory and Art of Teaching
Elements of Agriculture and Rural Economics	88	School Management	80			
Geography	82	Spelling	88			
History of the United States and Wisconsin	90					

Given at Dodgeville, Iowa County, Wisconsin, this First day of Sept 1922

No. 40

Provisions governing the renewal of Certificates will be found in Sections 39, 18; 39, 19; and 39, 20.

COUNTY SUPERINTENDENT OF SCHOOLS

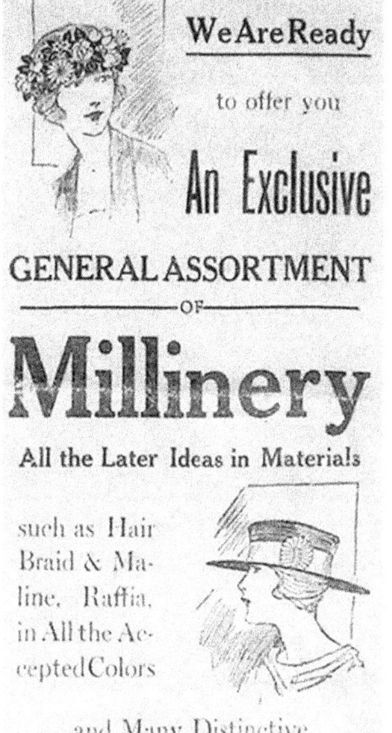

TEACHING CERTIFICATE. **Iowa County second-grade teaching certificate awarded to Pauline Kastendieck at Dodgeville, Wisconsin, September 1, 1922.**

MILLINERY ADVERTISEMENT. **Mollie Kastendieck and her daughter Pauline ran a millinery shop in Fennimore, Wisconsin, following the death of Andrew Kastendieck, in Missouri. Collection of Dee Willauer, great granddaughter of Mollie and Andrew Kastendieck.**

PAULINE KASTENDIECK.
Dubbed the "Hair Portrait"; this picture of a young Pauline dates to about 1918 at around the time the family left Billings, Missouri to live in Fennimore, Wisconsin.

VERDA KASTENDIECK.
The sister of Pauline Kastendieck sat for this portrait at about the time of her marriage to Oscar Brandemuehl in Grant County, Wisconsin. Verda taught school in Grant County.

COKER MINE NO. 1. **Cokerville mineworkers posed at one of several mines in the Grant County-Iowa County mining region near Livingston, Wisconsin. These men were representative of the area in which Pauline first taught school.** ***Lighty Photo, c. 1915; Library of Congress.***

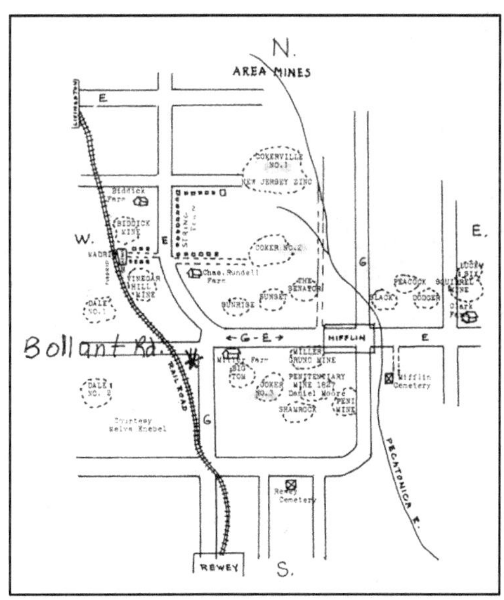

MAP OF COKERVILLE-MIFFLIN MINING DISTRICT. **An asterisk marks the location of the Brick School at Cokerville where Pauline Kastendieck taught second grade. Map not drawn to scale.** ***Courtesy of Melva Knebel and Cheryl D. Lemanski, University of Wisconsin-Platteville.***

COKERVILLE SCHOOL. **The first teaching job of Pauline Kastendieck was at the Cokerville School near Livingston, Wisconsin, where she taught second grade. The soiled overalls of a few of the boys come from playing on the mine pilings. Pauline is standing on the right.**

NORMAL TEACHER TRAINING SCHOOL. **Pauline appeared in this unidentified class photo probably taken in conjunction with Richland Center where Pauline trained and worked as a supervising teacher. She is in this photograph standing at the back, second from the left.**

18

Reflections on Nature

Pauline spent many hours on Point Lookout overlooking the Wisconsin River, gazing into the distant serenity of the Crawford County countryside. Fascinated by nature, Pauline was content, in her words, "to hold communion with her visible forms. By day there are the two great rivers which come together about three hundred feet below, and the prairie divided into little green, yellow, and brown fields spread like a patchwork quilt between the rivers and great dark blue ridges beyond with gray blue mists between them by night."[1]

Sometimes Pauline liked to sit there high above the river and imagine the people who lived in Crawford County long ago. She looked down at the Wisconsin River where Father Marquette's canoe, paddled by two stolid Indians, glided toward the Mississippi, thrilled with his discovery of the new broad river before him, only to sink with disappointment to find that it flowed south instead of west toward India.

In the distance, she could make out the town of Prairie du Chien about three miles up the Mississippi. At the edge of Prairie du Chien, she imagined Fort Crawford and envisioned a ball in progress, made pleasant by the presence of women whose manners and apparel would grace any court in Europe. It was a ball occurring amid the incongruity of the untamed wilderness populated by fur traders and Indians. Near the edge of Prairie du Chien, she imagined a mansion standing on a little knoll elevated above the city.

She could reconstruct in her mind the Indian mound that once graced the landscape, put there by ancient Native Americans who laboriously hauled soil on a crude raft from miles away to build it. The abandoned mound faded into the past as a sentinel of a lost culture, appropriated by a new culture that built a log palisade atop it to impound the French Fort McKay. A century of history punctuated by war lay dormant in the soil of Crawford County before the scene on the mound changed to one of ease and luxury. A coach and four horses drove up to the door of the mansion on the mound. Some women disembarked for tea.

The musings of Pauline on the history of Crawford County and the imagined lives of the people who lived there long ago always gave way to the pure awe of nature. Pauline wrote, "The sun, a great red orange ball, slowly, gently slid down behind the Iowa hills on the other side of the Mississippi, mists rose from the rivers, the patchwork pattern on the prairie faded, and the hills became darker. Soon the whole universe was blue like the hills, broken only by the stars like diamonds in a canopy of blue tulle, and the streetlights of Prairie du Chien like crystals on a blue velvet cushion. The wedge which is Crawford County could be made out only by means of the mists over the rivers like vapor rising from cold grape wine."[2]

The scenery alone was not what attracted white settlers to Crawford County. They first came for the furs and trade among the Indians. The whites pushed the Indians out, and the fur trade disappeared. Farmers sheared the ridges of trees and exhausted the land of its timber. As if Crawford County resented the loss of its forests, the rains washed away the soil and deposited it in the rivers. Someone made a gristmill on a broad powerful stream that flowed into the Mississippi and declared that the mill would begin one of the greatest cities in the United States. "The great river steamers will bring grain from the whole Mississippi Valley to be ground here, and our meal will be sold all over the world," predicted a settler. Such dreams became the machinations of folly. Drought reduced the powerful stream to a feeble little creek. In time, the mill became a faint groove in the meadow that was once the millrace. The old mill stone lay half buried in the sod.

Others came to Crawford County enticed by imagined riches that lay beneath the surface of the soil. Miners sank shafts in the hillsides and dug for gold and oil. The rich and powerful came, built great houses only to go broke, and abandon whatever failed enterprises seeded the Crawford County countryside. The old mansion on the mound became occupied by a professional guide who lured the touring public by means of glaring signboards and showed them Crawford County's remnant of old time aristocracy for fifty cents apiece.

Crawford County never achieved the status of its richer neighbors nor their storied reputations. Green County, Wisconsin, was Little Switzerland because its farmers raised cows and made cheese. Grant County called itself the California of Wisconsin because of its abundant harvests. No one ever called Crawford County Little Kentucky for its excellent tobacco. The county fell behind in its achievements beset by the intrusion of fickle seasons. A season of warm sun interspersed by refreshing showers one year became an onslaught of bad luck another year. Blights, killing frosts, and torrential rains that often seemed unique to Crawford County left farmers despondent and without means to raise a family. The lazy Kickapoo River became a giant of strength that pulled up the corn and tobacco in the valley, tore out the fences and bridges, hurled them into the Wisconsin River, and left nothing but a brown expanse of slippery, ugly mud and a lasting legacy of poverty.

For all of its shortcomings, Crawford County was home for Pauline for some of the most formative years of her education career. She took pride in the county, loved its people, and dedicated herself to the betterment of learning wherever there was a need in the rural schools that populated the countryside. Nevertheless, she acknowledged that progress was slow. Her career could well have ended in Crawford County without anyone ever knowing she was there. She once recalled, "When I was spending a summer away from [Crawford County] and was homesick and wanted a little news from her, I scanned the 'News from all around Wisconsin' column in the paper and only twice all summer was I rewarded with a word from Crawford County. One item stated that a murderer was suspected to be hiding in the wilds of the Kickapoo Valley, and the other that a woman in Copper Creek valley had found a rattlesnake in her kitchen floor."

Meanwhile, in the backwardness that defined Crawford County lay the oasis of Prairie du Chien. Steeped in history, Prairie du Chien dated to 1673 when French explorers first visited the area on their way up the Mississippi to Canada. Little more than a trading post, it passed to the British in 1763, following the French and Indian War. Largely dependent for many years on the fur trade, it incorporated as a city in 1872. Situated on a triangular plain, bounded by the Mississippi River on the east and the Wisconsin River to the south, a series of high bluffs ran east and northeast of the city. The plain ended toward the south where it melded into the wetlands of the Wisconsin River Delta. Backwaters of the Mississippi occasionally broke across the west side of the plain to form small islands. All in all a picturesque setting much different from the hills and valleys of the mining district at Cokerville and the patchwork of farms around Bloomington.

19

The Great Depression

Pauline's job as a supervising teacher took her to different schools in Crawford County, a job that required her to travel from school to school, sometimes in difficult situations. She recalled that she "climbed hills and waded through snow up to her waist to get to the schools."[1] She came to love the children of Crawford County dedicated in some small way to helping them rise above the circumstances of poverty that kept many of them from realizing their full potential. Pauline said, "I believed in her [Crawford County] and never flattered myself by thinking I was carrying the lamp of learning to her rural schools when I served them for five years as a supervising teacher. I only tried to turn up the wick a little in the lamp that already glowed there. She gave no 'medicine' to make me love her, but she tricked me, frightened me, and tried to baffle me and discourage me."

"She invited me with clear sky and bright sun to make a trip to the other end of the territory, only to send me back through terrific storms. She blocked my way with snow and forced me to drive along narrow ledges slippery with mud. She allowed me to drive my gasping Ford through deep mud to the top of a long hill only to find that I must skid down the next on a glare of ice. Sometimes when I became wary, she would lure me along for a few miles with a dry road and little specks of flying dust only to land me a little further along in a pool of bottomless mud. One day when weather and roads that were so nearly perfect that no one could be suspicious of anything, a weary looking little old man walked along the road whom I invited to ride with me only to find that he was a raving maniac.

"Sometimes it was impossible to drive at all, and I toured the county on foot. The way made weary with mud and snow, the road blocked with droves of pigs and cattle, and frightful with angry dogs, nevertheless Crawford County kept my soul at peace with its beauty. Whether dressed in varying shades of green for spring, red and orange and brown for autumn or in white and gray for winter, there was at every hilltop the temptation to stand too long and gaze."[2]

Through the perversity of geography, climate, and human nature, Pauline still believed in Crawford County, backward or not. She rationalized that in the county's long history, enough generations of people, both white and red, knew what was good for their souls to satisfy any doubting newcomer. Perhaps if the natives would only give back her lovely tees, Crawford County would remove the chains of privations from them and give as lavishly as she did in days of old.

Crawford County became a stop along the way for Pauline. During the summer, she added to her teaching credentials by taking summer graduate courses at the University of Wisconsin.

In October of 1929, the US stock market collapsed, plunging the nation and eventually the world into the Great Depression, adding new challenges and privations to places like Crawford County already teetering on the edge of distress. Job losses were catastrophic across the nation. Construction came to a stop, and crop prices from farming dropped 60 percent, aggravated by severe drought in the country's heartland. Mining wound down in southwest Wisconsin.[3] Unemployment shot up to 25 percent. Life in many parts of the country became a struggle for survival.

The Wisconsin State Legislature passed the first unemployment compensation law in the nation, an act that became a model for the rest of the country, and an act that brought much needed but insufficient aid to Wisconsin workers. The downturn in the national economy spread throughout Wisconsin with widespread economic devastation.

It was a perilous time for public education. With cash in short supply, parents were unable to meet even the basic expenses of clothes, supplies, and books to send their children to school. Taxes went unpaid, especially in rural communities, depriving schools of the necessary revenue to operate. School boards shortened school terms; teacher's salaries dropped to $40 per month for a five-month term, capping a teacher's income at $200 per year if a job existed at all.

Hard times descended on the smallest of enterprises. Mollie's old friend Lot wrote from Billings, "Did the depression reach you folks? It sure did us with eggs all summer selling at 7 and 8 cents, hogs at 2 ½ to 3 cents, chickens anywhere from 3 to 8 cents, cattle...well I heard one fellow sold a cow or rather shipped her and got $2.50 for her and it cost him $1.50 to get her to market." Lot revived old memories of Billings adding, "But 'taint no use to get strung up tight as a fiddle string. Might as well smile a bit and maybe sing. After all, the sun is rising most of the time and evening skies are glowing things of gold and red and life seems good after all is said, and that reminds me that we have had some marvelous sunsets and the stars have been a bit more glowing this winter and late fall than usual."[4]

Mollie missed Billings, and Billings missed Mollie. "Wish you were her tonight," wrote Lot. "We would roast peanuts make candy and talk and talk. Why not come back and see us all. Do and I'll fling a party and invite all our old cronies. Some have moved away but I believe the sight of you would induce any of them to return. Of course, Al Tippins is always here. He is a full-fledged lawyer now, but I never heard of him having but one case and he lost that."[5]

Meanwhile, Crawford County and Prairie du Chien were not exempt from hard times. If Pauline could not teach school, maybe she could go to school. Across the Mississippi River and down south a hundred miles was the State University of Iowa.

Wisconsin was not at the time known for the pursuit of higher education in its population. Prior to the Great Depression, fewer than eight percent of Wisconsin youth under the age of 24 went to college. Pauline had saved some money from teaching, paid off the $600 debt on the millinery debacle, and had no personal attachments. Now seemed like an opportune time to become an exception to Wisconsin statistics. Whatever the conditions and forces were that finally shaped Pauline's decision; she quit teaching fulltime and shortly thereafter, entered The State University of Iowa at Iowa City (present University of Iowa).[6] After years of working as a rural teacher supervisor, Pauline entered the University of Iowa to study for her degree in the fall of 1931 at the age of 32.

20

Back to School

After eleven years of teaching in the public schools, sometimes as an itenerate teacher working on provisional teaching certificates and often in difficult teaching environments, Pauline entered the State University of Iowa to obtain her degree. To no one's surprise, she proved to be an excellent student. She was older than the other students were when she entered the university, and far more mature than they were in both years and experience. Pauline was not a young student fresh out of high school but a mature young woman who dressed conservatively and did her hair in the closely styled waves popular with adult women of the time. Still very attractive, she nevertheless carried the aura not of an available young widow but of a confident professional educator. She looked like the educator everyone knew her to be.

Why Pauline chose to enroll at the State University of Iowa no one knows for sure. The decision apparently was more a matter of program choice than geography. Iowa City was a distance of about 100 miles from Fennimore, Wisconsin, while Madison, Wisconsin, site of another great university, was 65 miles across the state in the opposite direction from Fennimore.

It was about the same travel distance from her current teaching job at Prairie du Chien going to either the University of Iowa or the University of Wisconsin. She might have made a different choice had she known that the University of Wisconsin came into being at the behest of Wisconsin's first governor, Nelson Dewey, most likely a distant relative of the same New York Dewey roots as her late grandfather Austin Dewey whose birthplace was also New York.

Nevertheless, she chose the State University of Iowa, the first public university in the United States to admit students equally without regard to gender. It was an early signal from Pauline that issues affecting women would remain consistently at the top of her agenda during her entire life.

The University of Iowa had other qualities to recommend it. It established the first law school west of the Mississippi River and was the first to employ the new medium of television in education in 1932 while Pauline was a student there. The school also would have appealed to Pauline's creative interests as the first university to accept creative work on an equal basis with academic research. She most likely watched school officials lay the cornerstone of the Art Building in 1932. Her enrollment in the liberal arts college surely took her to the classes of Grant Wood, the celebrated American painter whose iconic painting, American Gothic, completed in 1930, ushered in a new Regionalist Art Movement, and helped land him a teaching position at the university.

The University of Iowa was home to an academic community unlike any other community experienced by Pauline before, far different from the rural public schools that were her contacts with education for almost a dozen years. Moreover, the Iowa campus dwarfed that of Springfield Normal School, in Missouri, where she first took college classes many years before, and the regional schools at Platteville Normal and LaCrosse Normal in Wisconsin where she obtained her Wisconsin teaching certificates.

The Pentacrest complex that anchored the center of the University of Iowa campus spoke eloquently to the belief that architecture should mirror the character of an institution. The Pentacrest was a cluster of five imposing structures that graced the bluff overlooking the Iowa River. At the center was the Old Capitol, its imposing facade visible from all quarters. Made of locally mined limestone, its distinctive gold dome rose above four Beaux-Arts Style buildings that flanked it symmetrically on four sides.

Less imposing but no less architecturally unique was the education building with its medieval-looking octagonal corners and Levantine style entryway. All of this no doubt made an impression on Pauline because it spoke of a kind of permanence and stability that offered reassurance in the troubled times of the Great Depression.

Upon entering the University of Iowa, Pauline discovered that the degree she wanted required a generous number of science courses. She was not a student of science, had never taken a science course, and did not look forward to it. She had two derogatory concepts of the subject. One, science, she felt, sought to kill the imagination, and secondly, science was a conceited and fickle knowledge, smugly confident that only that which science discovered was truth and all else was useless. Nevertheless, if she wanted a degree, it required taking science. She searched the catalog for what seemed to be the least formidable and potentially the least irksome. She settled on zoology. She said, "I secretly schemed not to take the course too seriously for fear that too much knowledge of animals would kill my love for them."[1]

Zoology opened her eyes to science. The course was in two parts: lecture and lab. The lecture affirmed many of her ideas about the circumstances of life. All life has its vicissitudes. She discovered, too, that the foregoers of science included some of the same superstitions that she had heard growing up in the rural environment of Christian County, Missouri. The desire to learn through science began with an inquisitiveness sometimes fed by magic. Why did tasks begun in the dark of the moon succeed, for example, while those in the light of the moon failed? To the precursors of science, the hoot of an owl, the swish of a bat's wing, or the wail of a wolf at midnight were omens of misfortune or death. However, a spider's web across the mouth of a cave, sunshine on the face when waking in the morning, or a rabbit's leap to the right meant success and plenty.

Science, the instructor said, was a desire by humankind to shed light on the traditions of life that anchored the knowledge of being in magic and superstition. A light came on for Pauline. She understood for the first time that her opinion about learning lay somewhere between science and tradition, in a perpetual war between the two. Of her first science lecture, she wrote, "I was spellbound with this story of knowledge and was impatient for the next science period when I could hear some more about it."[2]

Pauline soon learned that zoology incorporated more than stories about life. The second part of the course took place in the lab where examination of the physical side of life occurred. The professor gave her a grasshopper and instructed her to draw it four times larger than life size. After two hours of painstaking, tedious, nerve racking, eye straining measurement, she proudly presented her drawing to the instructor who upon a casual glance at it grudgingly proclaimed it "pretty good."[3]

One lab assignment that was particularly egregious for Pauline recalled a time growing up on the farm where around the pond sat those green-backed, popeyed, smiling frogs that were her playmates as she took her turn herding the cows. Zoology inevitably called for dissection. When the instructor handed Pauline a living but unconscious frog, it was a low point in her study of science. "I have always loathed a vulture," she said, "but science made a vulture of me." When she cut into the frog and watched its sturdy little heart beat its last few beats, the aspect became even more horrible. One night after class, she heard the singing of frogs and stopped a moment to listen, but only for a moment because the vision of the little frog in the lab came to her mind. She hurried on down the street, relieved by the blare of a radio. [4]

Thus, it went all year. The lecture hours invited Pauline's imagination to wander over the world, catching glimpses of the evolution of life and the consequences of scientific discovery. On the other hand, labs were another story. She usually left class feeling sad, morose, hopeless, and dull. In the lab, she did not dare to imagine or think, to only see, and do. Tiny creatures became objects not of how they lived and what they did but only about their construction. She summed up her passion for the humanities compared to laboratory science when she wrote, "Those periods were long hours of headaches, impatience, despair, and bursts of temper. Sometimes I wanted to dash the microscope on the floor and rush out into the fresh air." She took exception to the instructor's claim that science classes were the only classes that prepared a student for the world because they gave both information and practical work in the laboratory. Pauline fidgeted in her seat but kept silent.[5]

The science requirement for her degree had a reflective influence on Pauline. She came to see her experience as more than a preparation for life. It was a small copy of life itself. In what was likely a reflection on her life experiences at Billings,

Missouri, when the burden of great personal loss clouded her future, she wrote, "The lecture hours represent those parts of life when we are conscious of the present only by a glorious sense of wellbeing. We can look back over our past and smile at our failures as well as our successes. We can hope, plan, and know that somehow all will be well. The laboratory represents those times when life bows us down, humiliates us, chastens us—when the present fills us with dread and hopelessness. All the pleasures of the past are wiped out and we dare not think of the future." While her instructor and his science colleagues might take exception to her opinion, Pauline characteristically summarized the core of her beliefs that sustained her in her lifelong pursuit of learning.[6]

Life for Pauline living in a college dormitory presented another side to her many-sided perspective on human nature, the aspect of caring about others. As one of the more mature students at the university, she became used to a gentle, friendly, inquiring rap at her door. She casually laid aside her book and called, "Come in." A few minutes of counseling usually stretched into an hour or more of talking and fellowship. "It's such fun to come to see you," one young visitor said, "for you always seem so glad to see everybody."[7]

21

Cats

The sum of Pauline's education so far taught her to connect knowledge to experience. As she listened to a lecture on psychology at the university, her mind drifted back to her childhood on the farm at Billings and to the animals that were her companions. The professor informed the class that there were three levels of response. First, a single action to a single stimulus such as jerking the hand away from a hot stove; secondly, a more complex response like running away from danger; and the third level being the kind of response that requires thinking or reasoning, of which humans are the only animals with such capability, he said.

"Cats not think," thought Pauline? "Impossible!"

She remembered Ebony Tom, how Mr. Jackson took him away for his pet, how he ran away, and how she always imagined that their search for each other was one of the instinctive qualities of love.

She populated her childhood growing up on the farm with as many as 15 cats at one time, including a big black cat name Snowball, all gathered at dinnertime in the milk barn to be welcomed by Pauline, and affectionately appraised for their unique contributions to her cat entourage.

John was a great snow-white cat with round, unfathomable green eyes that alternately expressed hate, rage, sullenness, delight, or interest according to the many moods that make up cat life. He grew up a farm cat. When Pauline's father died and the family moved to Billings, they took John with them to live in town, first to a temporary lodging on the outskirts of Billings and then to more permanent housing across town.

John had a great deal of dignity. He never begged. He had a mind of his own. If he wanted to go into or out of the house, he sat quietly near the door until someone took note of his position and opened the door for him. If he were in a particular hurry, he stood erect and made the greatest effort to do what he saw people do to the doorknob that caused the door to open. He never asked for food. He never needed to because he did not depend on humans alone.[1]

Notwithstanding his waywardness—John was familiar with several households and visited a great deal—he was a contented and home-loving cat. When the family moved from the farm to the house in Billings, despite all neighborly manner of advice, warnings, superstitions, and derisions, they brought John with them. He resented the whole performance very much. In spite of all ample effort to make the new house attractive to him, he insisted on going back to the old house. Finding no one there, he took forlorn refuge under the porch. There Pauline found him day after day crouched in a dark corner, silent and sorrowful with his eyes like two balls of fire turned toward the hole in the wall where Pauline's face appeared. It took an endless amount of time, tact, and careful maneuvering to get him out. Lying on her stomach, trying to keep her voice sweet and pleasing, and her persuasive vocabulary exhausted, John sometimes tried her patience to the extreme. Eventually, his feline face finally appeared at the hole peering fearfully out as if he had never seen the light of day. Pauline well knew that if she gave way to her impatience she would have all her trying efforts to repeat, and probably would have to double them before she could get her hands on him again.

Pauline carried John across town so many times that people considered it commonplace. At first surprised and amused, they called their neighbors to see the big white cat riding in state in the arms of a half grown girl and viewing the world with the concealed interest of an aristocrat. After multiple trips, onlookers ceased to exclaim and gave the duo only a careless nod as they passed by.

It looked like John would never be content with his new home. Then one night a terrible storm came. The rain fell in torrents and jagged streaks of vivid lightning shot across the black sky followed by terrific booms and rumbling of deafening thunder. Between two great blasts of thunder, there came a most pitiful and terrified "mew" at the door. Pauline got up, ran to open the door, and in leaped John, drenched and terror-stricken. Everyone arose to welcome him home and to watch his exuberant expressions of delight at being safe at home in the midst of his family. He made the rounds of the family time after time, arching his back and rubbing against them, pausing occasionally to roll on the floor and all the while uttering purrs and meows of pleasure. Before that stormy night, he had always been John. After seeing him so humbled, so wholly bereft of his usual dignity, everyone with one accord without so planning began to call him Johnnie. Thus, it is that both cats and people often change their names in like manner.

On cold winter mornings after he had breakfasted and washed, Johnnie liked to sit on the window seat and watch the children go past on their way to school. One morning he grew very annoyed to find that a thick coat of white frost completely shut off his view. Pauline described what he did next. "Not knowing how to meet the situation, he did what anybody would have done under the circumstances; he walked the floor and thought it out. He heard a childish shout outside and knew he was missing something. His pace quickened, his ears turned back, and he gave the window a look of helpless rage. Suddenly, he thought of a plan. He raised a paw with claws extended and scratched the window, applied an eye to the scratch, and saw a tiny opening! Thus encouraged, he sat upon his haunches and worked desperately with both claws until he had cleared a place about the size of his face. He sat down to enjoy his self-earned portal with the enthusiasm of a sports fan at a game. His eyes glowed as he leaned far forward in order not to miss anything on either side. Occasionally when some daring child dashed across the street, he would rise to a half-standing position until the child safely reached the other side, whereupon he would settle down with a breath of relief."[2]

On pleasant summer days if John was not sleeping off the effects of the night before or not too much occupied with his own thoughts, he used to like to go down town with Pauline. The trips for Pauline ran the gamut from great pride of ownership to deep humiliation. On the way, Johnnie would trot quietly beside her or sometimes trot ahead on little tours of investigation, wary of his surroundings, his ears tipped forward and his tail sticking straight up. People they met along the way would say, "What a fine cat you have." When they reached Main Street where there were people and noise, Johnnie was like a different cat. He would skulk along near the buildings with his body near the ground, occasionally stretching himself to full height to stare fearfully in every direction. Then if people noticed him at all, it was only to laugh and say, "For heaven's sake, look at that cat!" As soon as they were out of the range of noise on the way home, he was himself again. When Pauline scolded him for his unseemly conduct down town, he would arch his back and rub against her, then dash into a lawn to crouch and pounce upon a harmless leaf that happened to move slightly in the breeze, which was his distracting way of saying, "Sorry I annoyed you. Now, let's just forget about it".

Pauline had a unique ability to draw convincing comparisons between animal and human behavior, and a singular gift to describe the links in writing. She wrote, "Cat and human natures are hard to understand. I never could see how the same two people could be the best of friends one day and the worst of enemies the next. Johnnie and a friend of his were like that. He had a good cat companion by the name of Mikey who lived at the photographer's house on the other side of the block. Johnnie and Mikey would eat from the same dish, sleep with the paws of one around the neck of the other, and sometimes gambol around like a couple of frolicsome kittens. Then again they would face each other with ears plastered close to their heads, back arched, tails switching angrily, eyes gleaming with hate and rage, and holding one paw up with all claws extended, ready to split each other's faces the moment their cat cursing vocabularies were exhausted."[3]

One of Johnnie's favorite diversions through the long summer nights was rat hunting. He never ate them, but always brought them home. It was common to find a big dead rat on the doorstep for two or three mornings in succession. At first, everyone praised him for his trophies. Nevertheless, they felt it proper to destroy the remains of his victims. He soon grew tired of having his property destroyed and ceased to show his catches. They thought he had abandoned his preoccupation with rats, until one day by means of olfactory organs they found a pile of his trophies in the woodshed. Pauline called him in and told him kindly but firmly that he could not keep them there, because not only she, but also the rest of the family and even the neighbors objected to the smell. He sniffed them over as much as to say he could not smell anything wrong with them. He watched Pauline bury them in the garden and stalked sullenly to the house without waiting for her. Pauline thought of all the satisfaction she had denied him. He could have taken groups of his feline friends to the woodshed, pawed over the rats, selected an unusually large one, and said, "Look at that baby. He sure gave me a chase. All the Toms in town had been trying for nights to get him, but I made up my mind he wouldn't get away from me—and when I make up my mind..." They saw no more rats for a week or more, but soon the same old smell wafted through the summer air. Pauline assured the neighbors it could not be coming from their place because she had buried the rats. Nevertheless, when no one was looking she searched diligently but found nothing. One day a neighbor from across the street called out, "I've discovered the source of the smell." Pauline's heart missed a few beats and she had a sickish feeling in the pit of her stomach. She managed to smile and offered a half-hearted "Good for you. Where is it?" The woman pointed to the roof of their house and there, near the eaves, was an ostentatious pile of dead rats!

Pauline remembered many human traits that she attributed to Johnnie, some admittedly imprinted by her imagination but others undeniably real. To amuse colleagues about her ideas on the congruence of human and animal behavior, she seemed always to return to the proof she saw in cats while growing up on the farm at Billings. For example, there was Old Benjamin, a big, yellow, lazy barn cat who went about in a state of annoyance at the kittens in the barn, especially when they amused themselves by playing with his tail. At first, he would switch a warning, but when they failed to heed it and only increased their rowdy and tantalizing frolic, he would turn, and, with all claws extended in one great paw, knock a kitten down with such force that it would land on its back with feet waving wildly in the air. One blow was enough to send them all scrambling to a safety zone to smooth down their rumpled fur and to think up something new to do. Pauline thought he was just a cross, mean old cat with no redeeming characteristic until a group of kittens became orphans by an accident, and Benjamin was the one who undertook their support. He would go out hunting and bring back a gopher or a mole and drop it among them, then stride away and sit down with his back to them, as much as to say, "Now, eat that. And keep still about where you got it."[4]

Then there was Spotty, a neat graceful self-reliant young mother cat, whose only kitten ventured forth on his shaky little legs, fell into the cistern, and drowned. Spotty could see him below, out of reach, but she knew that no amount of wailing of self-indulgences would make the little gray ghost real again. After sitting and somberly staring at it for a few days, she went out into the fields and found herself a baby rabbit to cuddle and wash and purr to and so eased her broken heart.

There were many lessons for Pauline in her interaction with nature but none more lasting than the memories of her cats. She genuinely believed that animals within the limitations of their existence could think and act in profoundly human ways. She once said, "It is probably true that of all the cats in the world many have to live by means of their physical agility alone. There are only a few who are intelligent, self-reliant, and well mannered—only a few who are able to manage themselves in such a way as to live honorably and easily without either toil or cunning, but—well, what of most of us?".[5]

PORTRAIT OF PAULINE JEIDY. **Pauline sat for this portrait at about the same time she started taking classes at the University of Iowa. Taken at the Brintnall Studio, the picture dates to about 1930 when she was about age thirty-two. William Brintnall had studios in Lancaster and Fennimore, Wisconsin.**

STATE UNIVERSITY OF IOWA. **The campus in two views as it appeared when Pauline attended as a student. Top, the Iowa Avenue Bridge looking east from the west side of the Iowa River toward the campus. Bottom, Iowa River Walk in winter viewed looking north.** ***Frederick Wallace Kent Collection, c. 1930. University of Iowa.***

Verda, Mollie, and Pauline Kastendieck. When Andrew Kastendieck died in 1912, Mollie and her two daughters left the family farm near Billings, Missouri, to move to Fennimore, Wisconsin. Mollie lived with Verda on the Brandemuehl farm near Fennimore.

Episodes of Change

22

Word Theory

Credited with two years of course work at Springfield Normal and summer courses taken at La Crosse and the University of Wisconsin, Pauline graduated from the University of Iowa in two years on January 31, 1933, with a Bachelor of Science Degree in School Supervision.[1] With degree in hand but without a job, she returned to Richland Center, Wisconsin, in the summer to contemplate her next move.[2]

Much of the breadth of Pauline's sensitivity to how children learn came from experience. She harbored a lingering desire for the arts and seldom missed a chance to participate whenever the opportunity arose. One time, during winter break from college, she joined a group of friends from Richland Normal and convinced them to enroll in the Fourth Annual Richland County Drama Tournament.[3] She assumed the role of both actor and coach. The group performed "The Flattering Word," the George Kelly story about the adventures of an actor on tour, resting upon the intriguing theme that you can cure a person of his prejudice against actors by extending him the flattery of comparing him to an actor. We do not know where Pauline's group placed in the tournament. However, it may be said with certainty that winning was not important. She valued most in people the qualities of expression, camaraderie, and the way they played the game.

She was approaching her 35th birthday when she graduated from Iowa. Nevertheless, her thirst for education was not yet satisfied. The Graduate College at Iowa accepted her for graduate study.

A professor in the English Department of one of Pauline's classes at Iowa made an assignment one day requiring the writing of a paper that would give an analysis of a certain character in literature. The professor, dissatisfied with the efforts of the class, said, among other things, that those who had to wear a dunce cap in school because they could not grasp traits of character from literature often had to wear a dunce cap all through life, adding pejoratively that they could not hold their own among real people.

Notwithstanding the obvious conceit of the professor's remarks, Pauline wondered: if concepts of character are difficult for university students to grasp from literature, they must be even more so for intermediate grade children. She knew that in reading we understand a word in proportion to our experiences with the object or idea that the word stands for. It occurred to her that perhaps the same was true of our understanding of people. We understand them in proportion to our experiences with them. Just as one can scan the pages of a book without being aware of the meanings implied by the words thereon, one can encounter people without being sensitive to the meanings back of their behavior. This becomes particularly noticeable in textbooks and courses of study where writers seem to consider the concept of character an easy one to grasp because they regularly embed lessons in biographical sketches. Pauline had the idea that the difficulties in understanding characters arose chiefly from students confronted by too many characters presented too briefly. She echoed the opinions of a handful of other educators who complained, "There are too many historical characters...Textbook writers apparently construct their books on the principle that the way to make a thing particularly elementary is not to say much about it. If the story is inherently simple, like the story of the Pilgrims and the settlement of Plymouth, it seems to be safe to devote three or four pages to it, and even to descend to details. If it is especially difficult, on the other hand, writers apparently must simplify it to a paragraph."

Pauline singled out another difficulty in the selection of characters for intermediate grade children to study. Children might learn more about the past, she reasoned, by studying a representative of the masses rather than studying the lives of kings and queens. Great men are no doubt in a sense representative. However, many who figure in school history books as representative are thoroughly unrepresentative.

Even if conditions meet basic circumstances of learning; that is, children are sensitive to the people about them to the extent that they have a fair understanding of human nature. Secondly, characters within their powers of comprehension appear in historical materiel with an abundance of details for visualization, there still stands between the mind of the reader and that of the author the printed words; symbols of meaning that frequently evade understanding.

Pauline told of an experience she had that suggested even teachers find it difficult to see accurately through these symbols. During an oral class exercise for a class of experienced rural teachers, a question about the identity of the United States foreign minister to Japan produced a range of answers from a Presbyterian clergyman to Catholic priest, and so on according to religious prejudice, not understanding that foreign minister was a political title. While intelligence obviously plays a role, ideas that are vague or altogether wrong make it even more difficult for children to understand them.

To this end, Pauline devised a study to investigate the ability of intermediate grade children to understand the symbols used to describe people of the past. Her purpose was to determine the extent to which pupils in the sixth grade understood words and phrases used in a history textbook to describe people.[4]

She applied a series of tests she constructed from extensively gleaning words and phrases from history texts broadly in use in Wisconsin. In a unique research model, she created three sets of descriptive terms: a list of 89 adjectives, 117 nouns, and 63 biographically descriptive phrases. These she arranged in a series of matching choices from which students picked the correct word that meant the same as the word used in a phrase to describe someone. The student participants were the thirty students of Miss Bertha Hogeseth sixth grade class at Richland Center, Wisconsin.

The investigation had the usual anecdotal sidebars of academic research. Children urged not to guess, guessed anyway. Those of the lower levels of achievement paid little heed. Pauline invited students who showed progress from test to test to comment if they knew how they had learned the meanings of words. The comments were not altogether encouraging from a teacher's perspective. "I don't know how I learned them," said one student. "I didn't know I had learned them. I like history and I worked hard on it." Another student concluded, "Well, it seems like when you see a word in a sentence, like in a book, the sentence shows you more than just the word by itself. And then once you learn a word, why you just know it." Logic had its adherents, too. "Well, when you see a word in a sentence you know just about what you want—anyway you know it can't be some of the others." When asked about his performance, a sixth grader responded, "I like to read and I read a great deal. I read every night. I don't know whether or not that helped my standing. I don't see how it could." When asked if he ever looked in the dictionary for meanings of words, he said, "Well, yea, I do once in a while if it is a rather short word and I think I shall have some use for it,"[5]

Despite a range of responses, Pauline was able to conclude from her study a number of findings, principally that children are not uniformly good test-takers. Nevertheless, she showed that meaning of a given term is heavily dependent upon the setting in which that term is used. Moreover, children do not understand a term as well as the teacher usually thinks they do. A Child may use words glibly with only a vague notion of their meaning and in a test may indicate as known that which she/he actually does not know.

One finding carried a clear message to textbook writers. The attempted method of simplifying the content of a textbook by rewriting the material in a vocabulary of narrow range does not significantly change the children's comprehension of it. Textbook writers should be careful, too, Pauline cautioned, that topics match the target grade level intended. Based on the references that she used in her study, Pauline discovered that advanced students performing at eighth grade level did much better on tests than students at the sixth grade.

The study formed the core of Pauline's graduate thesis, column after column of tabulated data manually typed in a 308-page tome that analyzed her work.

Taking courses off and on when she could, she finished the course of study at Iowa three and a half years after she entered graduate study and received her Master of Arts Degree in Education, with a minor in English, on August 20, 1936.[6] The subject of her master's thesis carried the title "A study of the ability of sixth-grade children to comprehend biographically descriptive words and phrases in historical content," a professorial-sounding title whose underlying content portended things to come.[7] It was the first of many publications to follow on the art of teaching, and a worthy introduction of a soon-to-be prolific writer and respected professional in the education community.

23

West Coast Journey

After graduating from the University of Iowa, Pauline took a job in Richland County, Wisconsin, one county over from Grant County, and about 30 miles east of Fennimore. Set amid the Ocooch Mountains, Richland County occupied a large section of the Wisconsin Driftless Region, a place name given to an unglaciated terrain of high hills, bluffs, and ridges. She lived in Richland Center, the county seat of Richland County. When Pauline first arrived there around 1935, it was a town of about 4,000 inhabitants.[1] There was a Wisconsin Normal school at Richland Center.

Richland Center had been her hub of operations when not engaged in taking classes at the University of Iowa. Pauline, like many teachers, used the three-month summer hiatus of the academic year to reconnect with family members in Grant County and to take time to add to her education skills. Over the course of her early career, she often enrolled in local colleges and the University of Wisconsin to take classes that improved her teaching knowledge.

The summer months were always a welcome break from the routine of the classroom. The long tradition of dismissing school to allow students to stay home and help with summer harvest continued unimpeded after the national organization of public schools, despite the changing picture of agricultural and workplace demands for young workers. Someone once asked a teacher what she liked best about teaching, to which she replied, "June, July, and August," the three summer months that schools traditionally were on vacation.

The town of Richland Center lay in a valley carved from the surrounding hills and bluffs by the Pine River. A scattering of shade trees accented its prairie setting that melded into groves of good timber. Built as an agricultural support community, Richland Center catered to the abundant timber mills that once drove the early economic development of the area. One of its celebrated citizens was the architect Frank Lloyd Wright, born in Richland Center in 1867.

We do not know exactly what Pauline did at Richland Center. Her education specialty was school supervision, but we know only that when she graduated from the University of Iowa in 1936, she lived at Richland Center, perhaps traveling Richland County to various schools as she had done at her previous job at Prairie du Chien, in Crawford County. Her name appeared in the 1936 *Fairman's Handbook* as one of the licensed Judges of Education from Richland Center, under the auspices of the Wisconsin Department of Agriculture and Markets.[2] Fair officials noted marked improvement in both attendance figures and cash income from the 1936 Wisconsin fairs over the previous year. They pronounced 1935 as the best fair year since 1930.

Nevertheless, it is unlikely that the Wisconsin fair circuit accounted for Pauline's livelihood fresh out of graduate school as an experienced educator. It is likely instead that she worked in some capacity at the Richland Center Normal school continuing her work in teacher preparation and supervision. County Normal schools offered post-secondary preparation for prospective teachers and taught the basic requirements to become a successful teacher.

The tradition of higher education in Richland County had deep roots. The first college of post-secondary education came to Richland Center in 1903. From a Normal School, it progressed to a Teachers College before going through various changes to become part of the University of Wisconsin System. It was a good step up the ladder for Pauline in gathering experience for future career opportunities.

After a brief time at the Normal School, fresh out of graduate school, and with good work experience behind her, Pauline decided to pursue her career elsewhere. She left Wisconsin for the West Coast in the fall of 1936, settling in Polk County, Oregon, to take a position at the Oregon College of Education at Monmouth, known locally as Monmouth College.[3] Monmouth was a teacher preparation college located 11 miles west of Salem, in the Willamette Valley of northwest Oregon. Pauline made a salary of $1,575 a year for the school year of 36 weeks, working a 40-hour workweek. It was a modest salary for someone of her qualifications. The median salary nationwide for elementary educators and teachers in 1938 was around $2,200 a year in the larger cities, a healthy improvement over the years of the Great Depression but low compared to the economic recovery of other occupations. Oregon, at the time, was among the lower paying states in the nation, paying an urban elementary teacher, for example, approximately $2,000 a year. Superintendents and principals—almost exclusively male—received three to four times the salary of a teacher. The school janitor was on a pay scale roughly equal to that of an elementary school teacher.[4]

Monmouth College began as a State Normal School around the turn of the century and progressed to a training facility for teachers—primarily for women, before becoming the Oregon College of Education in 1939 (present Western Oregon University). The Monmouth Training School of Pauline's era operated rural training centers in towns near Monmouth, where prospective teachers received classroom experience in schools under the direction of Training School faculty. The rural program was a model for other Oregon teacher training institutions.

Pauline's assignment as primary supervisor of teaching at the Rickreall training school began in September 1936, as a replacement for the supervisor who had resigned earlier in the year.[5] Teacher training schools like Rickreall followed the national model. Children bused in from rural neighborhoods became workshop subjects taught by student teachers under the supervision of faculty from nearby Normal schools. Practicing student teachers came to Rickreall from Monmouth College usually for a period of three months as part of final preparation before entering the teaching profession.[6]

At Rickreall, there were two supervisors, two bus drivers, and a janitor.[7] Pauline held a faculty position at Monmouth College as a supervising teacher while serving as the person responsible for student teachers in the primary grades at Rickreall. In her role as a "critic", Pauline was a member of the training school faculty that guided future teachers. Her duties were those of an education supervisor, although official forms often entered the cryptic occupation of "critic".

Pauline lived near the small town of Rickreall about five miles north of Monmouth on present Highway 99, and near the elementary school that served Monmouth College. Pauline found Oregon to be a different terrain from what she knew in

Wisconsin. The Willamette Valley was a broad region surrounded by mountain ranges to the east, west, and south. The flat fertile valley had a reputation for its agricultural production. Pauline settled into her duties and made herself useful in the community.

Rickreall was in some respects an itinerant community. There was no cadre of teachers, for example, that often forms a core of community-minded activists, because student teachers rotated out every three months.

Pauline took charge. She became the president of the local Community Club, a group of residents that met at the grade school building to plan improvements and devise entertainments to raise funds to pay for projects. The group thought there should be tennis courts in Rickreall and set about the task to get one built[8]. Plays in which Pauline usually appeared were mainstays of fundraising events. Her name was a frequent entry in the society pages of the press as someone associated with this or that community project.[9] Each year Monmouth College renewed her contract as primary grades supervisor, and each year the Community Club re-elected her president.

In November 1938, Pauline represented the Community Club that met with three other club representatives in the Rickreall Grange Hall as a four-person committee to plan the first Rickreall Christmas Pageant, "because the community lacked Christmas spirit."[10] Within a month, the project took form. The first pageant was in the Rickreall Grade School auditorium (later Rickreall Event Hall). The *Capital Journal* at Salem, Oregon, took note of its success. "An all-time record attendance was made here Friday night when approximately 450 persons from all parts of the county and state assembled for a Christmas pageant for which Rickreall's five organizations joined forces. A special lighting system was installed for the evening. Nearly 75 persons [made up entirely of community residents] participated in the program which included a candlelight processional by a vested choir of 30 voices." The article listed the principal cast that included Pauline Jeidy, "Angel of the Lord," a role she reprised in homage to her religious foundation first laid down in Christian County, Missouri.[11]

The Rickreall Christmas Pageant occurred every year, except for a couple of years during World War II.[12] Pauline was its first general manager. The pageant she helped to establish ended in 2015 after 75 years of yearly presentations of the biblical Christian story.[13]

Pauline followed the teachings of the Methodist Church in her religion, continuing three generations of a family that believed that people realized the lessons of Christianity through example and not by wearing ones religion on ones sleeve. She attended church regularly. Sunday mornings usually found her in Sunday school the same as it had for more than thirty years when her parents first instilled in her the value of Christian ways. She taught Sunday school if invited and delighted in serving wherever her journey took her.

At the University of Iowa, for example, the only organization to attract her attention was the Kappa Phi national Christian sisterhood. The organization began as a women's Sunday school class in a Methodist Church in Lawrence, Kansas, in 1915 and came to the University of Iowa in 1917 as an interdenominational Christian organization open to any university woman interested in its purpose.[14]

She did not often speak about religion because she did not have to do so. Anyone who knew her knew that within her flowed a wide river of religious faith. She shared generously of her time and money and regularly sent a portion of her paycheck home to Fennimore to help with family living expenses.

24

Being Pauline

In the spring of 1940, the census taker found Pauline living alone in a $15 a month rented house outside Rickreall. The census listed her as Pauline K. Jeidy, the K for Kastendieck. It was an assumed identity because Pauline had no middle name, at least not that she revealed. Parents sometimes gave middle names to their children that kids did not enthusiastically embrace, to the point that children growing up changed their names or insisted on different names. Her sister Verda's middle name, for example, was Evadna, a name one might exchange without her parents' fondness for Greek middle names. For the duration of her life, Pauline was Pauline K. Jeidy.

Rickreall became a popular destination for the people of Polk County, Oregon. People came for its excellent training school, the town's entertainments, and its continuous schedule of community events. The town grew accordingly.[1] The number of supervising teachers at the primary school rose from two to six, and included a six-week summer workshop session. Meanwhile, the highway commission planned to install an overhead beacon light at the intersection, one-step away from a stoplight; nevertheless, a sure sign of community growth.[2]

Rickreall fundraisers continued thanks to Pauline's tireless participation. She played Mrs. Lennox in "Good Gracious Grandma," hosted dinners at the Monmouth Hotel, and opened her home to guests when the need arose for a meeting place.[3]

Each year school shut down in June with a picnic in the grove, which closed school activities until fall.[4] Summer was a time to enjoy a change of pace from the day-to-day work of teacher supervision and community meetings. The Oregon College of Education at Monmouth asked Pauline to teach at the college. She was gaining statewide attention, easing up the career ladder. She drove from her home at Rickreall each day. School officials soon thereafter appointed her as delegate to the Oregon State Teachers Association and made her principal at Rickreall.[5]

At Rickreall, Pauline formalized her technique for motivating people to achieve their most creative ideas. Her organizational stratagem was a simple one: engage as many helpers as possible and give responsible groups focused responsibilities. For example, as many as 75 members of the Rickreall community engaged in planning the Christmas Pageant[6]. Each committee had a specific purpose that fit within the plan. Each year, the press hailed it as another success. "Scenes were well portrayed, each character taking their several parts in a most impressive manner."[7]

By 1940, the Community Club had $206.78 in the tennis courts fund, ready to take on a new project to put a new ceiling in the high school gymnasium. The club would stage a play to start funds for the work.[8] The club members unanimously elected Pauline president, again. They celebrated with a dinner party at her house. After dinner, they drove over to Dallas, Oregon, for a show.[9]

Three things happened about this time that underscored Pauline's scholarly presence and changed the trajectory of her career. Her colleagues recognized her as a leading educator; second, she began to wear eyeglasses, the inescapable symbol of professorial manifestation; and third, Monmouth College discontinued the teacher-training program at Rickreall.

One of the most prestigious organizations among educators was Delta Kappa Gamma Society, a professional honorary society of women educators.[10] Membership in Delta Kappa Gamma was by invitation only and considered an honor. Founded in Texas in 1929, the Society was 12 years old when the national executive secretary initiated Pauline into its membership. She may have joined the organization with a cautious outlook. A relatively small club, considering the number of women teachers at the time, Delta Kappa Gamma had a reputation of cronyism among its membership. Women teachers nominated women teachers based on "somebody knew somebody who knew somebody..." as much as on professional merit. The organization took on the aura more of a Greek sorority than a professional society, complete with a red rose symbol and heraldic crest. So much so, that an advisory appeared in the society's newsletter from time to time denying any identity with a Greek organization. Delta Kappa Gamma styled itself as an empowerment of women with a focus on promotion of excellence in education built on a professional foundation in a time when women were not encouraged to organize in any way other than a social manner. Collective association of professional women of like mind and circumstances offered much needed support in a man's world where the aspect of cronyism in education had its zenith. The best jobs in education went to men.

Pauline's initiation into the society took place at Portland, Oregon, to recognize a select few of Monmouth College women faculty. It marked the beginning of Oregon's first Delta Kappa

Gamma chapter of women invited to wear the fraternity's key in recognition of leadership in the teaching profession.[11] Pauline overlooked whatever shortcomings Delta Kappa Gamma harbored and embraced its charter: to join in united efforts toward better professional preparation of educators, to promote legislation to improve education, and to contribute to the Delta Kappa Gamma scholarship program that enabled many needy young women to attend college.

Pauline's physical appearance changed when she began to wear eyeglasses around 1941 at about age 42 when natural physiological adjustment in the eye causes many people to adopt vision correction measures, some reluctantly. Pauline, however, embraced the change, which gave her a decidedly more professional appearance. She was thereafter never without glasses.[12] Eyeglasses ran in the family. Verda wore glasses her entire life starting at an early age. In later life, Mollie likewise required corrective measures to read the many publications and letters that she so much enjoyed.

Delta Kappa Gamma notwithstanding, there was no stronger sisterhood than Pauline and Verda. They shared many private moments saying things to each other in confidence in a way that only siblings know. There were lighter moments, too, when the vicissitudes of personal feelings required secrecy.

Pauline was not prone to criticize others publicly or in private. She was not a vindictive person and only in the rarest instance held a grudge. Nevertheless, she was candid and did not take fools gladly. Some of her harshest words invariably landed on bygone acquaintances remembered from school days at Billings. In a letter to Verda, Pauline described one encounter with a former classmate in the inimitable style that made her recollection both sad and humorous at the same time. Writing to Verda, she pictured Bernice, a one-time acquaintance. "She is as brown as a nut, her hair is gray. She had a hole in her stocking, no girdle on, her stockings were rolled down, and there was a gap between them and her skirt." Such personal quips were necessarily restricted to the space between sisters. In the same letter to Verda, Arthur George came up as the subject of sisterly gossip. "He asked me if I was any relation to Verda. He used to go to school to her at Oak Hill", he said. "I told him I had heard you mention him, but I didn't tell him what you said."[13]

The prospects of World War II took a toll on schools across the nation. Monmouth College reported that registrations for fall classes dropped to 332 students, less than previous years because of work opportunities in the expanding defense program at good wages.[14] A scarcity of practice teachers from Monmouth forced the discontinuance of Rickreall as a training school.[15] It became clear that Pauline was ready for a job change.

Pauline worked at Monmouth College four years.[16] She left Rickreall better than she found it, widely appreciated for her work as principal of the grade school and president of the Community Club.[17] The *Capital Journal*, a Salem newspaper, summarized some of her accomplishments. "During her administration here the school grounds have been landscaped, tennis courts have been built, the Christmas pageant has expanded into an annual cooperative community activity, and the treasury has $120 on hand to apply on necessary improvements." One of her projects of personal pride was the number of birdhouses that dotted the school grounds. Small things sometimes meant the most.

She took a break at the end of the school year to visit Wisconsin, take some time to be with family members, and reacquaint herself with old friends. From there, she proceeded to Los Angeles, California, to enroll in a summer course at UCLA and to look for a new job.[18]

In a lengthy letter back home while in Los Angeles, she signaled a career move. "I finally got my money, but since you said that you were not strapped, I'm going to wait 'til I get to Oregon to send you some because I want to close up my small account there. Now, all I have to worry about is that it will last 'til Oct. 1, and that I can get a certificate to work in California."

She took time from classes at UCLA to tour Los Angeles with accompanying friends, and played the role of the usual tourist, visiting Hollywood to catch a glimpse of red carpet movie stars. "We couldn't get within gunshot of the place. We heard Jack Benny's and Maureen O'Sullivan's names called, but couldn't see them."

It was all new to Pauline. Never a shrinking violet, nightclubs, and fancy restaurants were nevertheless a new experience. "Last night we had supper at a place called Padua Hills. It is a Mexican place and while you eat their awful food, a beautiful Mexican girl dances around twirling her skirts and clattering castanets."

One of the highlights of her trip was a ride up the elevator with Shirley Temple and her mother. "She sure is a pretty and well-behaved child," Pauline wrote to Mollie and Verda.

This was not Pauline's first trip to southern California. However, this time she made the most of it. She indulged her curiosity for ethnic diversity and traveled on to Mexico for a short visit, bought the Brandemuehl children some gifts, proudly reveling in her letter home, "David's is to wear around his middle and is genuine hand-tooled Mexican leather." She ended her letter, "I sure will be glad when I'm settled down again."[19]

In August 1941, she completed summer study, returned to Rickreall briefly to pick up her household goods, and moved to Butte County, California. She had a new job as supervisor of Butte County rural schools.[20]

25

Mountain Letter

In September 1941, Pauline went to work as General Supervisor for the Butte County Public Schools, in California, a job similar to the job at Monmouth, Oregon, that required extensive travel to various rural schools scattered around Butte County.[1] She lived at Oroville, California, the county seat of Butte County 370 miles south of Monmouth, down the Pacific Coast in north central California.[2] A picturesque town of about 4,500 people, Oroville—City of Gold—sat on the Feather River just where the river breaks from the Sierra Nevada foothills and eases into California's central valley. During the California gold rush, Oroville was a supply hub for miners who worked the nearby claims. Pauline found a house in the upscale neighborhood of Canyon Highlands, in the foothills east of Oroville and settled into her new job.[3]

The politics of California education became apparent almost immediately. At the Feather River Conference of the California School Supervisors' Association, the fight was in full swing to keep art, physical education, and music as integral parts of teaching credentials. The Association urged the state board of education to abandon its plan to cut the arts, arguing that the arts were central to teacher preparation. Pauline had a vision of how to incorporate these subjects, as well as physical education, into the holistic learning experience of schoolchildren.[4]

Other changes were coming. At a meeting of rural teachers at Biggs Elementary School, she learned that recent California legislation made teachers responsible that all children secured a bus seat—no standing on the bus; also, the birthdays of Washington and Lincoln were now state holidays and not optional; and absence of a student for dental work was now excusable.[5] During the winter break, she drove back to Oregon to visit friends at Rickreall. Teaching was different in California, she told them.[6]

At Oroville, she began to build her plans for the improvement of Butte County schools. She met with a group of teachers at the Oroville Inn. Two things she wanted to do. First, to clarify matters concerning keeping permanent record charts of children throughout their school life.[7] Pauline understood from experience that teachers must know students well to teach them well. Every student, in her mind, was an individual who required individual attention. She decried the use of a student's record to create a stereotype, advocating instead for the use of a student record as a platform upon which to build excellence and success. Her approach to the permanent record did not necessarily accommodate the desire of military authorities at the time that wanted a picture of the person entering any of the services.[8] Nevertheless, she made suggestions in the spirit of assisting the military effort.

The second thing Pauline did was to guide the county in the development of social studies as a holistic topic that embraced multiple subjects under the umbrella of democratized education that fostered teaching of social studies, using the arts, history, and physical education.[9] Her knowledge and fondness for folktales was a primary tool. Serendipitously, northern California was rich in folklore.

Old-timers at Oroville liked to tell the story of Ishi, the last remaining Yahi Indian who appeared in Oroville in 1911 as the last surviving member of his tribe. Ishi was the last known member of the Native American Yahi people of the indigenous territory of California. White settlers wiped out all the members of his family in the late 1800s. For decades, he lived alone isolated from modern American culture until 1911 when he appeared out of the foothills of northern California. An anthropologist gave him the name Ishi. When asked his real name, he said he had no name because the Yahi tradition required that he not speak his own name until formally introduced by another Yahi. "I have no name," he said, "because there were no people to name me," meaning no Yahi survived to speak his name.

Ishi became famous as the "last wild Indian" in America. Anthropologists recorded his language, songs, and the primitive survival techniques of a lost culture. His ethnographic heritage was the subject of multiple books and articles written about him, of documentary films, music, art, and stage productions. He lived in the modern world but for a few years and died in 1916, leaving a wealth of ethnographic information that became the folklore of his mysterious appearance at Lassen Peak in northern California in 1911.[10]

When Pauline came to Oroville, the story of Ishi was still a story often retold among the local historians. Whether it was the story of Ishi that ignited Pauline's love of native culture, she had a knack for folktales and storytelling. She developed a strong interest in the education of the children of indigenous people.

Whether Mexican, American Indian, or some other claim to cultural diversity; Pauline saw in the language and folktales of the past an opportunity for a unique approach to learning. She pioneered the use of folktales to interest children in reading in much the same way European cultures used fairy tales. She saw that local folktales resonated with kids who identified with the characters of the tales with an eagerness that enriched their reading skills. Moreover, Pauline worked to ensure that all children received the same education opportunities as anyone else.

The responsibilities of a supervising teacher in the rural public schools of California took Pauline to places both picturesque and distressed. She saw America as perhaps few educators had the opportunity to do so. Each rural school had its own setting and often unique identity.

Her experiences accumulated over the years, starting in the mining camps of Cokerville, the outlying schools of Crawford County, at Rickreall, Oregon, and places in between. She saw education in a different way, as a patchwork of American values, cultivated, practiced, and passed to the next generation.

In a letter she wrote back to "folks in Wisconsin," she described what it was like in Butte County, writing from the small town of Forbestown, about ten miles up in the mountains from where she lived at Oroville. She wrote, "I am up in the mountains giving tests to the last eighth graders. When this is done all I have to do is give a demonstration at the college, make two commencement speeches, write a manual in reading and prepare a unit for social studies." She traveled around Butte County as part of her supervisory duties, giving tests, helping teachers prepare curriculum, and generally serving the education needs of the county.

The school at Forbestown reminded her of her days in Billings, bringing back memories of her school-day experiences twenty-five years ago. She said, "I wish you could see this school.

It looks a lot like the old Hale district where we went in Missouri, the one that Papa bought for a barn. It has six windows—two on each of three sides. The boards in the floor are 11 inches wide. The walls and ceiling are covered with ceiling boards. There is a rusty old box stove in the middle of the room. The seats and desks are battered old double ones. The building sits up on a hill and you look out into the tops of tall pine and cedar trees."

Saw mills were popping up in the mountains all over Butte County. The schools were getting bigger all the time. However, logging was not always Butte County's industrial means. It was once part of the gold mining craze, which swept California in the latter part of the 19th century, and later quartz mining. Forbestown once boasted five hotels in full swing. Schools went up even in the most remote places of the county to accommodate the families that came in large numbers to search for gold, in the valleys and high in the mountains.

Forbestown suffered a succession of fires and by the early 20th century was but a skeleton of its rich past. Many of the outlying schools became little more than remote outposts holding on to a few students in communities of dwindling populations. It was Pauline's job, nevertheless, to travel to every school. Of her visit to Forbestown, she wrote, "This is a ghost town. They say that once three thousand people lived up here. There was a big gold mining company working here. They also say that in those days everyone had a nice house, a well, and a rose garden. They used so much water in hydraulic mining that the water line went down. The wells went dry. Then there was not enough water for mining. The company folded up. People began to move away. Houses burned down 'til now all there is left is foundations, holes in the ground, mining tunnels, and an old lodge hall with a piano in it that came around the Horn."

She spoke fondly of those she met on these journeys out into the county, collecting folktales of native history as she was inclined to do wherever she went. "The teacher [at Forbestown] is an old timer," she wrote, "a pretty little thing with gray hair and a pretty complexion. She can remember some of the good old days. She just told me at recess that a man who lives close by has to go down to the Big Tunnel this afternoon and he said that she and I could go along. I'm sure glad to get to go. I'll tell you about it next week." The Big Tunnel was the Gold Bank Mine tunnel opened during the years 1935 to 1938 to work the low-grade ore. Forbestown briefly revived as a result but quickly fell into disrepair again when the mine closed. Pauline happened to be there about the time the mine first reopened.

Pauline had an allergy to poison ivy, a serious affliction for someone whose job required her to trek through wood and field to reach some of the schools she had to visit. After one excursion, she came down with a particularly harsh case. "I have been having quite a bad time of it this week," She wrote to her folks in Wisconsin. "I recovered from the trip last Sunday and felt pretty good for two days. Then the poison oak popped out on me. I went right to the Dr. and he gave me some shots. Today it is all dried up and peeling. That is a record cure as far as I am concerned."[11]

Exciting adventures in remote places, interesting people, and folktales of bygone times, interlaced with bouts of poison ivy; not a predictable description of a public school teacher, but such was the life experience of Pauline Jeidy.

PAULINE JEIDY. This undated portrait shows Pauline in her early thirties photographed at Mosher Studio in La Crosse, Wisconsin. Located two doors west of the Wisconsin Theater, in La Crosse, Mosher gave special student discounts. Pauline was a student at State University of Iowa from about 1929 to 1936. The photography company went out of business in 1939.

UNIVERSITY OF IOWA EDUCATION BUILDING. **Pauline made this building on the University of Iowa campus her base of research while studying for her master's degree in education.** ***Hawkeye Yearbook*, 1936.**

State University of Iowa

The Graduate College

Know all men by these presents, That

Pauline Jeidy

has completed the Course of Study prescribed by the Faculty of this College of the University and is therefore admitted to the degree of

Master of Arts

and is entitled to all the Rights, Privileges, Honors and Marks of Distinction thereto pertaining here or elsewhere.

In Testimony Whereof this diploma is conferred under the authority of the Statutes of Iowa by the State Board of Education. Witness the Seal of the University and the Signatures of its duly authorized officers hereunto affixed at Iowa City, Iowa, this twentieth day of August in the year of our Lord one thousand nine hundred thirty-six.

President of the University

President State Board of Education

Dean of the College

Secretary State Board of Education

Attest:

Secretary of the University

PAULINE JEIDY MA DEGREE. **Pauline received her Master of Arts Degree from the State University of Iowa on August 20, 1936.**

RICHLAND CENTER NORMAL. **This teacher training school located at Richland Center, Wisconsin, specialized in apprenticeship teaching. It was where Pauline began her work in teacher supervision.** ***E.C. Cropp.***

RICKREALL PRIMARY CLASS. **Pauline posed for this picture with an unidentified teacher and her primary students in her role as supervisor of teachers for Monmouth College.**

RICKREALL SCHOOL. **The teacher training school at Rickreall, Oregon, was the laboratory school for Monmouth College. Prospective students from Monmouth came here to observe classes. Pauline and her class occupied a room on the second floor on the right.**

HOUSE AT RICKREALL. **Pauline lived here during her time as supervising teacher for Monmouth College at Rickreall, Oregon. The house was midway between Rickreall and Monmouth. Bunched foliage in the tree is mistletoe.**

The War Years

26

Past Is Prologue

Pauline came to California knowing of the checkered past of the state on public education, and the historic lack of state support. Organized education did not come to California until statehood in 1850 when the framers of the first state constitution hotly debated whether there should even be public education before including the position of Superintendent of Public Education in the constitution as a political post filled by a statewide vote. The governor of California tried to strip the constitution of the superintendent clause, arguing that the clerk of the Supreme Court could handle education affairs in his spare time.

Meanwhile, the fight for high schools did not gain funding until 1902. Moreover, local public school districts only received funds for children in school, and not all children living in a district. The policy excluded many pockets of the indigenous population where schools were either not available or families opted out of the white man's schools. For many years, the California state department of education operated out of the superintendent's kitchen. As late as World War I, the superintendent's secretary was his wife. Not until 1921 did a recognizable State Board of Education take shape.[1] Against this background, Pauline entered the arena of public education in the state of California.

Pauline had a gift for writing; she could write in her best education administrator memorandum style, or she could write in elegant prose, beautifully laced with visual descriptions, whether telling of her own experiences or relating one of the hundreds of folktales that she knew and often recited. Nature in particular inspired her. Some of her best stories came from her time in Butte County where her job often took her into the rugged mountains and distant parts of the county.

She took a trip from Oroville up to Lake Madrone and Bald Rock, an outcropping of large natural granite batholiths in Butte County close to Lake Oroville. The place overlooked Sacramento Valley and the California coastal mountain ranges. About three miles east of Bald Rock was Lake Madrone, a picturesque gem set amid thick stands of redwoods and dogwoods in the Shasta Cascade region of California. Once home to the hunter-gatherer Maidu people, the small valley became a lake in the 1920s when a local mill owner built the Apple Tree Dam across Berry Creek.

It was where people went to enjoy an outing. Pauline wrote, "I went on a perfectly swell picnic last Saturday night. The teacher and some more folks up at Lake Madrone (twenty miles up in the mountains in another direction) planned it. We met at the Tradin' Post at the lake, loaded into a big cattle truck, clean, and bedded down with hay. We started across the mountains picking up more people as we went. Several of them were from Oakland and San Francisco who were up at their mountain cottages for vacations. They were all nice folks. We went up on Bald Rock and watched the sun set. We were so high and could see so far and the sunset was so beautiful that it was more than a view. It was an experience. Then we climbed down off the rocks, went to a beautiful little picnic spot with a fireplace and a spring, and fixed supper. We had everything good including three gallons of homemade ice cream for 15 people. I just ignored the matter of diet and went to town on it. After supper, a man entertained us with a guitar and a bag full of songs. At about 11, we loaded into the truck again and went off across the mountain to another high place—facing east this time and saw the moon come up. We were sitting on that big rock with a 3,500-ft. canyon right below us, and a roaring little river down there. That sure was something! About the same time the moon came up a wind came along. It was very beautiful, but sort of weird and awful, too. We got home at three o'clock in the morning and I had to get up for 9:30 Sunday school. I wouldn't have missed it for a lot."

Pauline always had time for students. One time after she had had an exhausting trip into the mountains the day before, a little boy came to her near the close of the day to tell her it was his birthday. He was seven, and he wished Mrs. Jeidy could come to his birthday party that his mother was giving at six o'clock. Pauline said yes, and he went away happy to have a special guest for his birthday. It was a large day for him and Pauline. Meanwhile, there would be several graduation ceremonies to attend at the different schools. She said in a letter postscript written from Forbestown that she "got a new white silk suit for the graduations."[2]

Far from Butte County, California, on the other side of the world another story was developing.

Adolph Hitler's Third Reich thrust Germany into war across Europe in the quest to build an empire. Meanwhile, the Japanese pushed beyond its island boundaries to take control of land and natural resources in an aspiration to gain economic and military dominance over East Asia. On December 7, 1941, the Japanese bombed the US Territory of Hawaii causing the United States to declare war, something the country had tried to avoid.

Americans felt the results of war almost immediately. Rationing of tires and gasoline went into effect in January 1942 to ensure enough rubber for military and vital civilian purposes. Local tire rationing boards issued certificates for tires or recapping upon application. People who depended on automobile transportation, which was practically every American, caught the brunt of the rationing policy. Pauline's supervisory travel required her to travel almost on a daily basis.

Rationing affected everyone, especially farmers and rural communities that depended on the automobile to move produce to market. The commuter who had no public transportation faced the prospect of losing a job. For instance, Cousin George Kastendieck whose job meant a regular commute between Springfield and Jefferson City, Missouri, lamented the circumstances. "We have tires enough for a while yet by being careful," he said. George was a veteran of World War I who fought in Europe. As a new war loomed ahead, he wrote to Pauline in 1942, "It is sure a mess having to go through all this mess again." He hoped his son, Bob, could stay in college, and not need to go to war. "I am afraid that if he has to quit he will never finish." As it turned out, the Army drafted Bob and sent him to the front of the European war zone where he received a serious head wound in the Battle of the Bulge. He survived and returned home from the war, and went back to college.

The early days of the War had many consequences, both abroad and at home. In January 1942, President Franklin Roosevelt repudiated Nazism and emphasized the dangers of racism. He said, "We must be particularly vigilant against racial discrimination in any of its ugly forms."[3] Nevertheless, upon entry into the conflict, the US government almost immmediately forced about 100,000 Japanese Americans into detention camps, primarily on the West Coast where Pauline worked. Roosevelt authorized the removal and internment of Japanese Americans and Japanese nationals from the West Coast military zone. Men, women, and children of Japanese ancestry ended up in one of several camps in northern California pursuant to an order from the president. A temporary Japanese internment camp went in at Marysville, California, about 30 miles south of Pauline, at Oroville. The detention camp was the topic of local and national debate.

As a student of John Dewey, Pauline shared his position on prejudice. Dewey observed in a speech before the New York Society for Ethical Culture at the outset of the war that people in the US condemned "the narrow, bigoted, and cruel practices of Nazism." However, he asked, "how far are we free of racial prejudice? What of our attitude toward Negroes, toward aliens within our gates, our anti-Semitism? And what are our schools doing to create tolerance, good will, and mutual understanding?" Dewey's words resonated with Pauline's deep interest in ethnic culture, which naturally turned to the plight of the impounded Japanese Americans. She began to think about the perception of the education of children regarding the moral consequences of war.

Meanwhile, the spring of 1942 came, and the excitement of war and Pauline's new job at Oroville gave way to sadness when Mollie suffered a stroke. Pauline dropped everything and hastened to her mother's side at the Brandemuehl farm outside Fennimore. Oscar and Verda had moved from the family farm at Mt. Hope to Fennimore in 1941 to be closer to the schools at Fennimore and the services that a larger town offered.[4] Ruth was in high school and David had turned 10 in December.

Mollie had suffered serious illness before but had always recovered. She had been in poor health for a while, under the watchful care of Verda at the Brandemuehl home but unable to work and keep up with her gardening. Mollie delighted in nature, studied it, and kept busy working among her flowerbeds. Many were the times when someone sick or shut-in in the community received a bouquet to cheer their day. She had a special interest in young people and did much to improve educational opportunities for children in the Fennimore community, always planning to do something to help or improve Sunday school. Having joined the Methodist Church at an early age, she devoted as much of her life to her church as her strength and health permitted. Few people knew that she was an active member of the Women's Christian Temperance Union and had been since her early days at Billings.[5]

She had a presence in the Fennimore community; her family and many intimate friends and relatives affectionately called her "Aunt Mollie." She became a subscriber and avid reader of the *Christian Herald,* and frequently shared her copies with friends and neighbors.

As time went by, Mollie's health began to fail despite the loving attention of Verda and Oscar in whose home she received every kindly care and consideration. Verda wrote to family and friends that Mollie's recovery was unlikely. She had her final illness on Sunday, April 19, 1942, when she suffered a stroke. She was never able to leave her home afterwards and steadily grew weaker until the end came on a Wednesday, May 13, 1942, at home with Pauline, Verda, Oscar, and the Brandemuehl children, the home she had nurtured and made her own for 18 years. Rev. G. A. Bird of Mt. Hope preached the funeral service with Rev. Lockhart at the Fennimore Methodist Church on

Saturday at 10:30 in the morning. They laid her to rest that afternoon in Prairie Cemetery.[6]

Mary Ann (Dewey) Kastendieck—Mollie—died just short of her 69th birthday. She made the most of a difficult life. Orphaned at age four and widowed before she was 39, she raised two daughters as a single mother and never wavered from her insistence that they have the best possible education. She saw to it that they went to college. Although burdened in her last years by poor health, she always found the strength to help others and to give of her talents and time to her church and community whenever she was able. At the end of her life, her epitaph said simply, "It can truthfully be said of Mollie Kastendieck, she hath done what she could."[7]

27

Remembering Mollie

Mollie's funeral, as all funerals are, was a time to renew family ties. Brothers Austin and Willard Dewey of Lancaster and Mt. Ida were still living. A large crowd filled the Fennimore Methodist Church to pay last respects to the venerable friend and neighbor much loved by all who knew her.[1] Rev. George Alfred Bird spoke as Mollie's minister and friend during almost her entire life at Fennimore. Rev. Bird served the Fennimore Methodist Episcopal Church for 22 years total in two separate periods of service from 1902 to 1909, and again from 1927 until 1942. He was at one time also minister at Mt. Hope and other locations in Wisconsin.[2]

They laid Mollie to rest on a beautiful sunny afternoon at Prairie Cemetery, near Fennimore, on present Highway 18, midway between the farmstead of Oscar and Verda and the town of Fennimore. The family did not return Mollie to Christian County for burial next to Andrew, her long-departed husband, on the gentle slope of Rose Hill Cemetery where many of the Kastendieck family lay at rest. Instead, they created a new place for her at Prairie Cemetery close to family and friends.

Tributes to her gentility and letter of admiration came from many places, including Billings, Missouri, where long estranged acquaintances remembered her as a special person in their lives.[3] Among the most caring condolences were those of the Kastendieck family. Andrew's niece, Mildred, who graduated from high school with Pauline, wrote from St. Louis, "I can't tell you how sorry I was to hear of Aunt Mollie's death. I had hoped that she would be able to come to Missouri and visit us all. We four kids will never have any but the very fondest of memories of her and Uncle Andrew. We had such wonderful times visiting you all on the farm. Mother had always wanted your mother to come spend the summer with her. She has talked about it for years."[4]

Cousin Katherine wrote from Milton, Iowa, to express her sympathy and to reminisce about the distress of the war. "It did not seem like 30 years since your father died but when I got to thinking about it, I knew it was. It has been three years now since my mother [Lizzy Kastendieck] passed away. Seems like time can fly...We wanted to go down home during strawberry time but guess the way tires are and gasoline maybe we are staying home We can get the tires but as you said there is lots of red tape to it. We are getting a couple of new ones but you have to wait for the certificate to come after you make application for them."[5]

Cousin George wrote from Springfield, Missouri, "We don't go down near as much as we used to before mother died...Then this tire situation has us rather tied down at present. We have tires enough for a while yet by being careful. If we only knew that we could get some more when these are gone. I am afraid this tire business is going to keep us from making our annual trip up to Kathryn's [*sic*] this Fourth of July." He added a prosaic note, "I know you are going to miss your mother but that seems to be the way things have to be and there isn't much we can do or say about it that will help much."[6]

The human kindness of Mollie's friends showed through, expressed in an awareness of her life's circumstances. One neighbor wrote to Verda, "How nice Pauline got home to be with your mother for a while. You girls surely have nothing to regret for you have been so good to her and always given her such excellent care and how happy she must have been, knowing she raised two wonderful women. All spring I have thought of her when I would pass my hollyhock plants for I remembered the plants she gave me one year, she was always so generous with all of her flowers."[7] Reverend Harold Allison wrote from Black River Falls, Wisconsin, to add similar reminiscences. "It is pleasant to think back over the many interesting and happy visits we have had with her. Her interest in flowers and other beauty and in the young people as well as her firm stand for things right will have its influence on all of us."[8]

In her letter to Verda, Katherine added, "I am glad Pauline was with you. Is she still teaching school? There seems to be a demand for teachers now days."[9] Only a few people knew of Pauline's growing success in education. Although she came back to Fennimore most summers, her work in Oregon and California distanced her from the day-to-day interests of the people of Grant County and from the wider circle of the Kastendieck family at Billings.

Nevertheless, Pauline never forgot her roots, whether when growing up at Billings, Missouri, or her meager career beginning in Grant County, Wisconsin. Lulu Adams, a longtime neighbor and friend from Mt. Hope, saw the poignancy of Pauline's determination to remain close to her family. She wrote, "And you could be with her, Pauline, when her need for you was the most urgent, but I'm remembering the days you were at home last summer when you brought to her and the rest of the family such a good feeling at the success you had attained. After all, it is the glad times that your mother lived to remember, and to talk about. Her family has given her many such times."[10]

Mollie touched many lives. An old friend wrote from Chicago, "She was always willing to do kind acts...no matter how she was feeling. Always a smile when we came to the home. I will never forget her."[11]

Pauline had many places in her calendar of memories that marked special moments. None more heartfelt, though, than knowing that those closest to her all died in the month of May: her father Andrew, husband Casey, and now her mother Mollie.

After Mollie's funeral, Pauline returned to Oroville.

There were many times when Pauline's thoughts went back to Missouri, remembering the good days in Billings when Andrew filled the house with his singing and the rhythmic clacking of a set of rib bones. She missed the times when he read aloud to her and the children, as he often did.[12]

By the time Mollie Kastendieck died, the old family had grown smaller. Of Mollie's five siblings, only two brothers survived her, Austin Dewey who lived at the county seat in Lancaster, Wisconsin, and Willard Dewey of Mt. Ida, Wisconsin. When her Aunt Lizzy died at Billings, Lizzy was the last of her Kastendieck generation to pass.

The passing of the old generation made way for a new one blessed with new offspring of Kastendiecks, Deweys, and Brandemuehls, to name a few. Nevertheless, in 1942, the living descendants of Mollie and Andrew Kastendieck numbered but four: their daughter Verda Kastendieck Brandemuehl and children Ruth and David Brandemuehl, and daughter Pauline Kastendieck Jeidy.

When Pauline completed her master's degree in 1936, she achieved the highest level of formal education of any generation of her family on both sides. The one to come closest to her at the time was her cousin Raymond Stone Kastendieck, who completed his architecture degree at Washington University. Most of her other cousins went to college but only for a year or two before moving into various careers. Still, a year or two of college for anyone of that era was more than many high school graduates of Pauline's generation sought to complete. Most young people were happy with a high school diploma, which usually marked a step up from the eighth-grade education of their parents. The exceptions in the Kastendieck family were noteworthy. Besides Raymond the architect, Mildred Kastendieck, Pauline's cousin and former classmate at Billings High School put both of her children through college after her divorce much like Mollie had done as a single mom after Andrew's death. Mildred completed four years of college and obtained her teaching degree. Her son, Harry Fulbright was the only family member later to eclipse Pauline's level of formal education achievement. He obtained his Ph.D. degree from Washington University and went on to become a highly respected professor of physics.

28

Kindred Spirits

In the summer of 1943, Pauline enrolled in the summer session at the University of California at Los Angeles, to use the break in the school year as an opportunity to freshen her education and add to her lengthening resume.[1] She became acquainted with Helen Heffernan and Corinne Seeds, two of the leading figures in education reform and in the politics of the California public school system. At the time, Miss Heffernan served as Chief of Rural and Elementary Education for the California State Department of Education and taught at UCLA. Miss Seeds ran the highly regarded University Elementary School at UCLA, a recognized innovator of elementary education across the nation. These two exceptional women reinforced Pauline's own ideas about education, which placed them at the center of a wide network of women educators in California for almost forty years. They were key figures in a concerted attempt to put the ideals of John Dewey's progressive education model into practice in a statewide system of public education in the United States.

Heffernan and Seeds were in step with Pauline's education values, which championed a child-centered pedagogy committed to a concept of education for democratic citizenship.[2]

As World War II raged in Europe and Japan, there was a heightened awareness of the morals of a democratic society. Heffernan understood that democracy rested on well-supported public schools that offered opportunities for intellectual and creative growth to all children regardless of gender or ethnic diversity; and, she believed, good schools required well-prepared and committed teachers.[3] She also believed that women should occupy leadership roles at least equal to their male counterparts. Heffernan's biographer, Kathleen Weiler wrote, "Perhaps most prominent is the feminist perspective that takes gender as central. Framing the lives of two women progressive educators around the fact that they were women and highlighting male power in the world in which they moved challenged conventional histories of the progressive education movement in which gender has largely been ignored as a category of analysis."[4]

These were ideas to which Pauline could relate. They greatly influenced her own emerging concept of public education. She became part of a movement that elevated California schools from a mediocre status in public education to one considered among the nation's best. California grew to be a model for school systems across the nation. Progressive education in the United States reached its height in the period between World War I and World War II. By 1943, progressive education implied both a pedagogical approach centered on the interest of the child and a political attitude associated with freethinking.[5]

It was into this encouragement of liberalism that Pauline found herself in the summer of 1943 at UCLA. She enrolled in the summer institute for teachers established by Heffernan to inspire teachers to envision themselves and their work as challenging and socially important.

For a while, since the war started, Pauline had observed children's reactions to the war, and wondered how much they understood about the act and consequences of war. Heffernan and Seeds saw in Pauline's work an example of their own progressive education model. They encouraged her to publish it.

"Reactions of Children of Different Age Levels in the War and Their Implications for Teachers," published in the *California Journal of Elementary Education* in August 1943, became the first of several published articles Pauline wrote that identified her as an innovative educator and a proponent of the Heffernan and Seeds school of thinking. She wrote from experience in a straightforward style that gave her work an informative and practical appeal.

The article revealed several things about child understanding of war. During the school year 1942-1943, Pauline observed and recorded behavior of students in classroom settings, including schools in Butte County where her job as General Supervisor of Schools took her to several different schools. She started with a series of questions related to school pupils' reactions to the war, that is, feeling toward enemies, confidence in the U.S. cause, allies, and leadership, and the hardships imposed by war. She wanted, among other things, to help teachers create teaching levels that addressed concepts and understandings within a child's comprehension of war. One of the progressive purposes of her study was to enable teachers to help children have mentally healthy concepts of war, and to be particularly cognizant of children dealing with stress because Pauline said, "Every child is under mental stress of some sort." Teaching about the war beyond a child's ability to comprehend it added to the problem.

Surprisingly, she found in her study evidence that primary children did not recognize a Japanese person as an object of hate despite the impoundment camps that singled out Japanese Americans. Kids applied feelings toward enemies to situations and not against individuals—anything bad was German or Japanese while anything good was American. One story underscored the finding. "It was soon after Pearl Harbor. One morning before school, ten or a dozen first-grade boys came running around the corner of the schoolhouse, each with an eager, intent look in his eyes and a stick in his hand. One boy said, 'Oh boy! Are we gonna get them Japs!' Two of the boys were Japanese."[6]

Older children tended to have more capacity for hating, which they expressed largely toward people they did not know or understand. Intermediate grade students could think of many reasons for hating the Japanese as a nation or as an army: because of Pearl Harbor, they are uncivilized; they kill women and children, and so on; reasons recognized in hindsight as likely motivated by parental influence. However, when it came to individual Japanese they had known, they liked as many as they disliked. Pauline concluded, "An understanding of a people tends to promote a friendly feeling toward them," a conclusion in step with her progressive idea of public education and the teachings of John Dewey.

In the upper grades, students had a better understanding of abstract ideas. Democracy, humanity, and freedom meant something to them. Expressions of responsibility in the war effort were reassuringly mature in scope, particularly the concern with buying war bonds and stamps, and gathering scrap. One girl wrote, "Just think, eleven twenty-five-cent stamps will buy one steel helmet. One twenty-five cent stamp will buy one month's feed for a carrier pigeon." The emphasis rested on helping Americans rather than on destruction of the enemy. How much of this thinking came from inherent student response and how much from local marketing is unknown because the government encouraged schools across the nation to contribute to the war effort by selling war stamps and bonds.[7]

Students in Pauline's UCLA study thought the war a worthy cause. They had perfect confidence in President Roosevelt as a war leader. A fifth grader said, "He's done O.K. so far, hasn't he?" Very few doubted ultimate victory. Students in the upper grades said, we were fighting for equality, humanity, and a better world. Yet they offered little indication of what a better world would look like, except to say, "After the war it will be a free world." They thought the allies should mete out no punishment to the people of enemy nations because in the words of a seventh grader, "They are as human as we are."

Pauline understood the qualities that teachers needed in the classroom, particularly during a period of potential stress like war. She strongly advocated for one of the pillars of progressive education, that is, a requirement to teach to a student's level of understanding. To this end, she recommended that teachers remain quiet, calm, and well poised in demeanor. The attitude toward children should be sympathetic but not emotional, and teachers should strive to show justice toward all in dealing with students. She cautioned not to ban war talk but to enter into conversations when necessary to clarify erroneous concepts of war. In the lesson on art, she said when a child paints a picture; evaluate the picture in terms of beauty and technique used, and not the subject it portrays. Pauline knew the value of self-expression. She knew, also, how to employ personal communication to benefit the teaching moment. In this way, she applied the best of John Dewey's theory of progressive education and took her place among the leaders of education change in California and across the nation.

Pauline understood, too, that kids will be kids and that good teachers should arm themselves with acceptance and a sense of humor. In her study, Pauline found that students exhibited mixed abilities in the knowledge of geography and where the war was. A first grader declared that he had "flown his planes to Germany, turned around, and come back."

Pauline's reputation as an educator grew at a steady pace in Butte County. She entertained in her home, was an honored guest at luncheons, and relished the opportunity to be part of the community.[8] School events often found her invited as a special guest, like at the annual grade-school pupils play day when Butte County schools gathered to play baseball, kickball, and ring tennis as part of the physical education program. Rewarded with ice cream bars, the winners received double servings.[9]

She developed an elementary school workshop that she taught at Chico State College in the summer. The workshop was a model that she would later perfect and see copied by multiple school systems. A main feature always provided teachers the opportunity to discuss problems encountered firsthand in the classroom.[10]

She had a visitor in the fall of 1943. Her idyllic descriptions of Butte County enticed her niece to spend the fall and winter with her in California.[11] Ruth, Verda's daughter, now a 19-year-old young woman excited to visit her aunt and experience an alternative environment to Fennimore, Wisconsin, savored the chance to visit her Aunt Pauline. It was a formative few months in the lives of both Pauline and Ruth. Their bonding led to a close family relationship that continued throughout the succeeding years. Ruth was, in colloquial terms, the daughter that Pauline never had. Her winter visits to California became a regular event noted in the society pages of the local press.[12]

Across the state, other events were transpiring. Dr. Violet G. Stone, director of elementary education of the Ventura County, California, school system, died in March 1944. The following month, the Soroptimist Club of Oroville installed Pauline as president, by proxy.[13] Her absence indicated a change was in the air. On June 28, school officials at Ventura announced that Pauline would be the new Director of Elementary Curriculum for Ventura County.[14]

29

Mission San Buenaventura

Pauline remained in Oroville, California, as school supervisor for three years, until August 1944 when she moved to southern California, to become Director of Elementary Curriculum for Ventura County. She made one last presentation before the California Teachers Association representing the Butte County Public Schools, her last appearance on the county's behalf before settling in Ventura County.[1]

Her reputation as a storyteller preceded her. The Toastmistress Club of Ventura lost no time in inviting her as a guest speaker. She quickly followed that appearance with a panel discussion before the Lincoln Parent Teachers Association at Sacramento, California.[2] She was starting to gain wide attention for innovative leadership in education.[3]

The cultural history of southern California was a natural fit for Pauline. Its indigenous people were rich with stories and storytelling, none remembered more often than the story of Matilaja's Daughter that originated in the earliest days of Ventura County.

In that story, according to folk tradition, the Mission of San Buenaventura cloistered the daughter of a local Indian chieftain. Indians attacked the mission in great force under command of Chief Matilaja to rescue his daughter, said to have been held at the mission against her will, or at least adverse to the desires of Olana, her lover. The raid was successful in releasing the girl. However, Spanish and Mexican soldiers from the mission overtook the Indians and in a pitched battle killed all of them except for the brave Olana who the devoted daughter found mortally wounded. After his death, she dug a grave for him and buried him. Like in the tragedy of Romeo and Juliet, they found her dead lying across the shallow grave she had made for her lover. An anonymous poet put the romantic story in prose a few years later under the title, *Amatil's Cross.*[4]

When Pauline arrived at Ventura, the art of storytelling was alive and abundant. Native Americans, like Alan Salazar a descendant of the Chumash Indians, appeared at events to lead spiritual prayers as his Indian persona Spirit Hawk. He relished telling stories about his alter ego, Running Hawk, a boy who dreamed of coyotes and bears and learned lessons from the animal spirits.[5]

Pauline's interest in storytelling did not stem from an ancestral spirit world such as Mr. Salazar's did. Nevertheless, she saw in folklore and storytelling a way to reach students and to teach many of the same lessons. Ventura was rich in cultural history.[6]

Located northwest of Los Angeles on the California Coast, the City of San Buenaventura (aka Ventura) is a very old and picturesque city situated between the Ventura River Valley and Santa Clara River Valley. The Pacific Ocean washes the southern boundary, the Ventura River edges the western boundary, a high hill looms on the northern side, while the fertile Santa Clara valley stretches out eastward.

The town of Ventura had a rich and storied history, which began as Mission San Buenaventura, a successful California mission founded by the Franciscans in 1782. After the Great Earthquake of 1812, settlers divided mission lands into private property to proceed with secular development of the region. By 1841, magnificent haciendas dotted the landscape along the Santa Clara and Ventura Rivers.

Nevertheless, for many years of its early history, Ventura County was a sparsely populated, penurious land. People were self-dependent with little outside contact. They built communities to serve their needs with little dependence on city life. They managed to put up a small school and have a teacher. They met once a month at the schoolhouse for a social time together. They brought their suppers along. The men talked of crops and farming, roads and prices, winds and weather. The women talked of canning and quilting, sewing and knitting, chickens, childcare, and favorite recipes. At these rural community gatherings, the children spoke pieces and played games. It was a time of neighborhood fun and understanding. Then the school burned, and they had no money to rebuild it. They kept in touch in other ways. A little newspaper called "The Headlight" began as an idea started by a woman to share local news. She wrote it by hand. Passed from family to family, it made the rounds of the residents who often added new items of neighborhood news as it went.[7]

The farms along the Santa Clara River were the lifeblood of Ventura County. The meat wagon regularly made the rounds selling round steak at eight cents a pound; and the best porterhouse at twelve and half cents a pound. Trade was by barter for eggs and butter. The water wagon carried barrels of river water to fill the barrels of the residents.

Travel to the town that grew up around the mission was hard, and people did not go to Ventura unless they had a whole day to spend shopping. A trip from the outlying community of Ojai, for instance, was an all-day trip by horse and buggy, crossing the Santa Clara River many times along the way. Farmers spent long hours carrying harvested crops to Port Hueneme on the Pacific Coast. A crop was loaded into a wagon and taken by a team of horses to the port. There it was loaded onto a ship anchored at the wharf. One time, a farmer had his corn loaded into the hold of a small sailing vessel, saw it cast of the anchor and move slowly away from the wharf toward the deep water of the channel. Then watched it sink within sight of land, with his year's corn crop lost.[8]

After the Civil War, more settlers came, buying land from the Mexicans or simply taking property at will. Railroad interests acquired vast holdings of land, and the discovery of oil attracted still more people. Up the Santa Clara River at the little town of Saticoy, the villagers built a new schoolhouse that had a stage and a balcony where visiting actors performed plays. The rich valley soil drew citrus growers along the rivers in a part of California where citrus grew better than anywhere in the state. Of even climate moderated by the sea, temperatures seldom dipped below freezing, a luxury very different to Pauline from Wisconsin winters and trudging through snow banks to reach remote schools. None of the disturbing forces of nature visited Ventura County, except earthquakes. The county sat atop several active seismic faults.

Being a popular destination came late to Ventura. California. In the beginning, fear of hostile Indians kept people out of the region. For most of its history, the town of Ventura enjoyed a leisurely, less crowded way of life compared to other West Coast cities. Accessible mostly by small ocean steamers, Ventura remained relatively isolated until 1887 when the railroad came. For many years, Ventura was a prosperous but isolated city. Entrance from the north was by way of a single road along the beach. Travelers came south by ship to Santa Barbara and then along the coast road to Ventura. Passengers traveling by stagecoach waited until low tide when the horses could cross the exposed wet sand. Inland, Ventura was accessible only across mountainous country and deep canyons. Northern access later improved when the Maricopa Highway opened in 1934.

The town stood likewise cut off from the southern part of the state. Not until well into in the 20th century was a trip to Los Angeles by automobile—a trip that Pauline often made—anything but slow and hazardous. Not until the last section of the Ventura Freeway opened in 1969 did Ventura become easier to get to from the south.

There were two Methodist Episcopal Churches in Ventura, the original church dating to 1867 and the South Church, organized in 1888. To that end, Ventura County was effectively crime free. Except for the brutality of white settlers toward the indigenous Indian tribes, Ventura County from an early date displayed a remarkably civilized behavior. The only lynching ever recorded in Ventura County occurred in 1873. So rare was the event that storytellers retold it many times as part of the unique folklore of the region.

As the story went, "George Martin took his team and gang plow as usual, and commenced tracing the lines around a certain piece of land that he had leased and occupied for the last three years. After turning around a part of the land he was met at one corner by a man named George Hargan, who had also leased a piece of land partly adjoining Mr. Martin's, so that the two pieces lapped each other by about twenty rods." Mr. Hargan claimed that he had measured his land and he, Hargan, needed to move the line to take a strip of Martin's land. A witness said, "Hargan went in front of Martin's team and stopped it and forbade Martin to run the furrow and turned the team off; Martin then said, 'Let me run the line out and you can have the land,' and started the team. When he had passed Hargan about ten feet, Hargan said: 'I have told you three times and will tell you no more,' and then fired a heavy load of buckshot, which took effect." Eight shot struck Martin a little to the left of the spinal column, under the shoulder, two passing through the heart. He fell forward on the plow and never spoke.

Hargan went to his home, hitched up his two-horse team, and drove towards the river. Local citizens overtook and arrested him. He made no denial. He said that he had left his house to kill Martin.

A witness to the event said, "The whole neighborhood turned out and consulted together and kept the prisoner closely confined and guarded until the testimony was heard before the Coroner's jury. The testimony was so plain and the crime so great, and as there was no officer present to take charge of the prisoner, the bystanders took him to the lone tree near the cactus patch and hung him."[9]

Such was a sample of the folklore of Ventura County when Pauline arrived in 1944. By that time, the city had a population of about 14,000 people. It was the largest town Pauline had ever lived in outside of her time at the University of Iowa. It was also the most culturally diverse.

PAULINE JEIDY. She resigned from her job as supervisor of teachers for Butte County, California, in 1944 to accept a position as Director of Curriculum for Ventura County, California. She posed for this picture about the time she moved to Ventura.

HISTORIC VIEW OF MISSION SAN BUENAVENTURA IN 1875. **The mission became the city of Ventura, California. Pauline came to Ventura as Director of Elementary Curriculum in 1944. Storke, *Memorial and Biographical History.***

BALD MOUNTAIN. **Bald Rock is a granite batholith located in Butte County, California, in the Plumas National Forest. Located close to Lake Oroville, the dome peak overlooks Sacramento Valley and coastal mountain ranges. It was a favorite weekend destination for Pauline and her friends while she worked as a teacher supervisor in Butte County. *Photo by Vladimirovich Albitsky.***

SAN FRANCISCO SHOPPING. **Pauline (left) and an unidentified friend from Ventura enjoy a weekend outing in San Francisco. The well-known pool playing business of Cochran and Palm Billiards is visible in the background.**

LOS ANGELES VISITORS. **Pauline was a frequent visitor to Los Angeles whether taking courses and teaching classes at UCLA, or sightseeing and enjoying the entertainment of the city. Seen here on the right with unidentified colleagues from UCLA.**

30

A Man's World

Ventura County mirrored the rest of California in the development of public school education, that is to say, public schools grew at a measured pace, distributed throughout the county, poorly resourced, and with no organizational vision for the future. Up until the turn of the 20th century in the earlier days of Ventura County, there were three classifications of schools: primary schools were available in the sparsely settled areas of the county; grammar schools were in more thickly settled regions; and there was a high school in Ventura, the only high school in the county.[1] Each of the kinds of schools identified with the number of grade levels taught at a school and the number of teachers hired to teach them, starting with a few grades in primary schools and advancing to a more extensive curriculum in high school. The public schools gradually improved, and by 1917, there were five high schools in Ventura County.

World War II brought a heightened awareness of illiteracy in the United States and in Ventura County. As of Aug 1944, draft boards nationwide rejected 4,217,000 draftees from military service. Of these, 250,000 men did not qualify for service because of illiteracy; another 681,000 did not qualify because of illiteracy but had other defects.[2] This meant that of the nearly 15 million men who reported for the World War II draft, approximately one in ten did not qualify for service due to an inability to read and write.

The plight of illiteracy extended beyond the draft to the general population in even more telling numbers. In the total population of persons above 14 years old who could not read or write, the rate was close to 3 percent. Among the black population, it rose above 11 percent, unacceptable in an educated society but much improved from the post-Civil War days when 20 percent of the adult white population was illiterate and 80 percent of blacks could neither read nor write.[3] The latter was not a surprising statistic in 1865 because white slave owners denied slaves access to education and severely punished anyone caught breaking the law against it.

California and Ventura County lagged the nation in English literacy skills, largely due to its American Indian and Mexican populations. As director of elementary curriculum in Ventura County, Pauline put at the top of her list of responsibilities the improvement of the program in reading.[4]

She rolled up her sleeves and reported to Mr. Dean Triggs, Superintendent of Schools for Ventura County. Here in Ventura she would spend the remainder of her life on the blue Pacific Ocean, far removed from the farmland of Billings, Missouri, where she grew up, and the rolling hills of Grant County, Wisconsin, where she began her career.

The politics of California education soon surfaced, sometimes in unusual ways. Shortly after her arrival in Ventura County, Pauline discovered that her salary was greater than that of her boss, Superintendent Triggs. Pauline received an annual salary of $3,800, $200 more than Triggs. Due to a quirk in California state law, her salary as director of elementary education topped that of the superintendent. Under the California constitution, county school superintendents ran for office as politically elected officials selected by county voters. Therefore, Triggs' salary came out of the county budget while Pauline's salary came out of state funds allocated and controlled by the state. By law since 1879, the constitution prohibited salary increases for locally elected officials during their terms until after the next election, in Triggs' case for two years until 1946 when the salary for his office was set to increase to $4,200. The only solution to the hiatus in the short term was to amend the constitution. Proposition 10 went on the ballot in 1944 giving Ventura County voters a chance to correct the pay situation and bring the salaries of the people they elected to office in line with current living costs and permit them to make more than their employees. Proposition 10 had a sunset clause. It restricted suspension of the constitution to the period in which the United Sates was engaged in war. Even so, the proposition barely passed 52 to 48 percent, and Superintendent Triggs and other elected officers got their raises.[5]

Pauline immersed herself in her new job just as she had done on each previous occasion when new challenges required new solutions. More recognition of her leadership in education added to her already substantial catalog of professional achievements. Her name soon appeared in the leading directories and indexes of education professionals and among the membership of California education associations, including California Elementary School Administrators Association, California Association of Secondary School Administrators, and California Society for the Study of Secondary Education, to name a few.

A milestone of dubious recognition was her membership in the National Society for the Study of Education. Her name first appeared as an active member in the association's *Forty Fifth Yearbook.*[6] The National Society for the Study of Education was an organization of professional educators founded in 1901. The organization gained a reputation for its two-part yearbook published annually with articles thematically centered on a particular education issue of interest to the public. The yearbook strived to provide a pluralistic perspective on the relationships between pedagogical research, policy, and practice in education.

The society professed to create a vigorous, inclusive dialogue that addressed educational problems. Although it gained praise for its yearbooks from academic and education communities, the society drew criticism for its conservative, overly cabalistic and cloistered board of directors. In Pauline's first year of membership, the entire yearbook comprised male contributors, not to mention the all-male board of directors, staff, and article contributors. This male-dominated presence varied somewhat from year to year, but the male authority of the organization often revealed itself by dismissing progressive trends in education.[7]

For instance, World War II precipitated a vigorous debate that encouraged greater attention to education for democratic citizenship. One scholar wrote in the yearbook, "If public education is to be conceived of as the cornerstone of the democratic order, it is essential that the school system itself be organized on a democratic basis...Democracy will not function effectively until all the people of the community recognize that all of the people are part of the community." Another contributor wrote, "The practice of democracy is a more effective teacher than mere talk about it."

Unfortunately, above the lofty rhetoric loomed a glass ceiling, keeping women from rising to the height of democratic citizenship. School administrators, invariably male, agreed that women should have equal pay but were slow to implement it in their systems, arguing that it contradicted the law of supply and demand, meaning there were more female teachers, thus they could be paid less. The conservative male voice allowed that women should receive equal pay for equal work, with some provision for family-load adjustment, meaning that the pay of a man as the breadwinner of a family should be more. They reasoned, "By and large, men have a larger dependency load than women, although women teachers are not without responsibilities of this nature." Yet another male writer concluded, "It is usually assumed that teachers of young children will be women, probably in recognition of the mother-substitute role which teachers of young children have to assume."[8]

It is difficult to imagine how someone of Pauline's progressive vision would subscribe to such points of view for very long, and her name soon disappeared from the membership rolls.

When Pauline first became a member of the National Society for the Study of Education in 1945, the society's total membership was a modest 1,583 members nationwide. Anyone could become a member by paying the $3.50 membership fee, plus an extra dollar initiation fee for first-time members. Membership dues were an important source of income for the society. After many years, the lack of members and other factors rendered the organization financially unfeasible, and it ended in 2008 as a membership society. The yearbook continued publication under the auspices of Columbia University.

31

Fable in Ethics

Coincidental with her move to Ventura, Pauline published an article that clearly established her philosophy about teaching. In a short piece titled "Fable in Ethics," she wrote in her typical parable fashion what a teacher should be, and not be.[1] Although the story was a product of her fertile imagination written in the prose of a fairy tale, it was unmistakably autobiographical. The characters closely resembled her cousins who graduated with her from Billings High School and who each entered the teaching profession with different career outcomes.

Cousin Mildred Kastendieck loved to play bridge, eventually divorced her playboy husband, and moved to St. Louis where she taught in the public schools. Cousin Katherine Kastendieck was an excellent student in Pauline's class. Katherine, Mildred, and Pauline attended Normal College, in Springfield, Missouri, to become teachers. Katherine entered the teaching profession briefly, soon married and settled into a good life as the wife of an Iowa veterinarian. The third daughter in the tale has all the qualities of Pauline herself. The following is a digest of the tale as Pauline told it.

The story was about a woman who once upon a time had three daughters. The first daughter was very beautiful. People admired her fair skin, deep blue eyes, and soft black hair. "What a beautiful child," they often exclaimed. "What lovely hair!" The mother doted over the first little girl and made sure she always looked exactly right. The first little girl soon learned that if her hair was messy, her face was dirty, or she tore her dress, no one said she was beautiful. Therefore, she did not run or play with other children.

The second daughter was not beautiful, but she was brilliant. She found the rough play of the children to be annoyingly repulsive. Someone was always yelling, "Hurry up!" or "Get out of the way!" She began to withdraw from the other children, to find refuge in her own vivid imagination. Everyone in her mind admired and loved her. Everyone in her mind listened to her. Grownups said, "What an odd little girl." However, she did not mind because someone usually said, "But they say she is terribly bright." It did not matter what people said about her. She could always sit alone and imagine.

The third daughter was neither beautiful nor homely. She was not brilliant, neither was she dull. She entered into games with zeal and gusto. She took the bitter with the sweet; she fell down; she bumped heads with other children; she scratched her knees and tore her dress. When differences arose among the children, she joined the side that she thought was right, and quarreled valiantly. When good fortune befell a friend, she was happy. When a friend was in trouble, tears stood in her eyes. Her mother spoke to people apologetically about her. "Isn't her hair a fright." or "You wouldn't believe it, but that dress was clean this morning." She did not mind her mother's tone because life was too rich, too full, for concern about such matters.

Misfortune befell the mother and forced the three daughters out into the world to make a living. There was a small teachers' college nearby where they could prepare to become teachers to make their way in the world.

The beautiful daughter, being the eldest of the three, went to college first. College presented no difficulties for her. All the boys in college liked her; hence, her social life was pleasant. When the other girls saw the interest of the boys in the beautiful daughter, they reasoned that if they were to enjoy the favor of any one of the boys, they must first win the favor of the beautiful daughter. They began to offer her papers already written, problems already solved, and advice as to which classes to take and which ones to avoid. The beautiful daughter graduated and soon obtained a teaching position.

The superior intellect of the second daughter made college easy for her. She found satisfaction in taking all the hard courses. Teachers favored her because of her clear thinking, her pertinent recitations, and her perfect papers. She considered the behavior of the students to be boisterous, and their thinking and conversation shallow. She found association with the instructors more satisfactory than companionship with students. Instructors invited her into their homes because they respected her opinions. She graduated, and their recommendations readily landed her a teaching position.

The third daughter entered college. Her friendly, straightforward attitude soon won a wide circle of friends. Other students followed her leadership. They named her the chair of committees, the captain of teams, and the leader of groups. She was not a straight "A" student but her class contributions gained appreciation of the instructors because they were honestly prepared and sincerely presented. She graduated and joined her two older sisters in the teaching profession.

All went well at first for the first, beautiful daughter. The children brought her flowers and complimented her. Mothers approved of stories told about her at home. She obtained status in the upper stratum of society, invited to clubs, card parties, and dances. She avoided professional organizations because they took money she needed for clothes. She did not study or go to professional meetings. They took too much time. She did not correct the papers that she assigned students because she did not have time to do it. When a mother inquired about her child's progress, the answer was always the same. "Oh! Just fine; she really is a lovely child." If the beautiful daughter heard a story, she tried to make herself more popular by repeating it at dinner parties and clubs. She entertained her acquaintances with stories of embarrassing situations of the principal and of other teachers. She shared amusing responses made by children to test questions, always adding interest to the tales by giving the names of the persons involved. One day the principal asked her to come to his office. He told her of reports that had come to him to the effect that she had given out confidential and official information that had harmed the school. She could not believe his crushing words. Her friends who had laughed at her stories had purposely done her harm. She had only tried to make friends. She resigned from her teaching position the next day and moved to a different town. She saw no fault in herself.

The second daughter approached her schoolroom with confidence, appropriate as the performance of someone who had made perfect scores in college. However, when she faced a sea of inquisitive eyes staring back at her, visions of her imagined childhood confused her. She saw a solid unit of potential enemies. She remembered warnings she had heard. "Don't let them get the upper hand of you. Let them know who is boss." She spotted someone chewing gum, called the suspect to the front of the room, and bullied a confession from him that he was chewing gum. Confused about what to do, she chose to show him and all the others that she had high ideals of behavior. She said, "Stick your gum on the end of your nose and stand in front of the room until you can remember to behave like a gentleman." The expression of the sea of eyes changed from curiosity to sullenness. School ended, and by four o'clock, everyone in town knew that the new teacher had made a child stand on the floor all day for chewing gum. The second daughter concluded that the way to keep children from misbehaving was to keep them so busy that they would not have time to think. She made up long tests and extensive assignments that few students could complete. She branded them as lazy and derided them by asking if they really had gone to school. She demanded to know what if anything their teachers had taught them. When someone in town asked her, "How's school?" She told them how bad it was. The second daughter honestly believed that the truth was how she saw things. In the spring when letters concerning next year's work appeared in the mailboxes, the second daughter's box was empty. She was not disappointed because she did not like teaching anyway.

When the third daughter faced her first class, she saw individuals—all potential friends. She looked forward to sharing their joys and their sorrows. She saw them in terms of her own experiences and thinking; hence, she dared to trust them. She gave them a chance to think, and respected their opinions. When a child needed discipline, she talked to him privately. She adjusted assignments to a child's ability. If a child did not show interest, she blamed herself. She studied all the available records of her children to understand their problems. She was distressed at some things she learned, but she kept her counsel. She made mistakes in dealing with her pupils, but they tolerated her mistakes because they understood that fundamentally she was their friend.

The third daughter considered teaching a dignified profession. She worked hard at her job and felt that teachers deserved to live on a level comparable to other professions. She joined forces with teacher organizations in working for higher salaries. She never belittled her profession by word or deed. Because of her love of people and her talents for leadership, she made a place for herself in the community, prelude to a long and fruitful career as a teacher.

"Fable in Ethics" appeared in the *California Journal of Elementary Education* in August 1945.

32

Quintessential Storyteller

Pauline added to her standing as a collector of American folktale stories and a master at telling these tales.[1] The richness of Ventura County in native folklore and her already considerable expertise in the subject blended to make her one of the nation's foremost experts in oral history. Consequently, she was in demand as a speaker. Folklore became her passion and an inauguration into the Ventura community. Telling tales was her hobby but it was more than a hobby. She often illustrated her talks with maps showing sectional types of stories, usually concluding with two of her favorite tales, "Brer Rabbit" and "Pecos Bill."[2]

These were sentimentalized stories that held an appeal for both children and adults. Pecos Bill was a character, bigger than life, and able to perform super human tasks. Stories about him accounted for much of the geography of the Southwest. According to legend, Pecos was born in Texas about 1835. On a trip with his parents in a covered wagon, he fell out of the wagon unnoticed by the family near the Pecos River. Coyotes found him and raised him; until his real brother found him and convinced him, he was not a coyote. Stories grew with Pecos's every deed. He was responsible for many of the landmarks of the Southwest. Said to have created the Gulf of Mexico, one time when there was a drought in Texas, he lassoed a storm cloud with his rattlesnake lasso and brought it to Texas. It rained so much that it created the Gulf of Mexico. Another time, he and his horse found themselves stranded in the desert and in need of water. Pecos grabbed a stick and dug the Rio Grande River. He rode a horse named Widow Maker because no other man could ride him and live. He had a woman friend named Slue-Foot-Sue who rode a catfish down the Rio Grande. After a courtship, Pecos Bill, enamored with Sue, celebrated by shooting out all the stars, except for one that became the Lone Star. Multiple variations of Pecos Bill stories appeared in magazines. Many of them traced to the fertile imagination of the writer Edward O'Reilly who first published some of them in 1917. Nevertheless, O'Reilly claimed he based them on old folklore passed orally from generation to generation. Storytellers like Pauline helped to make them a part of American heritage.

The folktale of Brer Rabbit, on the other hand, falls into a different category from Pecos Bill; that is, more akin to an Aesop fable meant to imprint on a young listener different layers of human behavior and the consequences of ones actions. Brer Fox made a doll out of a lump of tar and dressed it to fool Brer Rabbit. When the Tar Baby did not respond to Brer Rabbit's attention, he began to punch it out of rage. The madder he became the more he punched and became stuck in the tar. Brer Fox saw the entrapped Brer Rabbit and revealed himself. The helpless Brer Rabbit pleaded with Brer Fox, "Please, Brer Fox, don't fling me in dat briar patch," prompting the bad Brer Fox do to exactly that. The cunning Brer Rabbit, born in a briar patch and described as small but bright, used his home in the briar thicket to free himself from Tar Baby and escape the fox. Pauline often told this story to small children because they could relate to the antagonism between the rabbit and the fox, and cheered the quick thinking of the small but bright Brer Rabbit to outsmart Brer Fox. Folded into the story, too, was a warning about the consequences of rage. What Pauline did not tell, and unfortunately never considered relevant, were the racist overtones of the story. Told often in exaggerated Negro dialect, Brer Rabbit stories traced back to the trickster figures of Africa where similar stories figured prominently in African storytelling traditions. The incarnation of the story in American folklore disregarded its likely representation of enslaved black Africans. A reculturalized society caused the language of the *Uncle Remus* stories, of which Brer Rabbit was a centerpiece, largely to disappear from the lexis of American literature.

The unfortunate nature of many folktales was the ethnic bias embedded in them. For example, one source of Pauline's stories was *The Tree Named John* by John Sale, a 1929 book of collected tales based on his boyhood growing up on a plantation near Columbus, Mississippi. The stories had roots in slavery drawn from life and the superstitions that were implicit in them. Written in the truncated words of the African-American dialect, the book today would be undeniably racist in its tone. When Pauline told one of the stories from the book to the Soroptimists, the local press described it as a "fantasy devised by a southern mammy to amuse a little boy." Although of maligned origin, the morale of the story resonated with an audience. The "mammy" described he earth in the days when only animals inhabited it, and told how the rabbit outwitted the roaring lion, who previously dominated in the world because of his ability to frighten the other beasts.[3]

Ventura welcomed Pauline into the community. In her first year on the job, she was guest speaker at the American

Association of University Women, Delta Kappa Gamma, and Soroptimist, to name a few.[4] A new club that she particularly liked was the I-da-ka club, a community club similar to the community club she had known at Rickreall, Oregon. It started in Ventura as an auxiliary of the Lions Club to organize fundraisers for community projects. Pauline especially liked their club name I-da-ka, a Native American Indian term that meant, "We serve."

Pauline was in her element when clubs met in rural settings, one recurrent setting especially was the James Leonard ranch on Gonzales road near Oxnard.[5] Luncheon tables were set in the garden under a wisteria arbor, a lovely setting for Pauline, the Billings country girl, to tell her stories.[6]

There was much more to Pauline's affection for folklore than entertainment. Folktales for her were a tool for teaching. She often spoke before PTA gatherings at Saticoy and other outlying districts on the subject of children's literature, illustrating from folktales and her own experiences how children learned best by reading interesting things.[7]

Pauline thrived on the community work of all organizations. Her favorite club by far, however, was the Soroptimist, an international, worldwide volunteer service organization for women who worked for peace and in particular to improve the lives of women and girls in local communities and throughout the world. It was a particularly relevant organization, as World War II appeared to be edging toward a conclusion. She spoke often before the Soroptimist club. Within a year of moving to Ventura, the club elected her vice president.[8] The international group named her to the board of the 1945-1946 governing body.

As the school year loomed ahead, Pauline went into organizational mode. She brought with her to Ventura a teacher workshop model. Working with Superintendent Triggs, she retooled the annual fall teachers meeting into a different concept. The *Ventura County Star-Free Press* reported the anticipated change. "By using Ventura County as laboratory, at least 120 elementary school teachers in the county will be equipped to inaugurate a unique classroom program when their respective schools open next month. The program is planned not only to give youngsters training in the traditional three 'Rs' but such allied subjects as selling, principles of agriculture, simple manual arts and skills, and community living as well...Washington school students will take part each morning in a demonstration school. From 9 to 3:30, the teachers put in a full school day attending demonstration classes in the morning and methods and skills classes in the afternoon. Winding up the day are lectures and guest speakers."[9]

The Ventura workshop version had all the elements of the Rickreall model, and more. Pauline enticed Helen Heffernan, the chief of the elementary division, California State Department of Education, to be the workshop featured speaker. The visibility of activities in Ventura County was on the ascent.

On August 6, 1945, an American B-29 bomber dropped the world's first deployed atom bomb over the Japanese city of Hiroshima, immediately killing 80,000 people. Three days later, a second bomb fell on Nagasaki, killing an estimated 40,000 people. In Ventura County, the conversation grew somber. The use of the atom bomb suddenly to end the war changed the whole aspect of county business. At the Soroptimist meeting, a lively discussion of the Asiatic problem threatened to divide the membership.[10] Pauline took charge of the meeting and steered it back to its center, turning to the customary purpose of the summer meeting, namely, to collect books and games for the ship's library project, a project whereby the club provided reading and entertainment material for ships leaving Port

Hueneme. She read letters of appreciation from service members, a veiled reminder of the purpose of the Soroptimist.[11]

Pauline abhorred the war but she was not an avid political activist. She was an educator. When she spoke, it was not about war but about the relationship between the home and school, topics like "Comparison of New and Old Methods of Education" and "Education Today and Yesterday," always able to fold in a folktale or two that illustrated how folklore influenced early pioneers.[12] She made history not politics and war the subject. On one occasion, at a meeting of the Business and Professional Women's club in the Masonic temple, according to the local press, she "told of the relationship between the spiritual and physical, as well as the geographical problems of pioneers and the folktales, superstitions, and beliefs growing out of certain sections and groups."[13]

The first full year at Ventura ended. Christmas came, and with it memories of Christmases past. She reminisced in her mind about the holidays with family at Billings and Fennimore, and remembered the special times in the Rickreall Christmas Pageant. There would be celebrations at Ventura, too, but for now on a lesser scale. She joined the Toastmistress Club of caroling angels standing beneath snow-covered candelabra to set the holiday mood for the Christmas formal dinner at Pierpont Inn. Pauline highlighted the program reading the story of the humble little donkey that carried Mary to Bethlehem.[14]

33

The Jeidy Method

The days of uninspired teaching of the three R's to bored second-graders fell by the wayside in Ventura County schools under Pauline's leadership. She transformed a time when reading was just reading, writing was only writing, and arithmetic was, well, arithmetic. Before Pauline, there was something uninspiring about the presentation of the three R's in a classroom day after day in the same old way.

Pauline built her idea upon her concept of the integrated curriculum, in which multiple subjects, intermingled with social studies, made the three R's practical and interesting. "It provides subject matter, social growth, and experiences for youngsters;" she said. "For teachers, it improves instruction in social studies and skill subjects;" namely, reading, writing and arithmetic.

Holistic learning grew out of an interest for the overall wellbeing of children amid a national concern for faltering reading skills. One educator explained the social consequences of poor reading. She said, "The boy who cannot read adequately cannot attain objectives, the achievement of which depends to a greater or less degree upon reading; and this deficiency may seriously interfere with his success in such areas as social studies, history, geography, science, and reading itself...If the child cannot meet his basic needs, security, and pre-eminence; he tends to seek detours around his problems, and he becomes more or less maladjusted."[1]

Pauline was sympathetic and understating about the impact of instability on a young child. She took on the problem partly in response to the national anxiety about basic skills, but primarily of her own desire to improve teaching and learning.

She wrote a course of study in reading. In it, she illustrated how maladjustment in student behavior may have its inception. She described a little boy who had been adequate to the reading of simple first grade chart stories and pre-primers and who had seemed to enjoy a sense of power from making out the meaning of the "funny black marks." Then one day the child got his words mixed. The teacher frowned. She was angry and the child became unhappy. The teacher reproached him for not knowing the words. He was deeply hurt. The next day he tried again. He blundered once more and the teacher was cross. Now the fun was gone. The teacher had become someone to fear. With a change in his feelings toward his own ability and a change in his feelings toward the teacher, came a change in his feeling toward reading.[2]

Pauline's course of study in reading made learning fun. Although written specifically for Ventura County schools, educators acclaimed it across the country.

Her idea for holistic teaching went beyond reading alone. She believed that all of the skill subjects, and to an extent any subject poorly taught, had the potential to destroy a child's confidence in learning.

To develop her idea of integrated teaching, she began working on a teacher-inspired curriculum whereby teachers became the contributors to the new model. She began with a second-grade class study unit called "The Ranch," a class in which kids used basic skills to learn about animals, crops, and much more. For about an hour and a half daily, they studied about ranches and their equipment, how and when farmers harvested crops, about packinghouses and procedures. The plan allowed for and encouraged field trips to visit ranches. Schools planted trees and did other things related to the ranch. In game periods and singing sessions, they carried out the ranch theme by playing such games as '"Farmer in the Dell." They drew pictures of the ranch and ranch life. Each activity reinforced a previous experience and invited inquisitive minds to solve problems. Knowledge learned in arithmetic classes found applications in ranch data and outside projects like building a chicken pen or a rabbit hutch, all activities immersed in the social studies theme of "The Ranch". Teachers carried over the theme in creative writing assignments that encouraged students to write about their experiences in the social studies unit. Spelling, too, was unobtrusively interspersed in the lesson through compositions and introduction of new words like tractor and hatchery, part of ranch life not commonly part of a second grader's vocabulary but readily connected to the integrated theme of the ranch.[3]

The theme-centered teaching model became popular. The tradition of the Ventura County school system that began a new school year each fall with boring teachers' meetings ended, and reemerged in 1946 under Pauline's guidance as the Ventura County Teachers' Workshop. Her knowledge and experience overlaid the unique design of the workshop. Pauline extended the social studies model to other grades beyond second grade each with its own integrated theme, different in focus but serving the same purpose as "The Ranch". She made holistic learning a cornerstone of the opening pre-school workshop, redesigned to inspire teachers coming out of the workshop to enter the coming school year excited about teaching and armed with new ideas.

The workshop began each day with demonstration classes. Kids interrupted their summer vacations to voluntarily bus into a central location, in the same manner that Pauline had set up a similar workshop at Rickreall, Oregon, and Butte County, California. At the workshop, experienced teachers armed with Pauline's lesson plans for integrated social studies demonstrated the techniques of teaching multiple subjects. In the afternoon, art and music often dominated workshop activities. Teachers learned how to do folk dancing, singing, and construction, or whatever activities happened to occur in the morning demonstration classes.

One of the unique features of Pauline's workshop model was a session set aside each day to encourage teachers to make suggestions for improvement and in that way to demonstrate ownership of the workshop experience.

In the evening, a featured speaker addressed the teachers. At the very first workshop, Miss Helen Heffernan—Pauline's mentor, advocate of democracy in education, and freshly returned from an assignment with the Occupation forces of war-torn Japan—headed a cast of recognized professional speakers.[4] Pauline's preference for social studies and history themes taught in support of democracy traced to the outspoken opinion of Miss Heffernan who advocated teachers to get involved in politics. She said, "Politics is too important in a democracy to be left to the politicians." [5]

The workshop lasted two weeks. Coming in the post-war period, it helped to fill gaps in meeting the needs of teachers unable to get training elsewhere because of overcrowded university summer sessions oversubscribed by returning soldiers eager to take advantage of the GI Bill. Moreover, the workshop as a local program adapted to the specific needs of Ventura County educators.[6]

Pauline kept busy with a full calendar of speaking engagements in what seemed at times to be an endless number of clubs and organizations. She promoted her workshop to PTA members in outlying schools in Ventura County, extolling the benefits of home and school, or commending the benefits of health, happiness, security, and independence for young learners in school. She talked about religion, courtesy, and righteousness as needs for a well-rounded school environment, and declared that these things must also exist at home, as in school.[7]

She found time to serve as the new president of the Soroptimists, moving up from vice president the previous year. As president, she gained the additional perquisite of getting to travel to Estes Park, Colorado, for the organization's annual conference. [8]

She found time, too, for city business, welcomed at Ventura city council meetings as a representative of the Soroptimists. The mayor commented, "Maybe other service clubs will follow your example and send representatives to council meetings to see how we are spending their money."[9]

At Christmas season, she traveled around the county hosting institutes in the county to plan Christmas programs and decorations in the schools.[10] In addition, of course, there was always time to entertain the members of some local club with folktale stories; or, to spend an hour with a sixth grade class to tell them the story about Pecos Bill.[11]

Pauline opened the New Year 1947 with a nod to politics. She joined the American Association of University Women, an organization founded in 1881 to advance equity for women and girls united behind the common goal of breaking through educational and economic barriers for women. Her unyielding advocacy of women's rights closely aligned with the goals of the organization. Pauline harbored strong opinions about women's issues that she did not hesitate to inject into conversation. However, she also had a remarkable ability to skate around issues without stepping into a public controversy.

She found herself at the first meeting of the AAUW among women of like mind. Superior Court Judge Charles F. Blackstock told a large crowd that in his opinion "Woman is in every conceivable way equal to man and is in many ways superior to man." He never understood the reasons for the long period of subjugation of womankind. "America has not been too good to its women," he said.[12]

The AAUW selected Pauline as program chairperson, happy to have the woman known statewide for her storytelling programs in charge of entertainments.[13] Meanwhile, Pauline finished out her term as president of the Soroptimists and quickly replaced that duty with a new membership in the Business and Professional Women's club.[14] All of her club memberships were with women's organizations, not surprising because, despite Judge Blackcock's proclamation of equality between men and women, men's clubs excluded women.

A typical day for Pauline meant one or two speaking appointments. In one instance, Delta Kappa Gamma hosted a luncheon for girls from county high schools who had selected teaching as their future profession. Pauline talked about "Teachers for Tomorrow." She went from that meeting to the Business and Professional Women's club across town, dipped into her folktale collection, and delivered the improbable story of Nebraska's legendary hero, Febold Feboldson.

According to this story, Febold decided to adjust his crops to accommodate the climate of Nebraska whereby one side was always hot and dry and the other side wet and rainy. He planted corn on the hot and dry side and sugar cane on the wet and rainy side. Everything went along well until the crops matured. Febold Feboldson soon discovered that the hot side was popping all the corn and covering the ground like a blanket of snow. On the wet side, rain made the sugar cane soggy and all the molasses ran out of it. The molasses rolled in a huge river into the deep drifts of popcorn. It flowed right on, rolling up white puffy balls as big as houses. And, that is how we got our first popcorn balls. An attendee who heard the story reported that the delighted listeners were not kindergarteners but members of the Business and Professional Women's club. Pauline usually ended one of her stories with an explanation of its origin. "Mrs. Jeidy's extensive study of folklore and her artistry in repeating the tales have captivated the club's members on other occasions, the reporter wrote, "but Febold Feboldson's fantastic adventures proved spellbinding." Pauline explained that the early pioneers invented such whoppers as a defense mechanism against the hardships and unaccountable extremes of weather they encountered in settling the plains states. "The stories helped them to laugh at their troubles and gave them the courage to believe that the seemingly impossible task was, after all, possible of accomplishment," she said.[15]

PAULINE KASTENDIECK JEIDY. **This portrait dates to about 1946. It appeared in the *Ventura (CA) Star-Free Press,* along with an article published in conjunction with her selection by Gen. Douglas MacArthur to head the elementary school program in Japan during the Allied Occupation.**

Japan Occupation

34

The Year That Was

In the summer of 1947, Pauline skipped her usual habit of taking the summer session workshop at UCLA because she was teaching it. The university obviously knew her work and readily hired her to bring her workshop ideas to the Berkeley campus. She taught two courses in the summer session, both to serve elementary teachers. The first course was a special problems class that summarized her curriculum work up to that point; namely, newer trends and teaching problems in oral and written languages, spelling, handwriting, creative expression, arithmetic, health and physical education, art, and music. The second course adapted another of her workshop techniques to address problems in elementary education by means of group discussions whereby she used meetings, individual conferences, participation in creative activities, and observation in the UCLA Demonstration Elementary School. Emphasis was upon the solution of individual problems brought to the workshop by the class participants, a signature Pauline practice.[1]

All the while, she was busy rewriting elementary school curriculum, planning workshops, and attending community organization meetings. At the same time, she produced important scholarly studies, particularly in reading and reading behavior. One of her most influential papers highlighted her early interest in minority education, particularly of Mexican-American children in Ventura County.[2]

In 1947, her article appeared in the *California Journal of Elementary Education* and caught the attention of educators nationwide. Titled "First Grade Mexican-American Children in Ventura County," the article came at a time when school desegregation and perceived problems of educating mixed ethnic groups to attain social equality was beginning to emerge on the national political scene.[3] Inequality in schools was not limited to African Americans in the South. It also targeted children of the Southwest.

School boards throughout California resisted desegregation remedies for decades. For example, Oxnard, in Ventura County, built neighborhood elementary schools several yards away from each other to prevent Chicano children from venturing outside their barrio. Where budgets precluded the creation of separate Mexican schools, districts established segregated spaces within the schools, separating students in both the classrooms and the playground. Schools meted out corporal punishment to children who spoke Spanish at school, leading to tight-lipped confusion among Mexican children unable to answer teachers in English, and not allowed to speak Spanish. They remained silent, alienated, and marginalized; 50 percent of Chicano youths dropped out.

Blatant discrimination in California ended in 1946 with the precedent setting case of Mendez et al. v. Westminster School District of Orange County (California) et al., a lawsuit brought by parents of Mexican children. US District Court Judge Paul J. McCormick ruled that separate but equal educational opportunities did not satisfy the constitutional requirement for equal education by merely furnishing separate schools of equal technical quality. A paramount requisite in the American system of public education, he said, is social equality. Magistrate McCormick went on to say, "The entire student body instills and develops a common cultural attitude among the school children which is imperative for the perpetuation of American institutions and ideals."[4]

Into this milieu of political discord stepped Pauline. Her article gained a large audience, widely disseminated and read by teachers and parents across the country. She gave a firsthand account of her experience with the issue then before the political leaders of the nation; namely, the issue of mixed ethnic education in public schools.[5]

She addressed the question of segregation in the usual Pauline manner, first stating the issue in practical teaching terms without once alluding to the matter as a political topic. She began her article by acknowledging the problem and then secondly proceeded to direct her attention to its long-term solution. The integration of ethnic diversity in schools, she said, needed to begin in the first grade.[6]

For many years, separate but equal schools existed in California because children did not speak the same language. Anglo-Americans did not speak Spanish, and Mexican-Americans did not speak English. Pauline wrote, "School administrators and teachers sincerely believed they could do more for the Mexican-American children by teaching them apart from the Anglo-American children."[7] Because the governance of most communities was almost exclusively Anglo-American, the expectation was to encourage children in Spanish-speaking homes to learn English.

The problem occurred mostly in larger neighborhoods where social life generally revolved around associations of like cultures. The Mexican-American communities spoke Spanish; the

Anglo-Americans spoke English. Pauline pointed out that in smaller communities the social contact between ethnic groups made for freer use of English. She noted, "In the smaller communities with smaller schools, segregation of school children has never been practiced."

Educating Mexican-Americans and Anglo-Americans in the same schoolrooms with the same instruction and educational opportunities was largely a first-grade problem. She found in her study that an older child that moved into a community directly from Mexico could learn enough English with the help of a language tutor in two to three months to get along socially, and became reasonably proficient in one school year. However, unfortunately in the first grade, administrators often considered it an impediment to the progress of English-speaking children to place non-English-speaking students in the same schoolroom with them.

Pauline never mentioned in her article the desegregation court order of Mendez versus Westminster but conceded that one of the main reasons for dispensing with segregation in all grades included a desire that "the Mexican-American and the Anglo-American children arrive at a state of fuller understanding and appreciation of each other."[8] This was fundamentally the reason behind Judge McCormick's decision to end separate but equal schools.

Nevertheless, desegregation was far from perfect. Schools grouped first-grade children under the new rules based not on ethnicity but on reading readiness. This immediately introduced a discriminatory hierarchy between Mexican-American kids who spoke fluent English and those who did not. To ameliorate this, each classroom comprised both Mexican-Americans and Anglo-Americans. Separation into groups was according to reading ability and other common learning attributes and not

English-speaking ability. It turned out that six year olds, regardless of their ethnic backgrounds, thrived on playing happily together. Freed from the anxiety of the classroom, Mexican-American children quickly picked up the language of their Anglo-American friends.

Schools soon adapted Pauline's model of holistic teaching, using programs that developed social ease, language facility, and self-confidence. Teaching included a great deal of dramatic play, free conversation, and discussion in an environment where there were no inhibitions regarding speaking in any language. Both language groups profited from being together.[9]

With a successful publication boosting her reputation among national educators, Pauline quietly went about her regular routine of curriculum planning, teacher training, and community work. The topics of her addresses, however, took a noticeable turn away from the entertainment of storytelling and toward more sober subjects that embraced responsibilities within a democratic society. She spoke to a large crowd of PTA parents on how "Understanding Makes Good Citizens," an extension of her ideas on tolerance through the interaction of ethnic cultures.[10] She assembled a panel of experts before the AAUW to discuss "What Makes Good Leaders." [11] Her personal investment of herself in education was total. She used every opportunity to make that point. For example, she set up a special tent exhibit at the Ventura County Fair to show what went on in schools of the county. Students from each school across the county showed off their best accomplishments in classes from shop and science to art, music, and creative writing. The theme for the general elementary display was "School Prepares for Living in Democracy."[12]

In four short years since coming to Ventura as curriculum director for the elementary schools of Ventura County, Pauline led school leaders within the county to create work units that integrated social studies with history, geography, literature, art, arithmetic, spelling, composition, music, and dance, to name a few topics. Frequently writing the unit lesson plans herself, completed work units covered classes from the first through the eighth grade in themes varying from a study of the community, ranch, and industry to the westward movement and history of democracy in the United States. A new unit on Early California completed under her supervision, awaited publication by the *California Journal of Elementary Education* to circulate statewide to coincide with the state's centennial celebration.

Moreover, her summer workshops now attracted more than 175 teachers yearly. Her workshop model showed how new units could be taught, and demonstrated new methods and procedures in teaching. The workshop became a model for the UCLA summer session at Berkeley.

Working from her office in the Education Building within walking distance of her small house at 2009 Evans Avenue, the year 1948 winding down, Pauline looked ahead to plans to create new teaching themes and methods. She particularly had her sights on the development of a democratic educational program more representative of the meaning of the American way of life and the cultural diversity that she believed helped to shape it.

One day, a brown envelope came in the mail addressed to Mrs. Pauline Jeidy typed in bold letters next to the newly created eagle insignia of the US Department of Defense. She inserted her ebony wood letter opener and with one easy motion opened the envelope. It was a letter from the Foreign Service Office of the headquarters of Gen. Douglas MacArthur, in Tokyo, Japan. The writer of the letter wanted to know if she would join the Allied American forces in Japan, to help rebuild that country as head the elementary education division of the post-World War II American Allied Occupation.[13]

35

Assignment Japan

When news of Pauline's appointment to Gen. MacArthur's Japan workforce appeared in the local newspaper, it opened the eyes of many county residents who had not followed her work in reshaping the county schools. One citizen read the newspaper article and wrote a letter to the editor. "Our elementary schools must be pretty good, better perhaps than we thought. Otherwise, I don't see why General MacArthur's headquarters would have selected Mrs. Pauline Jeidy, director of curricula in our county superintendent's office to head his elementary school program in Japan...The assignment is definitely a compliment to the California educational system, to the way such matters are handled in our county, and notably, of course, to the efficient public servant named."[1] Nevertheless, when the editors surveyed the best stories covered in 1947, the story of Pauline's appointment made the list of the top ten but lagged behind the controversy over the construction of the Matilija Dam.[2] However, the press noted that the singular "high honor reflected the esteemed regard in which she is held in educational circles...The army had at its command the chance to seek in the United States any educator suitable for the important post."[3]

Pauline wrapped up her activities in Ventura and looked ahead to her new assignment. She took a one-year leave of absence from her position as director of curriculum with the intent to return to her job after Japan.

Her newly acquired local fame never changed her outlook on life. She ended the year 1947 with a Christmas program at the AAUW. Always the teacher no matter where she went, she told the club stories of Christmas that illustrated human virtues and rewarded those who did what they thought was right.[4]

Meanwhile, the education community recognized several factors in Pauline's selection in addition to her agreed worthiness for the post. Her appointment meant the army wished to set up in Japan a school system based on the California education plan. It also showed that there was an awareness in high circles of the modern elementary education program that she had pioneered in the Ventura County schools.

As head of the elementary school program in Japan under the army rehabilitation program, Pauline had the staggering task of preparing school curriculum including textbook selection, heading elementary school teacher education, elementary school administration, and supervision. Her duties as the head of elementary education extended to kindergarten education, education of handicapped children, and parent education.[5] She also had the responsibility of mapping out elementary school buildings and grounds.[6] Her job was to augment and carry out the details of the program started by Helen Heffernan who had gone to Japan to introduce the framework of the California system. Heffernan had gone to Japan as a textbook specialist and stayed on until December 1947.[7] She was one of several prominent women educators who joined the Education Department of the Occupation.[8]

Miss Heffernan, an attractive woman in her early 50s, was unmarried, free to travel, and like Pauline was highly respected in education circles. She held a Master's degree in education from the University of California and a PhD from Stanford University. A 21-year career veteran of the California education system—and creator of much of the California system—her friendship and guidance tempered Pauline's own career and philosophy of teaching. Heffernan returned home from Japan to resume her duties as head of the elementary division of the state department of public education in California. Although never publicly acknowledged, Pauline likely came to the attention of Gen. MacArthur's staff through the recommendation of Miss Heffernan who closely followed Pauline's work in Ventura County and knew the success of her work.

Miss Heffernan came to Ventura in mid-January to meet with Pauline to discuss the work in Japan. She went over the groundwork laid so far during her 14 months tour of duty as part of Gen. MacArthur's rehabilitation plan. Heffernan had a passion for the democratic model of teaching. "We have the best chance of building a democratic form of government in Japan of any nation in the world today," she told Pauline. "Most of the Japanese hope the Americans will stay until a democratic government is firmly established." Whether her appraisal of Japanese political sentiment was correct, the intense nationalism and militarism that developed in Japan from 1930 to the time of the war took a toll on Japanese education. Heffernan estimated rehabilitation would take another 10 years to revise textbooks for both students and teachers. Already plans were in the hands of the Japanese and the framework for an initial democratized system was in use in Japanese schools.[9]

Heffernan warned Pauline of the difficulties that lay ahead of her. "The education program is far from completed," she said. Conditions in Japan were bad due to economic difficulties: food, clothing and shelter, public health, education, all elements Pauline had long contended were basic to the learning process. Bombing by American bombers partially destroyed large parts of Japanese cities. The people of Japan sadly remembered a March 10, 1945, attack when more than 300 American bombers wiped out large sections of Tokyo, killing between 125,000 and 200,000 people in a single day.[10]

Almost 4 percent of the Japanese population—nearly 3 million people—died of war-connected causes. At the war's end, the major cities of Japan lay reduced to charred ruins; some 10 million people lived on the edge of starvation. The repatriation of 6.6 million Japanese soldiers and overseas Japanese citizens added to the country's suffering.[11]

However, Miss Heffernan was of the naive opinion that the Japanese forgave Americans and were grateful for American aid. They were working hard to rebuild their land into a bastion of democracy, she said. She told Pauline that her job involved the training of 12 million schoolchildren who, in her opinion, awaited conversion to democratic ideals in place of former nationalistic training. "There is plenty of democratic spirit in Japan, and we must see that it does not wane," she concluded.[12]

Pauline may or may not have shared Heffernan's zeal for political ideology. While she agreed that democracy was an effective and appropriate theme around which to build education planning, the success of teaching and learning required more than an overarching political scheme, especially in a war ravaged country as culturally different from the United Sates as Japan.

When the offer came to join the Japan rehabilitation effort, Pauline had been in Ventura County not yet four years; she was approaching her 50th birthday.[13] Tall, erect, graceful, and commanding in her presence, her soft-spoken manner invited listeners to lean forward to catch every word she spoke.

Pauline was a pioneer in interdisciplinary instruction. She showed how to integrate subjects like social studies, for example, through the entire curriculum from geography, history, and arithmetic to literature, art, dancing, and music. It was a new and insightful idea that soon elevated the California plan for elementary education as a model for the nation. However, she was never a one-size-fits-all administrator. The units of study she designed and taught in her workshops always varied according to the location of a school and its community.[14] Japan would be a special challenge. Gen. MacArthur and his staff picked her because they saw in Ventura County the best example of the California-type education system that the army wanted to build in Japan. At the time, the California plan was the most modernized educational program in the country, a plan that based much of its educational philosophy on the theme of democracy in action.[15]

On February 2, 1948, Pauline took the train out of Los Angeles bound for Seattle, Washington.[16] She arrived in Seattle and checked into the New Richmond Hotel across from the city's two railroad stations on lower 4th Avenue. The New Richmond was an impressive nine-story hotel in Neoclassical Revival style built of concrete with terra cotta facing and all the amenities of a onetime excellent destination. When Pauline arrived, it was under rehabilitation. The US Army took over the building in World War II and rented it for use as a hospital. Only recently had it returned to service as a hotel.

The luxury of the New Richmond was brief for Pauline. She wrote, "Our baggage had to be in the lobby of the New Richmond Hotel by 8:00 a.M. We were warned to eat a good breakfast, which we did. Our baggage was transferred to the pier ahead of us. A rumor came to me that I was to fly over. The passenger list was too long for the boat by two items. Because of rank, another woman and I would get to fly. I waited around for a while but was not called. Heard afterward that two dependents were chosen for the air trip."

She described her debarkation experience, which gave a glimpse of what was to come. "We were hauled to the port at 10:00, lined up, showed our AGC cards, got meal tickets and were shown our state rooms. Mine was B6, very small, with two metal lockers, two folding chairs, two portholes, toilet, washbowl, and shower, and beds for four. There was a great pile of luggage, but on examining the tickets, I found that they all belonged to one person, which gave me a feeling of security, which I learned later, was false because the woman had two sons, aged three and four.

"I took a tour of the boat and was having a wonderful time on the top deck when an orderly came along and told me that space was 'off limits' for passengers.

"After we—the civilian personnel—were settled the 'dependents' moved in on us. Such a deal of nervous scolding names and bawling babies!"

The ship was the US Army Transport *Thistle*, an aging craft scheduled for demolition in the near future. The trip to Japan started as an adventure of memorable possibilities.[17]

36

On Board the *Thistle*

Pauline wrote a series of letters about her journey to Japan, sometimes humorous, usually typical of her sardonic wit, and always insightful. The letters provided an eyewitness account of events as they happened in post-war Japan, a sensitive description of the day-to-day life of the Japanese people struggling to revive a decimated school system. Official accounts of her work are in government reports and books written about the American Occupation covering the years of the MacArthur rehabilitation plan. Her personal thoughts, however, reveal the more human side of her story in letters she wrote to the Soroptimist club, Ventura County schools office, and family members at Fennimore, Wisconsin. The letters presented here allow Pauline to tell her story in her own words, minimally interrupted for clarification of location or circumstances related to the depictions of her experiences.

"We moved out at 11:30 with confetti, paper streamers, and an army band making horrible noises. The day was perfect and the colored paper made us look a little festive.[1]

"Those of us who sat on deck and watched the shore, soon learned that we were cruising around in a small circle. Rumor said that the compass was out of order, then that we were having engine trouble. Every once in a while, a tug would bustle out and a man or two would climb aboard. Then in an hour or so, it would bustle out and take them off again. When dark came we were still circling. Rumor said that our boat had just been in dry dock for ten days and that this was its last trip, and that it was to be junked if and when it finished this trip."

The *Thistle* was originally the Steamship Munargo, a commercial cargo and passenger ship built in 1921. It served as a troop carrier for the War Department during World War II. The army converted it into a hospital ship in 1943, and then designated it a US Army transport ship engaged in relocating army dependents and personnel. The trip Pauline took aboard the *Thistle* from Seattle to Yokohama, Japan, in February was one of its last trips. The army declared it surplus in November 1948.

"Three o'clock in the afternoon we had fire drill. Sailors grabbed the hoses and put out the imaginary fire. Passengers all had to put on their life jackets and rush to lifeboats. The babies looked the funniest of all. The jackets were nearly full length for them. They looked like big baseballs with hands on them.

"After dinner, I wanted to read a while. Got my *Readers Digest* and went to the so called 'ladies lounge.' It was full of soldiers, sailors, girls, smoke, and confusion—not one vacant chair. I went to the deck. It was cold and dark. Then I found a deck chair and dragged it in by a heater in the hall. Everything was lovely for about a page. Then a pink faced boy carrying a billy club came and told me there was to be no 'loitering' in the halls. I asked him to suggest a place for me to go to read. He suggested the 'ladies lounge'. I picked up my chair and started, but he said, 'No, I could not take the chair.' I took him to the door of the 'ladies lunge' and showed him the situation. He said there was a small lounge up on the next deck. There it was; a lovely room with leather covered furniture and one lone girl sitting, writing a letter. I rushed in, and said. 'Ah! at last a place to sit down and read.' The girl looked up coldly and said, 'No, this room is for ships' officers only.' I crawled out, took one last look around, and went to my stateroom. I have always thought that 'stateroom' implied a certain elegance and privacy.

"My roommate had thought she was to have the place alone. She said her husband was a major and she was entitled to better accommodations. She thought it was an imposition on a mother to be housed with a stranger. The children empathized her attitude by sticking out their tongues at me. The room was hot as a furnace and our portholes opened only onto an enclosed deck, where noisy games were going on. Thus, the first day ended.

"I arose early and was out on the open deck in time to see the sunrise. Sometime in the night, we had struck out to the west. The sun came up directly behind us. We were in the Alaska passage with mountains on each side of us. The weather, the air, the scenery were beautiful. Everything is lovely as long as you can stay on open deck.

"We had our first casualty at lunchtime yesterday. A woman put her hands over her face and started screaming and crying. Someone led her out and we have not seen her since. Last night we had a movie, Allan Ladd in *Calcutta*. I do not like Allan Ladd but I stayed as long as I could stand it because the movie was set up just outside our stateroom and it would be impossible to sleep with all the racket, and the lounge is full of the blaring of radio, and the crying babies.

"During the night, the boat began to pitch. One end was always up and the other end down. In addition to the teetering, a vibration from the engines makes everything rattle. At the climax of each pitch, the boat itself creaks from end to end.

"When you stand on deck and look toward the stern you can see only water and the next moment all you can see is sky. The dear children in our stateroom wake up at about 4:00 and start screaming. One of them bit a neighbor's finger this morning."

The *Thistle* was a relatively small ship 430 feet long with a beam width of 57 feet that accommodated 230 passengers. Nevertheless, its size made for a steep pitch angle in high seas rising up over the crest of a wave and then plunging down to repeat the movement with the next wave. Its steam turbine, single-propeller propulsion system pushed the *Thistle* along at a speed of 16 knots, about 18 miles per hour, or roughly the cantor speed of a good thoroughbred mare.

"The waves do strange things to you when you go upstairs. For a few steps you can fairly fly, you feel so light. Then for a few steps, it's all you can do to pull yourself from one step to the next.

"Not many people showed up for breakfast this morning and some left hastily when they saw food. The 'sickness' seems to hit people very suddenly. They can't even make it to the railing. Up on the decks they don't scrub but once a day. It's a mess, dark, wet, rainy, foggy, windy, and filthy, but it's the only place where you can get any fresh air.

"The MPs on the ship are sure nice kids. One of them was telling me how he dreaded a storm. I asked him if it made him sick. 'No,' he said, and his homely face took on a look of great concern, 'I dread it on account of the passengers. It makes 'em so sick.'

"I have found a place to read. One of the MPs let me have a chair, which I can put by a heater under a light just like I had the first night. I can sit as long as I like with no disturbances.

"It was cold and wet on deck this morning, snowing a little. In addition to the up and down movement, the boat has taken on a side roll—enough to make my chair slide back and forth as I write this.

"There is a decided difference between the army wives and the gals who are going over to work. [The 'gals' were part of the Occupation force en route to Japan] It's the army wives who fold up card tables and chairs and hide them behind the piano so they'll be sure to have them when they get back. They keep the chaplain and the officers busy with complaints and requests. They are snooty to the help and keep them on the run all the time. The working gals just grab the hand rails, propel themselves about and say little. The MPs take care of the babies and do a better job of it that the mammas. They can lay the babies over their shoulders and pat their behinds as well as anybody. They are probably more effective because they don't scream at the babies. The mamma in my room repeats over and over a ritual something like this, 'Why won't you mind me. I don't get any rest. I'm almost about dead. Why won't you be good just once. I could just cry you try me so. Get back into bed or I'll spank you. This time I mean it. Just wait 'til we get to Japan, I'm going to bed for a month and let your daddy take care of you.'

"We had good weather for a few hours this morning and again for a couple of hours at sunset. The wind was blowing a gale and the waves were high. It's hard to see where the winds come from when the sky is clear. The chaplain had church this morning. He made the lounge look a little like church. I was surprised to find that as Mark Twain said of Father Marquette.

'He carried equipment for explaining hell to the Indians.' He had an altar covered with dark red velvet, candles, portable organ, hymnbooks, and printed programs. It was quite nice for the moment, but did not do any good in the end. People put on good clothes and sang well together, but immediately after the services, they grabbed for bridge tables and good chairs. At the table, the first ones there grabbed for the biggest salad. The chaplain is better on the run than standing still. His sermon was good but he rushed so and looked so anxious to finish-as if he had to meet a dead line.

"Last night was the worst night of all for rough seas. Several times when the boat seemingly stood on end then fell with a groan, I expected the loud speaker to blare, 'Man the life boats.' At the end of each downward pitch, a sudden stop scooted me about six inches out of bed. The night was spent in scooting out of bed and working my way back. The ranks were thin at breakfast. The sea seemed quieter this morning. Yesterday's report showed we were about one third of the way to Japan."[2]

37

MacArthur and GHQ

The reconstruction of Japan came under the military authority of General Headquarters (GHQ) commanded by Gen. Douglas MacArthur. It was a relatively small organization at first, but its size grew rapidly after 1946. At the height of the Occupation in 1948 when Pauline arrived, it had more than 6,000 members, nearly 65 percent civilians like Pauline. Civilians outnumbered military people several times over. A sizeable number of staff were Japanese. Ninety percent of the GHQ work force for reconstruction was American civilians and Japanese, exclusive of other Allied countries.

To take on the task of administering occupied Japan, the US government established an organization of special civil staff sections to oversee specific areas of government. One of these was the Civil Information and Education section (CIE) put in place to direct the rehabilitation of Japanese schools. Ironically, when MacArthur set up the Military Government Section of the GHQ to operate the civil administration of Japan, his organization did not include a division of education.[1] Planners quickly corrected that oversight with the establishment of the CIE.

Unfortunately, at the outset, the execution of CIE programs by inexperienced junior military officers led to the impression that the Americans had few real qualifications for their work. Japan's postwar education minister complained, "Many of those who carried out the occupation administration of education were persons of extremely limited knowledge and experience in the field." The historian Ejii Takemae wrote, "Japanese educators had little use for the idealistic American reformers of lesser background and experience."

However, after the beginning in 1946, the qualifications of education professionals coming to Japan improved significantly. The United States sent many of its best and brightest leaders. An examination of American educators who followed the initial wave of rehabilitation revealed a different story from its beginning. "By and large the civilian corps of civilians was people of outstanding character and merit," wrote Takemae. Most possessed administrative skills and expertise in some field vital to the tasks of military government." At the time Pauline arrived in 1949 to take up her post in the CIE, the Occupation depended largely on non-military experts like her to staff the rehabilitation effort.[2]

Pauline's journey on board the *Thistle* continued, as the old steamer limped unhurriedly across the Pacific. As she neared he coast of Japan, Pauline's life at sea presaged the experiences that awaited her in the Orient. The most miserable aspect of serving in Japan came down to the act of getting there. The reward for swaying back and forth to keep her balance was seasickness.

"I dragged me out of bed, dressed me, and went and lined up with many others outside the doctor's door. They handle people quickly, efficiently and humanely there. It did not take long to work my way to the doctor. A brisk, clean healthy looking nurse sat me down in a chair, put a tin wastebasket beside me and told me not to use it if I could help it.[3]

"Its warm on deck today but cloudy and damp. It was just announced over the loud speaker that *B* deck was off limits because of rough weather. I have been on *A* all afternoon. It's quite a sight to see the big splashes. Dark slate gray water becomes aqua and white as the waves break.

"This morning a ship was sighted; the first sign of life since we started. Everybody was quite excited. We were supposed to get into the bay this evening and dock in the morning. Then about noon, a terrific wind came up and slowed us up to less than 3 knots an hour. We really have big waves now. They look like mountains. We perch up on top of one then pitch down into a deep, deep trough. The spray flying through the air looks something like a blizzard. All decks are off limits.

"We made it. This morning we were surprised to find we were standing still. The water used for ballast was being pumped out so that we could sail in shallow water. We pulled into port at Yokohama at about 10 and there were the army husbands, all lined up bearing gifts and flowers. A snappy colored band was playing and all was joy and gladness. The husbands came aboard and took the families away. Then civilian personnel came aboard and gave us our hotel assignments and meal tickets and changed our money to army script, which is all we can use over here. Japanese boys took our luggage and we were herded into buses for the trip to Tokyo. On the way we saw about every type of transportation propelled by man, beast, or motor.

"I have a single room, with shower down the hall. The food is good and nicely served.

"I saw Gen. MacArthur Saturday. There was much blowing of whistles, stopping of traffic, scurrying to line up, and snappy saluting. Then the Gen. stepped out of a mile-long black car and with an air of casual dignity ascended the steps. The door closed behind him and everything settled back to normal. They say it happens twice every day, including Sunday."[4]

The occupation of Japan operated under a strict command structure headed by Gen. MacArthur, the Supreme Commander for the Allied Powers (SCAP).[5] His General Headquarters was in Tokyo, decorously called the GHQ, an acronym sardonically adopted by the Japanese to mean "Go Home Quickly."[6] The complex super-government of the Army Occupation, although ostensibly under Allied control received its orders from Washington.[7]

MacArthur personified the Occupation not only to the Japanese but also to the world at large. He was age 65, known affectionately as the Old Man war hero. A Gallup Poll taken in April 1946 placed the general higher in public approval ratings than either President Harry Truman or Prime Minister Winston Churchill. MacArthur cultivated an aloof, imperious image to supreme effect. He interpreted his mandate as SCAP broadly, occasionally working behind Washington's back to apply policy directives to suit his own purposes. He had a reputation as a loaner. Takemae summarized how most Japanese viewed him. "He isolated himself, worked seven days a week, including holidays, arriving at his office in a black 1941 Cadillac. He abhorred staff meetings and remained inaccessible to most of his subordinates. There was no telephone in his office, and only a handful of aides could see him without appointment. He had a deep distrust of the media. He ordered several journalist expelled for their liberal reporting." Takemae's blistering appraisal of MacArthur claimed an even more sinister side to the general when it came to the Japanese people. "He was a racist and a nationalist who believed in the innate superiority of

American values and civilization over those of the Orient. He had a smug paternalism beneath which lurked a racialist impulse." [8] According to a witness, he once cursed the President as that Jew in the White House.[9] He allegedly had a desire to Christianize Japan.

In spite of his detachment and conceit, MacArthur radiated a charisma that could charm even his fiercest critics. A spellbinding speaker, he inspired listeners with his frank and disarming eloquence and cultivated in his staff a fierce devotion.[10]

Pauline was neither an avid follower nor devoted student of Gen. MacArthur. The demilitarization of Japan did not come under her charge of responsibility. Her work focused on revitalizing the Japanese education system. She settled into a hotel graciously furnished with real beds and bathtubs. She unpacked a few of the things brought from home to remind her of the comforts of Ventura, and turned her attention to the job ahead.

"I have met Mrs. Viney who teaches the Crown Prince, and have the promise of an interview with her, when she will tell me how royalty is taught.

"I took a jeep and driver today and, with the head of education for the handicapped and an interpreter went to visit a school for the deaf. If I am able to judge, the children are getting a swell deal there. The teachers [Japanese] were poised, vivacious, graceful, and had a great deal of personality. Their relations with the children were friendly, respectful, and businesslike. The children in the upper grade could lip read and talk 'til you would hardly know they were deaf. They asked me, through an interpreter, where I lived, when I came over and why, and if I had ever visited schools for the deaf in America. This school is in a residential part of the city which has not been bombed. Houses, flowering trees, gardens, hedges, and narrow streets were very pretty.[11]

Takemae described the state of handicap education in Japan before and after Pauline's arrival. "Previously, many disabled pupils, particularly those with mental and emotional difficulties, were kept at home. Implementation lagged considerably due to a shortage of teaching materials and qualified staff, but by May 1948, there were 74 schools for the blind and 64 for the deaf and mute, with a total enrollment of 12,400."[12] It would be presumptive to believe such a dramatic change could occur because of Pauline's appearance in February 1948. Nevertheless, the structure of the schools and her firm belief in the empowerment of children through interaction in what schools came to call "mainstreaming" in education had the distinctive imprint of her philosophy of learning. She organized conferences and workshops among primary school educators and helped develop teaching materials for students with disabilities under the Japanese Fundamental Law of Education that spelled out the rights and goals of the Japanese system.[13]

The Fundamental Law of Education was a statement of principle that set the objectives for each level of education. It also provided for special education, making districts responsible for assuring students with disabilities the same level and quality of education as other children.[14] At the invitation of the Occupation, Helen Keller visited Tokyo to give a boost to government efforts to enact another law, the Law for the Welfare of the Physically Disabled.[15]

NEW RICHMOND HOTEL. **Pauline traveled by train from Ventura, California, to Seattle, Washington, and stayed in the New Richmond Hotel prior to embarking for Japan. The hotel was under renovation after being in the service of the US Army during the war.** ***Photo by Asahel Curtis, University of Washington Special Collections.***

USAT *THISTLE* **The US Army Transport steamship *Thistle* traversed the route across the Pacific from Seattle to Yokohama, Japan. A Department of the Army civilian colleague of Pauline took this picture on the day it sailed. Pauline sailed to Japan aboard this ship on one of the last trips it made. Her stateroom was on Deck B. Photo by Elizabeth Terry.**

GEN. DOUGLAS MACARTHUR. **In 1945, Gen MacArthur became the Supreme Commander of the Allied Powers overseeing the Occupation and rehabilitation of Japan following Japan's surrender at the end of World War II. MacArthur and his staff selected Pauline to direct elementary education programs for the Japanese Ministry of Education.** ***Library of Congress.***

MACARTHUR COMING TO WORK. **Gen. MacArthur arrived at his office at General Headquarters in a 1950 Chrysler Crown Imperial limousine. Pauline's office was in the same Tokyo office complex as MacArthur's headquarters.** ***MacArthur Memorial Foundation.***

OCCUPATION VISITOR. **Helen Keller visited Tokyo in 1948 to boost government efforts to enact the Law for the Welfare of the Physically Disabled. She came at the invitation of a Japanese organization for the blind. At the right is her Scottish companion and guide, Polly Thompson. Pauline had a part in the 1949 passage of the disability law.** ***Courtesy of Takemae, Inside GHQ.***

Letters from Japan

38

Cherry Blossoms, Tea, and the PTA

Pauline approached her job as a participant observer, an anthropological study technique whereby a researcher learns about her subjects by becoming one of them. She understood that she could accomplish little without the trust and cooperation of the Japanese people. While her letters carried the aura of a tourist discovering a new and interesting place, they revealed an amicable and inquiring visitor respectful of the Japanese culture while recording the kinds of human experiences she believed to be at the center of a successful education program. She painted a portrait of an individual embracing the people of Japan as a person wanting to know about the vision and needs of the Japanese and less as a government official who had at her disposal the ability to change education in Japan. Her visual writing style weaves a story that is at once respectful and thoughtful while charming the reader who may have a weakness for Mark Twain.

In one letter, she speaks of the Mombusho, a name that referred to the Japan Ministry of Education. The ministry retained a strong hold on education reform after the war and was frequently at odds with the Civil Information and Education section of the Occupation.[1]

"I've been to a Cherry Blossom Festival and have attended ceremonial tea.

"Last Sunday Miss Kunugi from the Mombusho offered to guide me on a shopping tour to Kamakura. She said I should not buy anything; it was only an orientation trip.

"We took the train near this hotel and had a beautiful ride for about an hour and a half. The cherry, peach and plum blossoms, and trees of camellia against a background of green grass, grain and gardens of black soil, pine trees, and nice, homely little houses with thatched roofs made beautiful scenery all the way. Most of the way we were in a narrow valley, with orchards and gardens on the hillsides where they were not too steep.

"Kamakura is a lovely little city on the seashore that escaped the bombings altogether. We found to our surprise, when we got off the train that it was Cherry Blossom Festival Day and there were crowds of people in town. Most of the women and many children, both boys and girls were in kimonos. Colors were gay and many materials were gorgeous. Little boys with close haircuts and fat cheeks sure are cute in gay silk kimonos down to their heels and wearing wooden sandals.[2]

"We fell in with the crowd and followed a band down the street, under an arch, which shows you are approaching a shrine, down a lane lined on either side with cherry trees in bloom, into a little park, and there was the shrine against a hillside. It was a brilliant red small building with ornate gold decorations. We climbed many steps to get to the shrine, which is guarded by two large carved figures with sword and bow and arrows. There was a pile of paper money in the shrine, which people had tossed in, in order to bring some good fortune. We did not follow suit, for we did not think we could get much of a fortune for a dime, and did not feel like risking any more.

"We came across a tea ceremony being solemnized inside an enclosure of canvass. Miss Kunugi asked if I could go in and was given permission to take me. This was an outdoor ceremony so we sat on stools at small tables. Tables were arranged in a circle and people sit facing the inside of the circle. The colors of the costumes, the grace, and precision of serving, the ritual of the tea-making were very dignified and lovely. I tried to drink my tea just as the others did. You take your bowl in both hands, raise it about even with the forehead, and bow your head just so. You finish it in three small drinks and your last sip must be noisy. Then you turn the bowl in your hands, wipe the edge with your fingers, and set it down just so. The host stood right behind me watching. He patted me on the back and said something that meant I had done well. I think he was only flattering me. I was the only American there and felt big, awkward, and drab.

"After a few hours, we left the park to do the shops of the village. All this time I've been waiting to see real Japanese silk. There is none on the market here. All that is made is exported, but I was told that many of the Japanese have had to sell their good kimonos and obis. I could leave the kimonos without too much pain, especially since I learned that a woman of my age should wear nothing but black with only a bit of subdued elegance near the floor. It seems that the Americans have notoriously bad taste about such things. Brides and babies can have bright colors.

"After the kimono lessons we went to the beach. The waves roll in just as in California, but the shoreline is very different. We were at the edge of a small bay lined with vegetation and nice homes. There is much rain here. Even the walls of stone are bright green with moss."[3]

"I made my first PTA speech today. I was asked to go to a district out in the suburbs of Tokyo where there was to be a delegation from five PTAs to talk about what a PTA can do to help the school. I made up a speech that dealt mostly with child guidance (small g). People in CIE thought it was good. The people who had asked me to go thought it was good and asked if they might translate it, mimeograph it and pass it around. I protested enough to comply with modesty, but not enough to discourage them.[4]

"At noon today, I asked for a jeep to make the trip, but I learned that jeeps cannot stay out after 5:00. I asked for a sedan and found that they must be asked for 24 hours in advance. I was trying to figure out what to do next when someone took pity on my ignorance and got a sedan for me.

"A nice Japanese lady came to go with me, show the driver the way, and to interpret for me. She was educated in Baltimore and has seen more of the US than I have. We got on very well. She invited me to a tea in the Imperial Gardens Sunday. Double cherry blossoms are to be out then.

"We were in sight of the school at about ten minutes to 3:00 and were feeling smug about arriving at just the right time, when the muddy path we were on dwindled into nothing and a hedge loomed up ahead. The driver backed around and one rear wheel dropped into an irrigation ditch. In no time at all, some men and boys from the neighborhood were there with poles, which they used most effectively to pry the car out. We passed cigarettes and with much bowing and smiling and many goodbyes and thank yous we went to find another way to approach the school house. We found another footpath and started on it, but it was lopsided and we slid into the ditch again. This time we were in shouting distance of the school so we got out, spread our umbrellas, and walked the rest of the way.

"There were hundreds of getas (wooden sandals) in neat rows in the hall, but we were assured we could keep our shoes on. It makes wiping the feet an awful responsibility. Even though we were a little late, we had to go to the principal's office for tea. Then we had to take a tour of the rooms, which were as bare as picked birds, a little shabby, but very neat and clean. The view from the windows made up for lack of beauty inside.[5]

"When we got to the assembly room we found it crowded with over 200 people. I gave my speech, and then the interpreter gave it. She wanted to do it that way. She did a good job. I could tell by the way she looked, but the people just were not interested in my nice speech. They wanted to know how a PTA operates and who is in charge of it.

"The meeting was over at about 5:00 and we went to the principal's office for more tea. Then we were invited to the president's home for tea. The sedan was waiting at the door for us. The [PTA] president rode with us to show us the way so we felt quite confident, but soon came to a bridge that was only half there. We backed out this time without trying to turn around. My companion pointed out a high wall that surrounded the house we were to visit. That was my first experience in a Japanese home and it is something to remember.

"We got out at the gate and walked into a dream of a garden. I did not have time to take a good look for we soon were at the door where the wife of the president was on her knees, with her forehead nearly touching the floor. We were not really introduced, but were told who she was.

"I started to kick off my shoes at the door, but was told that I could wear them to the step up into the house, two paces ahead. I placed them neatly beside another pair of shoes, but someone had to turn them around for us. I had left the toes toward the house. They must be turned toward the street. When we left, I found it was much simpler to put them on when turned that way.

"We went into a room beautifully furnished with very comfortable western style furniture. All the overstuffed furniture had been covered with Chinese embroidered linen. We had tea in little covered bowls which set on lacquer stands about four inches high. We also had delicious paper-thin wafers, made of sweet potato they told us.

"Then we went into the less formal of the two tearooms in the house for more tea and food. I was given the honorable cushion at the head of the fourteen-inch high table. The others sat at 12-inch high tables. We began with thick green tea served formally, which meant that each bowl was brought separately and served from a kneeling position. After tea, we had two balls of rice about the size of a walnut with the hull on. Looked something like it too, for they had been rolled in something dark and sweet, which I learned, was made of beans. These were eaten with small sticks, about four inches long, which were used as forks. Then more tea, pale green this time. Apples came next, quartered and carved for beauty. These, too, were eaten with a stick. Last came coffee.

"All the while they asked questions and I told them how democracy works in the PTA, the voting, the discussions, the committees, etc. Sharp claps of the host's hands punctuated this occasionally when a woman would run in from somewhere, drop to her knees, bow her head, listen to his order, and run to do his bidding.

"The nicest thing about the position at the head table is that it faces the garden. The garden is the most studied and carefully arranged informality you ever saw. Stones, evergreens, shrubs, and flowers are in just the right proportion. The whole side of the house facing the garden was of glass, in panels that could be moved aside in summer.

"We left at about 6:00 in the universal manner, with much chatter, invitations to come again, holding each other's things while putting on shoes, and so on. I left with a beautiful big bouquet of flowers—magnolia, camellia, plum blossoms, daffodils, hyacinth, and more that I could not identify, also two exquisite small pictures that a man in the district had painted. They are simple and beautiful in a fragile sort of way. I prize them very highly."[6]

39

Art and the Occupation

The Civil Information and Education section of the Occupation contained various divisions. The Education, Religions, and Information divisions performed the bulk of CIE's work. However, two other groups, Arts and Monuments, and Analysis and Research divisions, also did important work. Arts and Monuments, set up in 1946, had the principal task of upgrading museums and making works of art available to the public. In 1947, Sherman E. Lee, curator of oriental art at the Detroit Institute of Art took control to work with eminent Japanese scholars to democratize the state museums in a program that broadened public access. The new model followed the prototype of US institutions, but not always to the full satisfaction of the public.[1]

The US Army exercised strict control over all aspects of Japanese culture. They practiced censorship and encouraged self-censorship. Ejii Takemae expressed the hypocrisy of US censorship when he wrote, "It was not a perfect model of democracy in action...The peculiar circumstances of the defeat and occupation profoundly changed the political, economic, social, cultural, and ideological contours of the land."[2]

Pauline's vision of holistic education depended heavily on incorporating the arts into the learning process, especially at the elementary level. Her own childhood experiences in school plays, acting in community productions, and elevating storytelling to an art form itself told her of the intrinsic value of creative expression.

Play-acting she believed satisfied a desire for dramatization that seemed to be rooted in the nature of everyone both children and adults. Even when people do not perform in a play themselves, they watch plays and movies performed by actors and read plays and books.[3] The desire for dramatization formed a basic principle of Pauline's teaching method. The impulse of a child at play to imitate an adult's life was a main tool for learning social studies. She advocated role-playing in problem solving, and for the best learning effect whenever possible to place students in actual problem-solving situations. Children who gather knowledge in solving a problem and understand the procedure they used have a learning experience not forgotten for the rest of their lives, she said. Problem solving in this way was not only a method to acquire knowledge about a subject but also a method of living. Moreover, children learn the benefits of studying together and spending time together. Nevertheless, she also believed it was essential that students learn to practice problem solving on their own and preferably at an early age, at least throughout the first grade. She strongly recommended tours and school trips as part of the problem solving process.[4]

In a letter she wrote to the Ventura County school office, she described her visit to a Japanese Normal school where 200 kindergarten teachers were observing demonstration teaching. "I was amazed at what they were doing." She wrote. "One room was having rhythms...one room was doing market." The children were buying and selling at a great rate. They had a flower show, an art shop selling pictures, and other commodities. Some were painting with black paint on old newspapers. "It was all the paint and paper they had, but the youngsters were making wonderful trains, houses, flowers, and people." The third room was dramatizing the activities of a railroad station. "It was wonderful! They bought tickets, loaded baggage, boarded trains, blew whistles, and called stations. They even had one section of the train labeled US Army." All other labels were in Japanese.[5]

Pauline wrote a letter to her friends in the Ventura Soroptimist club asking for supplies to use in classrooms. She needed things like paintbrushes, crayons, paper, and paint for the children to use in the schools. Clubwomen took up a collection to buy a plentiful supply of materials.

She visited a Japanese department store to view a school display of social studies material. She wrote home, "Mobs of people were treading on each other's heels trying to see it all."

The store manager asked her if it would be possible to get a similar display from America. He was of the opinion that everyone in Japan would be happy to see it. The Japanese people would value their schools more highly, he thought, if they were like those in the United States. Pauline asked Ventura County officials to ship the county schools fair exhibit to her, pledging that the interest in it would be greater than in Ventura County.[6]

It was immediately clear to Pauline that Japanese schools already knew the value of including the arts in a child's education. The integrated method of instruction was already at work in Japan awaiting only the resources and carefully modulated classroom planning to cement the activities into a progressive, stepwise process to achieve the highest potential of each student. That would require the democratization process in which every student had access to quality education. To do her best work in that regard, Pauline needed to understand more fully Japanese art and culture.

"I went to two Japanese plays tonight, and it's different from anything I've ever seen. One was written about 250 years ago and the other in the 15th century. The costumes and stage sets were out of this world...All lines are recited in falsetto and many speeches were long. Their interpretations through facial expression and bodily movement were most accurate. The theatre had been redone by the US Army and was modern and beautiful.[7]

"I went to a puppet show tonight. The paper said it was given for the benefit of Japanese girl scouts and was going to dramatize Japanese folktale stories. Imagine my surprise to find that they were doing the *Musicians of Bremen.*[8] The scenes were wonderful. The musicians of Bremen did things they have never done before to my knowledge. The cat and dog were always picking a fight and the donkey was the peacemaker. They gave the impression that the musicians were walking a great distance by rolling the scenery along behind them. As houses, bridges, trees, and fields went by, it gave the impression that the animals were travelling.

"At the end of the program, an American Catholic priest said a few words then a Japanese priest did the same. Then everybody stood up and sang, 'Stand up, Stand Up for Jesus.' The Japanese sang in their own language and we sang in ours. It all sounded quite harmonious.[9]

"I went to the Imperial Gardens this afternoon to see the double cherry blossoms, which are at their very best just now. I know I have written so many superlatives that they don't express a thing any more, but again the sights to see were out of this world...There were cherry trees nearly as big as elm trees covered with double flowers about as big as a half dollar. The colors ranged from the faintest pink to deep pink. Besides the flowers, there were pools, streams, arched bridges dotted with gay kimonos, evergreen trees, and maple and willow in the early spring, pale-green stage.

"The occasion for opening the gardens was an exhibition of the Bugaku, an ancient ceremonial dance which is given just once a year. The dance is not a lively one, but seems to require a great deal of precision even to the fingertips. Again, the costumes were such that we can never see at home. The music was played on ancient instruments, which looked much like ones the couple from Ontario brought to workshop last year. In addition, there was an immense drum, which had a lovely blood-chilling primitive sound.

"Tomorrow we go to hear the *Voice of the Turtle.* You probably have the impression by now that I'm not doing any work, but let me assure you that such is not the case.[10]

The work of the Allied Occupation force was secretive and heavily censored; Pauline's letters seldom alluded to her duties as head of the education department, and then only in broad terms. Materials related to the Japanese Occupation, GHQ/SCAP, take up more than 800 linear feet of file space at the National Archives in Washington, D.C. A file contains Pauline's official correspondence, internal memoranda, and reports dated from March 1948 to January 1950. Pauline's unofficial personal letters mostly covered trips and encounters with the Japanese people that she experienced in the process of carrying out her official duties.[11] Her letters home painted the true picture of Japanese culture at the time of the Occupation.

"I spent the evening in revising some of my clothes. I had bought a new suit, which was as usual too narrow in the hips. I can't win. It was some help to have the skirts grow longer, but no help at all to have them narrow from top to bottom. I had a dress made by a Japanese dressmaker who does pretty well at most things and especially well in hand work, but cannot make a hem. She never cuts the material evenly at the bottom. She just measures the place where the hem ought to be and rolls all the remaining material into it. I am not good at it, but can make improvements on hers.

"Last night I went with a party of sixteen people to a kabuki play at the Tokyo Theater. Kabuki is wonderful, a great improvement over the Noh plays in my estimation. Noh plays are classical and very stilted and dull. Kabuki has life and zest to it. It originated much later than Noh. Kabuki is only about five hundred years old. It has some of the elements of the Noh plays in the chorus and the orchestra, but is much more understandable.[12]

"There were three one-act plays which lasted from six to eight thirty. We took some sandwiches to eat during the intermission. The first play came near being a tragedy, but wasn't. Two brothers met the man who had killed their father, and the younger more innocuous brother wanted to kill him in revenge, but the older brother persuaded him to control his temper. The old man was wealthy and gave them a fine home for the rest of their lives, so the whole thing ended happily. The younger brother's show of bad temper was very funny. We have been told that the Occupation will not allow them to put on the gory plays with suicides and murder in them. When I think of our Saturday night westerns and our so-called mysteries, the order is hard to understand.

"The second play was a comedy which had a gambler, a landlord, a street cleaner and a corpse in it. The gambler and the street cleaner took the corpse to the landlord's house and scared him into donating quite a stack of food and drink to them. It was funny and not gruesome, because the corpse looked much like a live man playing dead. He was tall, angular, and homely, which made quite a scene when he was carried around by the short, fat gambler. They tied the corpse on their backs, just as women tie babies on their backs.

"The third play was a dramatization of a famous fairy story of Japan. An angel comes down from heaven and takes off her heavy wings and hangs them on a tree while she walks around on the earth. A fisherman found the wings and wanted to keep them. The angel comes back, begs the fisherman to return her wings, but he is stubborn about it. He finally promises to return them if she will do a dance for him. She does a beautiful dance and he gives back the wings. He enters into the spirit of the affair and does a dance himself, which she admires for a while before flying back to heaven. An interpreter said they need to pull the angel up with wires, but it was considered unsafe, so she just whirls herself off the stage in a graceful dance.[13]

"Today is Army Day and we have a holiday. Another woman from this hotel went with me to the Imperial Palace grounds and saw the generals review the army. It was as spectacular as it could be with nothing but brown uniforms. The Palace Grounds with pink cherry blossom, weeping birch just turning green, pine trees, stone wall, green grass, and moss made a lovely setting.

"I love to see the US Army march. There is as much precision and uniformity as in any army, but at the same time a casual, easy, comfortable sort of swing to it. To give you an idea of how dressed up they were, I'll quote from two of our neighbors. A woman in a seat above us said when the MP's with gleaming helmets went by, 'Uh-uh! They must have been spitttin' and polishin' for a week.' A soldier to the right groaned when his own company went by, 'Ah-h, My God, you could cut your hand on the creases in those pants.'

"There was a British company in the parade. I learned today that there are 5,000 Russian soldiers in the Occupation. I asked an American soldier why they did not join the parade. He turned his hands upside down in a gesture of complete ignorance. We walked back along the top of the wall and had a fine view of the palace grounds."

40

Boy's Day

Today is a great day for the Labor Unions," wrote Pauline. "The Occupation went to work as usual, but there was a sense of dread in the air. Miles of men singing marched down Avenue A to the Imperial Palace Grounds. Each man carried a little red flag. At noon, we heard sirens and rushed to the windows. It was a small division of the army fully equipped going full speed down the street. Everybody dreaded something, but nothing happened. They tell us that the red flags mean nothing more than that they like the color.[1]

"Today is Boy's Day. Big carp fish made of silk are flying from high poles. When the wind is right to billow them out they really look like big, wide-eyed, sturdy fish as they are supposed to look. Because so many people lost their treasures, or were displaced by the war, the carp are not as numerous as they used to be, they say. The number of carp on the pole indicates the number of sons in the house, and the relative size of the carp shows the relative sizes of the sons.

"For days, the store windows have featured boys' dolls. The dolls are all sturdy, thick-legged little rascals and all seem to have some significance in history or folklore.

"This evening four of us were invited to a Japanese home, where there are two small sons, to celebrate Boy's Day. The father and one son met us at the station and guided us to the house. It was a nice folksy little neighborhood just up the hill from the station. The street was narrow and unpaved with no sidewalks. There were many wholesome looking men, women, and children. Small shops, mostly food, line the street on both sides. In all available space, there were flowers, fruit trees, and lush gardens.

"When we arrived at the house, we met the wife, the grandmother, and the smaller son. The father and some wore western clothes, but the women were prettily dressed in kimonos. They were most gracious hosts. It's hard to believe now that we couldn't talk to each other. I never realized 'til I came over here how much communication can be carried on without words.[2]

"We took off our shoes and were ushered into the main room of the house and invited to sit on the cushions on the floor which surrounded the twelve inch high table. The table was perfectly bare at the start. We were served a beautiful and delicious dinner which lasted for about two hours and we had the privilege of seeing it develop right before our eyes. First came tea with sweet somethings made of rice and beans, then some tasty, pretty, solid, round, black-eyed beans in one dish and bamboo sprouts, onion, and carrots in another. Next came soup with mushroom, egg, and green vegetables in it. This was served in covered bowls of gleaming lacquer. At about this point the host brought in two little charcoal cookers, which he put on the table, and he and his wife proceeded to make sukiyaki. It was most delicious. All the while beer and sake flowed freely.[3]

"After that came the bowl of rice. We could dip into the cookers and get hot liquid to pour over it and was it good! Last came tea followed by a big orange.

"During dinner, the grandfather joined us. He is a rather tall, dignified gentleman, a dentist by profession. He was dressed in a kimono, too. Men's kimonos are dark, drab, and dignified, while the women's are pretty and gay.

"On some terraced shelves covered with green silk was the traditional Boy's Day display, which features dolls, iris, flags, and carp. After dinner they let us try on the wife's wedding kimonos. There were three, the pre-wedding, the ceremonial, and the going away. The first was sand colored with beautiful brocade, the second was white with beautiful brocade, and the third was black with the same. All three were lined with red.

"We left with regret just in time to make the train before dark. We came to our station about nine and walking to the hotel [where we] got to see another angle of Boy's Day. Many boys in short kimonos were pulling a cart loaded with a big barrel-like drum. Many more boys were beating on both ends of the drum. The rhythms were wonderful and the sounds were exciting. People were gathering from every direction, falling in line behind the drum, and following it down the street. We followed for a block or two, but were too tired to go far from home.

"Today was a wonderful day! I was invited along with a friend in the textile business to the Tokyo Theater to attend some Japanese kabuki plays. These were given for Japanese audiences and were much better than those given for the Occupation. Those for the Occupation went in for fancy costuming, but these were down to earth realistic plays. There were three of them. One was about a sword smith, one about a rickshaw man, and the third was a tiger dance. Two of the most famous actors in Japan performed. The acting was wonderful. Again, I can hardly believe that I couldn't understand the words. Our host, the owner of a silk mill, had rented a box so we were near enough to see the expressions on the faces of the actors.

"One of the princes was in the box directly across from us, but I was so busy watching the stage I forgot to look at him. The plays lasted a long time (3:00-7:00) so everyone took food. Our host had box lunches and we took candy and nuts. Every time the lights went on, we ate. After the plays, we were invited back stage to meet the actors, but I had a ticket to *Madam Butterfly* at the Imperial Theater and did not want to miss it.

"Our host was a very efficient man. He guided me out through the thick crowd, hailed a taxi, told the driver where to take me, and away I went. The taxi was a charcoal burner and great sacks of extra fuel were carried in the car.[4] The driver was a good one and delivered me to the right door with speed and accuracy.[5]

"*Madam Butterfly* was beautifully done! Such stage sets, such costumes, such grace, such music! Cho Cho San and her maid were so beautiful and graceful! Pinkerton was a somewhat discordant note. He played the part as he thought an American would act. There was enough accuracy in it to be a little embarrassing. I guess they just cannot imagine an American doing anything gracefully.

"Today being Sunday, we went by train and electric tram car up into the mountains. The scenery is much like the mountains in Northern California, only more concentrated. At no place could you see the ground. The whole area is a maze of small farms, big trees, rocky ravines, and dashing brooks.

"This particular area is famous for hot mineral springs, so it is dotted with many bath houses. We were invited to take off our shoes and look into one, which we did, and saw to our surprise that the place was full of naked men. The girl in charge explained that both men and women use the pool, but no woman happened to be on hand today.

"Tonight we went out to the edge of the city to a small Japanese theatre to see a Noh play. The first one was a comedy and was very funny. The second was more ritualistic. The theatre was interesting. It was a real Japanese one, so it had to be entered without shoes. There is no scenery, no furniture, and no nothing on the stage, but the simplicity is beautiful.[6]

"Tonight, three of us took a notion to go for a walk after dinner. We went on a street that I had not seen for a long time and it was amazing to see the changes that had taken place. It was a little narrow street made for walking and not for driving. The last time I had seen it, which was in the middle of the summer; there was scarcely a sign of life. The visible signs of life did not, at that time, indicate any prosperity. Tonight the street was in a blaze of light and business was going on at a terrific rate. The street was broken up and full of holes so that one had to watch the feet carefully in order to keep from falling, but otherwise all was prosperity and gaiety. One of the women had taught in mission schools over here before the war. She said that that street was back to what it was before the war.

"The shops were full of foreign goods. There were a few American shops but we passed them by. Most of those shops were filled with American trifles, such as nail polish, shoestrings, buttons, and the like. We spent our time studying goods from China, India, and Java. They had some of the most fascinating materials made from cotton. At least they said it was cotton, but it was as soft as pongee silk...A piece of cotton material big enough for a bedspread cost thirty-five dollars. I guess the south sea islanders are getting wise to American ways. They had little pieces of common burlap with the most interesting designs painted on them. A piece about six inches by eight inches sells for a dollar. I couldn't see that much money in burlap, no matter how much paint and artistry. It still smelled like burlap.[7]

"The Japanese must think we are plumb crazy in the way we handle money. Somebody sees something she wants but does not have the money to pay for it. She asks the shopkeeper to put it away for her. He insists that she take it home and pay for it whenever she likes. She protests, but decides to take it. Someone else in the crowd thinks the shopkeeper is not getting a square deal and offers to lend the money. The deal is made. Then the one who lends money sees something she wants to buy and there is not enough money in the whole crowd to pay for it. She takes the stuff home and the first gal to buy something is supposed to pay her debt by coming back to the store and pay for the last purchase. Do you follow me? It never seems to confuse the Japanese, and I have never seen one of them write down anything about the transaction. When the first one goes back to pay for the purchase, the shopkeeper will say, 'Ah, yes, four thousand yen for obi for lady with brond hair.' Brond means blond.

"One hears the most amazing things about markets for Japanese goods. I shall be interested in what the customers say when I get back to the states. I heard yesterday that the market for silk yardage had gone to pieces in the states. I asked the reason and was told that the goods were so full of faults that the American women would not buy it. The story went on to the effect that at first everybody was glad to get silk and flocked to buy it, but when they discovered how shoddy it was they did not return for more. If that is true the Japanese are certainly not doing their best, because the stuff that we find in the stores here, which is made up especially for kimonos, is most beautiful and is free from faults.

"There are several theories to explain it. One is that when the buyers come from a foreign country the Japanese show them a fine grade of material and quote a low price on it. The buyer places a large order. Then the Japanese discovers he cannot come out even on the price he quoted. He does not want to lose face by admitting he has made a mistake as he plans to come out even by making a poor quality of material.[8]

41

The Mombusho

During the Allied Occupation of Japan, reformist policies generally came under the overarching rubric of two broad divisions—demilitarization and democratization. The common policy under each of these was to eradicate the will to war by dismantling authoritarian structures and promoting liberal ideals through the legal and educational systems.[1]

The education arm of the Occupation of Japan resided in the Japanese Ministry of Education, the central administrator of the education system in Japan that dated to the 19th century. By 1945 at the war's end, the old Japanese education system lay in ruins.

The defeat of Japan discredited prewar thought about education, and a wave of foreign ideas swept into the country in the form of the postwar military occupation. Through a series of social and cultural reforms, the Occupation decentralized and restructured the old education system to instill democratic ideals.[2] American authorities abolished the prewar educational framework and established the foundation of Japan's postwar educational system. Pauline's team in the CIE oversaw the revision of curricula and textbooks, replaced the nationalistic morals course with social studies, introduced the election of local school boards, and established teachers unions.

Accomplishment of the goals of the CIE required dismantling and reconstructing the Japanese Ministry of Education—the Mombusho. As the member of Gen. MacArthur's staff in charge of elementary education, Pauline oversaw the Mombusho as it worked to implement the Americanized school policies. In addition to writing and reviewing classroom textbooks and materials, she trained Mombusho staff and arranged conferences to deliver the new curricula to schools. With this responsibility came the opportunity to travel from one end of Japan to the other.

The primary station of the military component of the Allied forces was on the Island of Okinawa, Japan. Meanwhile, the CIE operated out of Gen. MacArthur's headquarters in Tokyo, on Honshu Island. Therefore, travel to distant parts of Japan meant long trips through the Japanese countryside. Pauline recounts one of eight such trips she took with representatives of the Mombusho. In her correspondence, she refers to the Normal teachers. Japan established Normal schools for teacher training in the late 19th century. Organized similar to American Normal schools, higher Normal schools trained elementary school teachers while more advanced Normal schools trained secondary school teachers. Although the Allied Occupation abolished the traditional Normal schools and directed the CIE to inaugurate new post-WW II education reforms, the teachers Pauline encountered during this trip were products of the old system.

"Today we arrived at Kure, a small city on the famous, beautiful Inland Sea. The British are occupying this area. We are billeted in an Australian YWCA. It is a white stucco, southern

California type of building located on a side hill and furnished in excellent taste. The five of us have single rooms. There are plenty of baths and showers and their living rooms are big, homey, and attractive. Aside from the fact that we shall have tea, tomatoes, and spaghetti for breakfast, the food is far superior to anything else in the Occupation I'm sure. Their idea of a day's food suits me exactly—breakfast at 8:00, tea at 10:00, lunch at noon, tea at 4:00, dinner at 6:00, and supper at 9:00.[3]

"The little city spreads over a small valley and extends up the hillsides on each side. The mountains are behind it, the bay and the islands are in front. From here, it reminds me of Berkeley.

"This is wheat harvest time, and the smell of ripe grain is in the air. Everyone is working at it. The fields are very small. They cut it with a small cycle and lay it neatly across the little ridge on which it grew. They gather it up and carry it to the roadside where they flail it, beat the grains out over the edge of a table, or pull the wheat head through a sort of iron comb. They winnow it by tossing the grains up in the air from a wide basket. Then they sift it through a small sieve. Tonight we saw an old lady hulling the grains through a little mill with a hopper that would hold about two gallons.

"Today we saw Hiroshima for the first time. It is a pitiful sight, but nothing like it was two years ago they say. The area where big buildings used to be is mostly covered with little makeshift shops and houses. Our meeting had to be held at a little elementary school across the river and across the tracks because the Normal schools were bombed out. A girl's Normal school was destroyed and about three hundred girls were killed. An elementary school was destroyed with all the children in it.

"There are people on the streets and some in our meeting that have horrible disfiguring scars. Most of the schoolchildren seem normal, but a few have vacant far away expressions, which made me wonder what they were thinking. In a small town nearby, I had the awful experience of having small children cry and run away when they saw me. They did not say aloud, but their faces puckered in an expression of fear and dread and they ran home or hid behind their mothers' skirts.

"Our meetings are not as good as they should be. Americans have not quite worked out a way to make ourselves understood. The Ministry of Education people are submitted to a great deal of needling because of shortage of money and materials. I had a young man by the name of Ono leading my section who knew how to take it. He is calm, good-natured, shrewd in human relations, and has a ready tongue.[4]

"The sixth grade demonstration was done by a homely, colorless little fellow who was more frightened than the children. He was not a Normal school teacher, just an elementary teacher. All the observers were Normal teachers and certainly gave the poor lad a bad time in the discussion period.

"The first grade was pretty good. There were 55 youngsters. They romped all over the schoolyard in dramatic play showing how tramcar transportation works.

"Today was an eventful day. At nine, I had an appointment with a girl from the Hiroshima Publishing Company. She took me to the publishing house where I met her boss. He is a calm, serene man with a look of wisdom and a quiet smile. He had one of those awful scars. The girl told me that he was injured by the bomb and had been in bed for months. His place of business was completely destroyed except one small section and that part was pushed 12 inches down into the ground. He started to give directions for rebuilding before he was out of bed. The first time he walked out of doors, he saw a group of schoolchildren under a battered old roof, with no walls, no furniture, no books, trying to have school. He was so moved by the sight that he resolved to revamp his whole publishing house and print nothing but children's books. They print the nicest things I have seen in Japan—children's books and magazines with colored pictures. They want more and more American books for children so they can see how they are made.

"I mentioned the many scars on people. The girl said that only a few are seen on the streets, but when the doctors come, as they do periodically, perfectly awful looking people are brought out.

"I went back to the meeting and laid all the cards on the table—told them the meetings did not seem to be going too well and asked for suggestions. They were frank, but courteous. They said they would like smaller groups so they could have more discussion. We laid out plans, which they approved. Their suggestions will be tried out at the next stop, which is on the most southern island of Japan.

"This afternoon some of the Mombusho boys took us on a boat trip to Miyajima, one of the beauty spots of Japan. The trip included a natural bridge, a park full of maple trees, a shrine with Torii out in the water, a tea room overlooking the bay, a potter using a wheel, and a sacred horse who has to spend the rest of his life in a small pen.[5] It was all very beautiful, but the best part of it was the friendliness, sincerity, appreciation of the beauty of their country and just plain fun of the Mombusho men. These were all young men. This was the first time on a conference for some, but they certainly gave a good account of themselves.

"We arrived at Miyzaki after an uneventful train trip from Kure which afforded a high scenic level, but the comfort level was low. There were ocean, mountains, forests, and neat little farms nestled in the narrow valleys. The trains were run by coal and were not air-conditioned, which seemingly gave us a choice of being dirty or hot. But in reality we were both.

"Miyazaki is an unattractive town on the coast of the island of Kyushu. It looks a little like towns on our western plains. We are staying at a Japanese hotel, which means that all our indoor time is spent with our shoes off—a custom that I like very much.[6]

"The people of Miyazaki are friendly, cooperative, and hospitable. We have had tea and entertainment at every pause in the program. The Japanese teachers are a talented group. They speak in meetings with ease, grace, and courtesy. When time comes for entertainment, one after another volunteers to play the piano, dance a bit of ballet, tell a story with dramatics to rival Kikugoro, or sing.[7] Then they expect something from CIE, and we are so lacking in talent. We happen to have a small Japanese-British man traveling with us as an interpreter, who plays the flute very well. He comes to our rescue in such a case. We have come to call him or Average Raiser.

"Yesterday after 4:00 we were taken to a small peninsula which is exclusive because it has on it tropical plants which grow no place else in Japan. It also has most peculiar rock formations.

"Our conference here is in the groove. Everybody is happy, questions are deeper, answers are more intellectual, and the demonstrations were of a higher quality and more sincerely done than at other conferences.

"The education officer here is a friendly, sincere, adjustable person who has made firm friendships among the Japanese educators. The Japanese 'school inspector' is a fine, energetic, wise, correct little Japanese woman who lost her husband, an army officer, and her sons in the war. She seems to have turned all her interest and energies to serving elementary schools. She is highly respected and very effective.

"The Army Officer in charge gave a party for Americans last night. Everyone had to go, but no one seemed to enjoy it. Nobody could think of anything amusing to do, but everyone promised great hilarity as soon as the guests got a little drunk. This state was reached at about 10:30 when several of the men leaped to the middle of the floor and started yelling and dancing. The education delegation left about that time but I'm sure were not missed. Hours later we were awakened by the breaking up of the party. As far as I was concerned, the party was not a total loss. The Major had arranged a fishpond at which both the sheep and the goats (Army and Civilian) could fish. I drew a nice little basket which I have used for cosmetics, towels, etc. ever since.

"The Japanese vice governor gave us a dinner party. It was more fun. One small cup of sake will bring out all sorts of talent. We had delightful singing and folk dancing."[8]

PLAYGROUND VISIT. **Pauline encouraged playtime and role-playing as an important element of her teaching philosophy. Pictured with a class of Japanese first-graders, visits to schools like this one in Kamakura, Japan, were a major part of her activities as director of elementary curriculum for the Allied Occupation forces.**

LESSON IN AGRICULTURE. **Pauline encouraged Japanese schools to increase the frequency of field trips as a teaching tool, especially to augment early childhood experiences. Japanese children watch with mixed responses.**

MOMBUSHO COLLEAGUES. **Pauline worked alongside members of the Japanese Ministry of Education, known as the Mombusho. She posed her with two unidentified Mombusho staff. As an officer of the Occupation of Japan", she directed the policies of Japanese education. which the Ministry of Education then carried out.**

JAPANESE DINNER. **Pauline was a frequent guest in Japanese homes. Her position in the Occupation of Japan force as an education leader brought her many invitations for tea. She welcomed each opportunity to interact with Japanese culture and warmly described her experiences with the Japanese people in her letters.**

Ground Zero

42

Christmas

The Japanese people accepted the conquest of Japan with mixed reactions. The horrific bombing of Japan by the Allies killed enormous numbers of people in acts of war seen by many as murderous atrocity. On the other hand, the Allied rehabilitation of the country promised long sought improvements in Japanese life. Takemae wrote, "The relative beneficent nature of the Allied Occupation stood in sharp contrast to the oppressive policies the Japanese themselves adopted in the areas they had occupied throughout war-torn Asia...For many Japanese, 'defeat' became synonymous with 'liberation'."[1] The leaders of prewar Japan had geared the education system to produce obedient subjects ready to lay down their lives for the Emperor. A tightly regimented society denied the people basic civil liberties, and subjected them to rigid police controls.[2]

Forward-looking Japanese women and men stepped up to implement Occupation goals long suppressed by the old regime. A surge of creative energy flowed from the people without which the rehabilitation reforms could not have occurred. Among the most immediate and significant changes was the instatement of women's rights guarantees and the reorientation of education and the health and welfare reforms proposed by CIE. The cadre of American women leading the CIE, including Pauline, fought for the inclusion of women's rights in the Occupation reforms.[3]

The CIE proposed the introduction of Parent Teacher Associations, and the Social Education Law legally mandated them in 1949. Roughly, 90 percent of the country's school districts established PTAs. At the same time, prominent women educators and feminists worked to start the Japanese Association of College Women. After Pauline arrived, the name changed to the Japanese Association of University Women. The organization endeavored to upgrade the academic standing of its members and improve other institutions of higher learning for women.[4]

Meanwhile, the seriousness of the many tasks before Pauline and the CIE gave way to the levity of the holiday season, to welcome in the incongruity of an American Christmas celebration in Japan.

"CIE is in a state of confusion over a Christmas party. Some want to have a big general party and some want to have a lot of little parties. Some want to invite the Japanese and some do not. Our own division has decided to find out what all the others are doing and then at least match the best if not out-do it. That's a fine example of Christmas spirit isn't it?[5]

"Today at noon, we had a little excitement in our dining room at the hotel. It is a dark rainy day—a proper setting for a mystery. While we were eating, two big MPs came in, sat down at a table, and started eating. It was most unusual to have them there and all the more so because they wore their hats and overcoats and carried clubs. I suppose everyone in the dining room thought he or she had broken a rule and were about to be nabbed. We found out afterward that they had brought a prisoner to consult with a lawyer. You may have read of the case.

The young man was caught last December smuggling drugs and selling them in Yokohama. He managed to get to the US where he consulted a lawyer and was advised that if he came back to Japan as a civilian trader, the Military Police could not touch him. The lawyer was mistaken for they nabbed the fellow at the airport as he came in and threw him in jail where he has been ever since, waiting for trial.[6]

"This afternoon another woman and I got a recreation sedan and rushed out to do some last minute shopping, just like people do in the states. The only difference being that we had a Japanese driver and paid twenty-five cents an hour for the use of the car. The activities on the streets are mostly American with groups of Japanese watching them. Our festival days are sources of great curiosity to them. In honor of the Americans, or to invite business, or because the owners are Christians many of the shops had Christmas trees. They were horrible to behold. It is very strange that a people who seems to have so much natural aptitude for art could make such a mess of a Christmas tree.[7]

"This afternoon from four to six our commanding officer had a cocktail party. Many people, including me, went from a sense of duty, but stayed to have a good time. Everybody was gay, but on good behavior. The whole affair was one of the nicest parties of its kind I have ever attended. Many others who are much more experienced than I said the same.

"The day dawned dark, damp, and chilly. The hotel was pretty crowded all day, but quiet. The management started serving eggnog at ten in the morning and kept it up all day. I do not know where they got the stuff to make it, but it was very, very good. The lobby was resplendent with an immense Christmas tree.

"In the afternoon I went with the Santa Paula Judsons to deliver some Christmas presents to the Japanese. It was a very interesting venture. Mr. Judson had worked with a Japanese radioman who died last year. His wife was left with four small children to support by teaching school. And if you think the salaries are small over there, you should see them over here. Anyhow, the Judsons had bought two beautiful golden haired American dolls for the two middle-sized girls. The older girl is thirteen and they assumed she was too old to want a doll. They saw their mistake when they looked at her face when her younger sisters got their dolls. They went back on Christmas day to deliver another doll to the older girl. They were right in bringing it to her. You should have seen her. She took it into her arms as if it were the most precious thing in the world. She did not say anything, but went and sat down on the floor and looked at her doll. The other two girls, who had gotten their dolls the day before had them strapped on their backs just like live babies. It really was something to see those golden haired, blue-eyed dolls with straw bonnets on their heads peeking over the shoulders of those Japanese girls.[8]

"The mother was not at home. She was teaching school. We could not talk to each other. The grandmother who takes care of the children was as nice as could be. We did a great deal of bowing and smiling and took our departure.

"On the way home we stopped at the home of an American Major, and my, what a difference. They had a big Christmas tree with loads of presents under it. Kids were playing on the floor with the most elaborate mechanical toys. The grown folks were sitting around with drinks and candy within easy reach.

"Dinner at the hotel was quite a gala affair. The Army went all out and furnished everything in the traditional Christmas dinner. Every one made up small parties and reserved tables. I was in a party that was arranged by a gal in industries. She is from Louisiana and she brought some southern style traditions into our party. She stirred up some sort of devil brew at the table and set fire to it. It burned with a beautiful blue blaze, which attracted quite a lot of attention, especially from the Japanese waitresses. They were dressed in kimonos and obis. It was quite a sight to sit in front of that devilish blue blaze surrounded by all those wide-eyed kimono-clad girls. You will be interested to know that when the glasses cooled down so we could drink the stuff it was right tasty.

"Tonight a group of us went to the Ernie Pyle Theatre to see the *Snow Fantasy*. A number of the Occupation in honor of some girl produced it. It was a stupendous affair as far as costumes and scenery was concerned. I do not know where all the money came from, but I never saw so much satin, velvet, and sparkles on one stage at one time. It was rather pretty and there were a few wonderful children in it. But there was also something incongruous about it. The whole thing gave you the impression that it should be done by grade school kids, but six-foot GI's took most of the parts. If they didn't look like sissies with those little white satin ruffled panties and flowers behind their ears. I must say they went through their routines with a right good will. There must have been a powerful gal at the head of the thing. I'll bet their mothers could never have made them do it.

"Today the Mombusho boys brought in the first draft of the first language book for blind children. They had really done a swell job. The vocabulary control was excellent. In fact, in some pieces they had allowed their concern over words to destroy all the interest value of the book. We talked it over for a couple of hours and they took it away to work it over. It certainly brings home the limitations of the blind when you think of the things you cannot put in the book because they cannot experience it; and when you think that you cannot depend upon the pictures to give meaning to the content. It may not be perfect when we get through with it, but it will be the best they have ever had."[9]

43

Nagasaki

The calendar turned over to the year 1949. Pauline began her second year in Japan. The Occupation command asked her to continue as head of the CIE elementary education section, extending what originally was to have been a one-year appointment.

On January 7, her travels took her to Nagasaki, ground zero of the atom bomb. An estimated 200,000 people, mostly civilians died because of the two atom bombs, one dropped on Hiroshima and the other on Nagasaki.

The Japanese historian Takemae called the bombing, "The most cruel effect humanity has ever known...The use of history's most hideous weapon against non-combatants in crowded cities was indeed an unpreceded atrocity, and it represented America's moral nadir, for the bomb negated the very values the United States claimed to be fighting for." Gen. Eisenhower reputedly said, nothing could justify the use of so terrible an instrument of destruction. MacArthur supposedly felt appalled and depressed by "this Frankenstein monster."[1] The US military confiscated photographs of the destruction.

The loss of the war in such a hideous manner was an affront to the national pride of Japan, impossible to forget and for many to forgive. Nevertheless, the irony of the degrading loss of autonomy also liberated the nation. An authoritarian regime that had repressed the civil and political freedom of its own citizens, and savagely invaded and tyrannized its neighbors ceased to exist. The Allied Occupation led by the United States and acting for the most part alone rewove the social, economic, and political framework of Japan, changing its national priorities and redirecting its path of advancement. [2]

Unbeknownst to Pauline, there was a family tie to the atom bomb. Harry Wilkes Fulbright, Jr., the son of Cousin Mildred Kastendieck Fulbright, Pauline's classmate at Billings, held a key position in the Manhattan District Project that built the atom bomb. In the period from 1942 until 1944, he was in charge of Washington University's cyclotron under contract to the Manhattan Project. When he graduated in 1944, he transferred as a group leader to the Los Alamos Scientific Laboratory in New Mexico where physicists built the bomb. His part in engineering the bomb remains a secret. So secret was his work at the time that no copy of his doctoral dissertation survives. He spoke of this later when Washington University could not find a copy in the university's library collection. As Harry described it in a 1998 letter to the Washington University archivist, "Wartime secrecy had prevented its normal appearance…The thesis topic was a study of Neptunium 239 decaying to Plutonium 239…to establish an energy level scheme for Plutonium."[3] Plutonium 239 was the primary fissile element used for the production of nuclear weapons. Dr. Fulbright left Los Alamos in the summer of 1946 to accept a teaching position at Princeton University.[4]

Pauline described what it was like to stand at ground zero.

"Our young guide in Nagasaki took us first to see the place, which is just below the Atom Bomb Center, where they have planted young trees and made a little park dedicated to world peace. Just below the Center, there is a big plaque, which lists the bomb damage and classifies the damages. One class is listed as being due to wind force. A school building just across the ravine was destroyed by wind force. It is, or was, a concrete building with steel reinforcements. The front walls were pushed against the back walls at about a 45-degree angle. Nothing has been done to it. It is a gruesome sight.[5]

"Nagasaki was bombed at eleven in the morning, August 9, 1945. It was a cloudy day and our guide told us that for that reason the bombardiers missed a little. Nagasaki occupies a bowl surrounded on three sides by mountains. It has overflowed into smaller surrounding bowls, and it was into one of these smaller bowls that the bomb dropped. It reaped a great harvest of schools, churches, hospitals, and one prison; also many homes but very little in the way of industries. A school with hundreds of children was completely destroyed and all the children killed. A prison full of prisoners disappeared with all killed. A hospital with all its patients and doctors was wiped out. It fell near a Catholic church, which was completely destroyed. A frame church has been built on the grounds. Some women were hauling the bricks and debris from the old church. They were using bare hands and wheelbarrows. This little valley looked more devastated than Hiroshima, because less had been done in reconstruction.

"We went to a shipyard where nothing was visible except the iron or steel framework of some buildings. Everything that would burn was gone. This damage was the result of incendiary bombs, not the A-bomb. But, they had a ship building industry underground in a side hill which was unharmed and was going full blast. At present, with the blessing of SCAP, they have two ships in dry dock. One was a small freighter, which was just getting finishing touches before being launched and sent to the Philippines, and the other was a big American tanker which was being repaired.

"Our guide pointed out a cross on a hillside which marks the place where twenty-six Catholic missionaries where crucified in about 1600. The Japanese government resented their influence and had them murdered by pouring scalding water in their mouths and hanging them on crosses.

"In the afternoon, we went to a Chinese temple. The most impressive thing about it was a big, black, gorgeously clad god who guards the gates of hell. Connie McCullough said, 'It was always so. Those who guard the gates of hell are the best-dressed people. It is the angels of heaven who have the gold leaf peeling off their noses.' Another point of interest was a great iron kettle about eight feet deep and the same in diameter, which had been presented to the province of Nagasaki bout two hundred years ago, along with a shipment of rice, to tide the people over a famine. The guide said, 'The sun did not shine for a year and the rice could not grow.'

"We went down the hill from the temple, across the city, and up the hill on the other side where there was a lovely old Catholic church. We tiptoed up to the front of the church to look at a wonderful painting of the twenty-six satyrs on their twenty-six crosses. There are more Catholics in Nagasaki than in any other place in spite of the fact that 40,000 of them were killed by the atomic bomb. Which proves that an idea is not killed by killing people.[6]

"From there we climbed further up the hill to the Butterfly's house. I was a little surprised to learn that *Madam Butterfly* was a real person and a little relieved to learn that the man in the real case was a Frenchman, not an American. The garden on the lower terrace is the original garden and the rear of the present house is the original house. It is now occupied by an American major. His very pretty, vivacious wife showed us through the house and gave us the background.

"Connie and I had a hasty breakfast this morning, went across town and picked up the interpreter, and boarded the eight o'clock train for Kumamoto. We got there at four in the afternoon and found to our surprise that they were not expecting us. What a blow! One thousand people were assembled at Nagasaki and we foolishly expected the same thing here. We were faced with a cold day with nothing to do and the poor Japanese were faced with the problem of getting a crowd together by Monday. Things do not look so bright at the moment. It rains and snows by turns and the sky is dark. We drew a Japanese hotel where it is our privilege to shiver in dignified, austere elegance. Every little while we are driven to pull a hand out of a pocket to point out some new piece of carving on door or window. One feature of comfort is the bath, which is neck deep and as hot as you like.

"This morning seven Japanese gentlemen called on us to plan the meeting for the next day. We learned what jobs would be represented and what the customers wanted to have discussed. In the afternoon, they came by for us in an old Dodge converted into a charcoal burner and the nine of us went sightseeing. We went to the ruins of the old castle of a feudal lord. There was only one watchtower left. They took us to a park where a Japanese mountain range had been built in miniature. The small mountains covered the park and were so much like the real ones that we could identify some of the peaks. From there they took us to a pottery plant where they had the most beautiful things. Time after time, I have asked folks to kick me if I buy any more china, but I did it again! The little potter was a most gracious man. When we were about ready to leave, he made ceremonial tea for us with all the careful precision of a real tea artist, but with none of the pomp which sometimes goes with it.[7]"

44

Textbooks and Train Trips

As part of Pauline's assignment, she had charge of producing a series of elementary textbooks. Besides visiting schools and making speeches, she held conferences with professors who were writing books for use in the Japanese schools. She recounted one such meeting with four Japanese professors who were working out plans for a schoolbook destined for publication by the Japanese Ministry of Education. The evaluation protocol required her to review books word by word. She wrote, "The reviewing of books is a big job, but the writing is much harder for the Japanese. They have to submit everything in both Japanese and English. If I approve it, it then goes to a reviewing board who can read both languages. They look to see if the Japanese says the same as the English."

Translation often produced amusing results. For example, "Taro and his father went to shop early in the afternoon, because later the traffic is devilish though." When telling of Edison's work on the light bulb they mentioned that he had experimented with more than 1,600 kinds of materials, then exclaimed, "what a hell of efforts to make!."

Pauline praised the Japanese writers. She acknowledged, "In the Japanese, the idea is expressed in dignified, beautiful language. They are only trying to translate it so we [Americans] can understand it."[1]

The approval of a new textbook garnered a celebration. Her staff threw a party each time the government approved a book. She remembered the first such party. "At first I, thought the party was over before it was." She explained a number of courses came interspersed with entertainment. She said that the Japanese served dessert first, usually a helping of cookies. This they followed by a course of raw fish, which Pauline thought was the main course at her first such party. To her surprise, a course of chicken came next, followed by steak or sukiyaki.

These multi-course dinners functioned as more than just parties to the Japanese. Pauline came to believe that the dinners gave her Japanese staff the opportunity to fill their stomachs. "Because of the low rations of food at home during this time," she explained, "They appreciated a good dinner."

Pauline's sensitivity to the Japanese people and their culture was one of her chief assets. Her reciprocal friendliness made her a favorite of MacArthur's staff. She was the soft-spoken American who always noted the gratefulness of the Japanese people for the food furnished by the United States for the Japanese school lunch program. She often heard them talk about it, many times with tears in their eyes.[2]

Keeping order in the Japanese Ministry of Education was difficult. The Mombusho contained two distinct and competitive factions. On the one hand, the conservatives who were primarily holdovers from the old regime wanted to retain the educational traditions of the past. On the other hand, the more progressive wing wanted a new education system more like that of the United States. Pauline often found herself in the middle of a debate.

The large number of Japanese employees was significant, and in some staff echelons, such as CIE, they outnumbered Americans. Many of these individuals, although occupying subordinate positions, were highly qualified for the tasks they performed and firmly committed to the ideals of reform. Serving as the eyes and ears of the staff sections, these Japanese brought various issues to the attention of American officials and kept them advised of Japanese views and reactions to CIE policies.

Takemae tells a story about Pauline in her role as a CIE leader. "In 1949, CIE Elementary School Officer Pauline Jeidy asked her Japanese subordinates about an attempt by a conservative pressure group to introduce traditional calligraphy into the elementary school curricula. The group claimed that calligraphy improved artistic ability, penmanship, and moral character and was as indispensable for Oriental children as knives and forks for Westerners. Japanese staff members told her flatly that such assertions were nonsense. Jeidy consequently opposed the measure, demanding that the lobbyists substantiate their arguments."[3]

The many conferences and trips to Japanese schools could be grueling. There were no special transportation arrangements for Pauline and her staff. She used the same accommodations the people of Japan used in the course of their day-to-day lives. A trip from Tokyo to distant points of the country meant long, often uncomfortable train rides. However, there were exceptions. She recounted one travel adventure in a letter to the *Ventura County Star-Free Press*. One day, she was to go by train to Maebashi for a meeting, but she found there was no room in the second-class car for her and no standing room in the third class car. Her interpreter solved the problem. He found the train crew was running a "test car" that day. The "test car", Pauline found out, denoted a trick often played in order to furnish a comfortable, roomy ride for the boys who worked the train. She found herself riding in style in a heated, clean car designed to hold 88 but which on that trip carried only 11. That, she said, was one of the most comfortable rides she had while in Japan.[4]

Another time, she found herself riding around in a Cadillac. That was when she went to a meeting in Nobeoka. The president of the school board met her and her interpreter in the mayor's car. The mayor's car turned out to be a Cadillac bought with public funds and lined with white linen, ruffled at the edge. The mayor's resentful voters referred to the car as "the problem car."

While on another trip to visit schools, she rode around in an ambulance because all other vehicles were in use. During that trip, her host cooked for lunch what was supposed to be one of the delicacies of Japan—fish heads. When it came time to eat, Pauline found that she could not forget the sight of the cook boiling the fish eyes. She found herself nibbling around the eyes and missing them. Her host, she wrote, tactfully remarked that she did not care much for the eyes herself.[5]

While in Nobeoka, Pauline discovered that she was uniquely a person of interest to both children and grownups. The children followed her because she looked queer—a tall woman who towered over many of the small-size Japanese with whom she worked. The grownups followed her to see what she looked for in the shops. Some high school girls followed along because they were studying English in school and they wanted to hear her talk.

During the trip to Nobeoka, one of her Japanese staff members riding with her and her interpreter pointed out a great monument on a hillside. He told Pauline that the monument was made of stones and that each stone represented one country of the world. Over the stones was a roof-like affair, which represented Japan. The monument meant, he said, "the entire world under one roof, Japan being the roof." Then, the speaker added with a sheepish grin, "now called peace tower."

Wherever Pauline went in Japan, she often heard the same questions, not significantly different from her experiences with the schools of Ventura County.

She wrote, "Today we had the first session of the Kumamoto meeting. There were about two hundred men and five women there. They asked the usual questions:

"How can one operate a core curriculum?

"What is done about discipline in an activity program?

"Are the skills neglected in an activity program?

"Would one have a daily program, or should he follow the children's interests?

"Is intelligence a proper basis for grouping children for instruction?

"Who is supposed to make the unit of work, and how is it done?

"The same questions come up everywhere we go. They were a nice group. We had a good interpreter, Connie and I work well together as a team, and everybody was happy.[6]

"After school, Dr. Pederson, the education officer took us shopping and I saw a little jade goddess that I thought I could not live without, so Connie, the interpreter, Dr. Pederson, and I pooled our yen and got it. Now I'm in debt again; but she is worth it.

"This morning Connie and I went to school to meet the supervisors from the prefectures office. They had planned their activities as supervisors and wanted us to evaluate them. They were good, but in their efforts to be democratic, they had listed most everything that would meet emergencies for the moment, but had neglected to do any long term planning. We both commended them for what they had done, but I tried to tell them the idea of a five-year plan.

"At 12:30 Connie went north to Saga where she will meet members of our staff and run another meeting with them. At 4:30, the interpreter and I went south to a small town where we spent the night. The GI quarters were none too good, but again there was a wonderful Japanese bath. For this bath, they had hauled in some big rocks and stacked them in the corner of the room in the most natural way. This bathtub was built in a quarter of a circle around this pile of rocks. When you sit in the tub up to your neck in water, you could imagine you were in the great outdoors, if it were not so hot.

"The trip down here was beautiful with assorted seacoasts, pine woods, mountains, orange trees loaded with oranges, fishing boats, and neat little houses with thatched roofs. In this area a goodly proportion of the roofs are of tile painted white. The interpreter tells us that is a sign of wealth.

"This morning we had to leave at eight o'clock by Japanese train with none of the usual luxuries such as heat, cleanliness and a place to sit. We were assigned a little corner in the front of the car just behind the engine. It was the place where some of the train crew usually sits. I wrapped us up in my red blanket from Santa Paola, but even so, it got awful cold, especially on the feet. When we went through a tunnel, and there were many of them, the smoke rolled in through the doors, windows, ventilators, and cracks. It got so thick we could not see 'til the wind blew it away. Our faces became as black as tar. There is a smoking volcano in that neighborhood, and between the tunnels and smoke, we could see it plainly. The mountain is high and seems to rise up right out of the ocean. The smoke is slow, black, heavy, and ominous looking.

"We were met in Miyakonojō by my favorite GI and a delegation of Japanese whom we had met in June. They took us to a nice new Japanese hotel where we washed up and ate a big American meal prepared in our honor. It was better than the usual American food cooked by Japanese cooks. I have often wished they would stick to Sukiyaki. They can make that taste so good. It was cold and windy with little flurries of snow in the air. Our GI friend had driven up from the coast where it is warm most of the time. This morning was exceptionally cool and he had come away without a coat. I lent him my red blanket, which he folded around his shoulders and wore for the rest of the day. When he wore it into the conference room and followed me up to the stage the Japanese nearly split their sides laughing.[7]

"There were about a thousand teachers there and we had a fine meeting, in spite of the cold. They had a hibachi with three lumps of charcoal setting near me. It was fine for the hands, but did nothing for the feet.

"We left for Miyazaki by Japanese government car, an old Buick, at about four o'clock. The road took us over a mountain range and down on the coastal plain where it is much warmer.

"We had not gone more than a half hour before we had a flat tire. The Japanese supervisor knows her territory as well as the best of 'em. She took us into the farmhouse nearby to wait. This was a typical one with the south side all open to the air and the public. The floor is elevated around two and a half feet and in the middle of the floor there is a metal lined pit, which serves for a fireplace. There is no chimney and no hole in the roof. Some of the smoke blows outdoors and some of it gets in your eyes. This house was as neat as a new pin. A neat homemaker, some shining kettles, and two fat cats surrounded the fireplace. We were invited into the other rooms to sit around a beautiful blue hibachi. I asked to sit at the kitchen fireplace with the cats. The lady served us tea, and when the man of the house came home he served us with something like sake but not so good. It seems you show your most friendly feeling by flipping the dregs from your cup into the fire and offering it to someone else to drink from. The GI went through the gestures with gusto and offered me his cup, so I did the same and offered him mine. It was a gala occasion, but the taste value of the drink was not high. Crowds of kids came to stare at me. I said, 'Hello' in my best manner and got no response. I bent my head and said, 'Konnichiwa', and all the heads went down politely, and everyone said Konnichiwa.[8] They seemed a little amazed. It is my color and my size, which seems to throw them.

"Arrival in Miyazaki was like old home week. There were so many friends from last summer. The Japanese were very friendly and the Americans were all anxious to hear some news from Tokyo."[9]

45

Going Home

Days were getting shorter as the seasons turned into fall. The Ventura County school office collected Pauline's letters into a file and eagerly awaited her return from Japan. Meanwhile, at home in Fennimore, Wisconsin, Pauline's letters circulated among friends and neighbors and came back eventually to the Brandemuehl residence to be neatly place in a desk drawer.

The letters arrived with the same pride of sharing with which the writer wrote them. On a late fall day, writing from Tokyo to Verd—she always called her sister Verda, Verd—and to Ruth, her niece, she addressed a letter to "folks in Fennimore."

"Nearly two weeks ago when I was out visiting schools, I found a sixth grade room that was studying America. The children asked me some questions and then wanted to know if I had some pictures I could lend them which would show them what daily life in America was like. I brought some children back with me and lent them some books from the CIE library. They were mostly textbooks, but showed many pictures of life in America. Last Saturday two children brought the books back and had some more questions to ask. They were mostly about church, which surprised me a little. They wanted to know how many churches there were, how many people belonged, why people joined a certain church, what the churches do for people, how they teach people not to steal and do things like that, and so on. I was a little reluctant to try to answer some of them, but made a stab at all of them.[1]

"Saturday afternoon I went to the PX to have a permanent. They gave me the works, permanent, shampoo, wave set, hair do, and manicure for $7.50. The whole process takes only about three hours. They have the place organized so that the customer has to do no waiting. After the permanent, I went to a dressmaker who is attempting to make me a dress out of an old haori coat [traditional Japanese hip- or thigh-length kimono-style jacket]. The material is beautiful—black with some shiny threads, called lacquer threads in it. It looks quite encouraging up to now, but I have learned it is best not to expect too much.

"Tuesday noon a Japanese lady who went to school at Berkeley came to have lunch with me. She has a private kindergarten and sort of a missionary school for older children where she teaches them English. She invited me to come and spend a night with her sometimes. I agreed to go and she asked me if I could come this coming weekend. I looked at my book and announced that I could. She looked delighted and said she had been praying for someone to come next weekend for she did not have a speaker for church or a storyteller for Sunday school. So for the first time in my life I shall be an answer to prayer. And in the meantime I hope the lord will put some ideas in my head as to what to say.

"In the afternoon, I went out to talk to a group of college professors about 'The curriculum of the elementary school.' The interpreter was scared to death because another interpreter had told her that when she interpreted for one of the men in CIE, the professors had yelled at her and criticized her interpretations. They were a sour looking group. I told them in the beginning that they looked as if they did not expect to believe a thing I said. They laughed heartily and became quite cheerful and friendly.

"Wednesday morning I went out to talk to about 200 Tokyo teachers about visual aids in the elementary schools. The interpreter says that the elementary teachers are the nicest people we talk to. I complemented her on her observation and assured her it was so in my country—apologies to anyone else who may read this. At this time of year, these Tokyo schoolhouses are mighty cold—especially if you are on the side of the house away from the sun. Today we were sitting in perfect comfort in one of the schools with the sun streaming in, when a sudden wind and fog come up, and it suddenly became like a refrigerator.

"On Wednesday morning, two of us were invited to one of the big department stores to see an exhibition of educational materials. They had gone to a great deal of trouble to install machinery on the fifth floor of the store so that they could show the public how pencils, Crayola's, and brushes are produced. We were especially interested because the idea of mass production was only evident to a certain extent. People turned handles, or pushed and pulled things, and pencils, or Crayola's came out by hundreds, not by thousands, or millions as they do in America. They were using cedar from America, lead form Korea, rubber from India. Only the metal around the rubber came from Japan. On the first floor, they had set up a loom and a ragged skinny little man was weaving silk. I could hardly tear myself away from that.[2]

"Tuesday evening all of CIE were invited to see some pictures from America. They were slides showing scenes in America and are to be shown in Japan and Korea. Perhaps you have seen them. They are prepared for circulation by *Life* and *Time*. They are shown on an immense screen that covers the whole front end of the room. In order to change slides one slide is put on top of the other and the two merge for a moment before the picture changes. It really is quite restful and effective.

"Last night three of us went to see the famous all girl opera troop. They are wonderful. Their headquarters are down near Osaka, but they came to Tokyo to perform for Billy Rose on Tuesday. Since they were here, they let the Occupation in on it, too. It was most enjoyable. Especially so because everything about it was so new, colorful, gay, and vigorous. Their costumes were gorgeous and they were all pressed and new. The papers say that they are the most popular entertainment and make the most money of any entertainers in Japan.

"Today is Saturday and a beautiful day. I think I'll set out doors for a while.[3]

Across the Pacific Ocean far from the shores of Japan, in Ventura, California, school officials were entertaining Japanese guests. In the fall of 1949, two officials from Japan's Ministry of Education visited California. Ichero Takeda, head of elementary education in Japan, and Rentaro Ono, leader of social studies, took a three-month trip to the United States to observe the operation of public schools under the democratic system of government. They were there specifically to study the schools of Ventura County. They both had been working in Japan with Pauline as head of elementary education for the US Occupation.

The Japanese visitors came to the United States and to Ventura County because of Pauline. They said they had worked with her in compiling a course of study for Japan's elementary schools and reported that the course of study contained many features similar to those of Ventura County. They wanted to see how Ventura county schools operated and to meet persons with whom Pauline had worked. The two paid high compliments to her, saying, "She is doing a wonderful job in their country, that the elementary schools have improved because of her work and that they hope to keep her longer in Japan."[4]

However, that was not to be the case. Pauline completed her work in Japan, and in the spring of 1950, after two years and three months working for the CIE, she finally got her chance to fly across the ocean, an experience previously denied her when she came to Japan. That time, officials bumped her from a flight in favor of military personnel, relegating her to ship travel and a vexing journey aboard a creaky old vessel that was on its last leg.

This time, she took time to vacation briefly in Europe, traveling west from Japan until she reached the shores of the Atlantic. She flew out of Shannon, Ireland. She briefly toured Ireland, collected pictures of the Hill of Tara in County Meath, and visited other nearby sites whose lush countryside captivated her country-girl curiosity.[5]

Ireland was a special place for Pauline because Bridget Ford Kastendieck, her long-deceased grandmother, emigrated from Ireland. Bridget died long before the birth of Pauline. Nevertheless, the opportunity to embrace the land of one of her ancestors beckoned her.

Shannon, Ireland, prospered as the gateway between Europe and the Americas. It had a history of pioneering in global aviation as the site of the first transatlantic proving flight in 1945. During the war, limited aircraft range necessitated refueling stops on many journeys. The military made extensive use of the Shannon airport both during and after the war. Shannon became the most convenient stopping point before and after a trip across the Atlantic.[6]

Pauline traveled light for someone who had spent almost two and a half years away from home, weighing herself in at a healthy

165 pounds and three bags of luggage filled with the necessities of travel and a generous supply of oriental keepsakes and gifts. On the evening of April 16, she boarded the plane for the overnight flight to the United States. She flew aboard a Boeing 377 Stratocruiser, British Overseas Airways Corporation model G-AKGH. The Boeing 377 was a large four-engine plane considered one of the most advanced propeller-driven transports of its time. It was also among the most luxurious. Its design was patterned after the B-29 Super fortress of the military with innovate features that included two passenger decks and a pressurized cabin, a relatively new feature in aviation. Typically, it carried fewer than 100 passengers on the main deck and a dozen or more in the lower deck lounge.[7]

Pauline seemed to have a custom of finding herself amid historic circumstances. In this case, aviation stood out. Boeing delivered the last 377 to British Airways in May 1950, the month after she flew out of Shannon. She did not know it at the time, but problems with catastrophic failures of the propellers of the 377 hastened its demise as a commercial carrier.

The 377 cruised at a speed of approximately 300 miles per hour. After some ten hours flying over the Atlantic, the calendar rolled over, and the plane touched down April 17 at New York international Airport, commonly known as Idlewild (present John F. Kennedy International). Pauline arrived amidst another piece of airport history. The day before, April 16, 1950, the first jet airliner landed at Idlewild, a new airport that had opened two years before in 1948 in anticipation of future advancements in air travel.

OFFICE BREAK. Pauline seldom confined herself to an office routine. A typical workday usually found her somewhere enjoying time with Occupation colleagues, traveling across Japan, delving into Japanese culture, or at a Japanese school talking to teachers and parents about the future of Japanese education. This photograph shows her at an outdoor cafe in Tokyo with unidentified members of her CIE team.

PAULINE K. JEIDY. **General Headquarters, Tokyo, Japan.**

ATOM BOMB MUSHROOM CLOUD. **The city of Nagasaki suffered the same fate as Hiroshima in August 1945. The devastation wrought at Hiroshima was not sufficient to convince the Japanese War Council to accept unconditional surrender. The United States proceeded with an already planned drop of a second atom bomb. The bombing of Nagasaki was the last major act of WW II.** ***US Army AAF photo, Library of Congress.***

NAGASAKI AFTER THE ATOM BOMB. **Nagasaki was a major shipbuilding city and a large military port. It was not a favored target for the atom bomb because it had been bombed five times in the previous twelve months. Nevertheless, it became a secondary target when bad weather prevented dropping the bomb on the city of Kokura. The Nagasaki Prefectural Office put the figure for deaths at 87,000 with 70 percent of the city's industrial zone destroyed.** ***British Broadcasting Corporation.***

PAULINE AND FRIENDS. **Visits to Japanese schools were high on Pauline's list of favorite things to do as director of elementary education in the Allied rehabilitation of post-war Japan. Photographers often found her on the playground engaged with kids awestruck by her size and American persona.**

BOEING 377 STRATOCRUISER. **Pauline flew out of Shannon, Ireland, aboard a British Overseas Airline plane like this model G-AKGH. The airline industry considered the Boeing 377 to be the luxury model of passenger planes. Pauline's plane landed at New York International Airport on April 17, 1950.** ***Charles M. Daniels Collection, San Diego Air and Space Museum.***

Golden Years

46

Advice to Teachers

Things had not changed much in Ventura County after her two years and three months of Allied Occupation work in Japan,[1] Pauline returned to her job with the Ventura County school system; however, this time as Assistant Superintendent of Ventura County Schools instead of Director of Curriculum. Her job did not substantially change, only her title.

Meanwhile, her reputation as a scholar grew. Her early research on Mexican-American children became a landmark study that received widespread academic attention. (Scholars continued to cite it into the 21st century, recognizing it as an influential article about minority education in America.)[2] By 1950, Pauline Jeidy was a respected authority on childhood education. More of her articles and chapters appeared in journals and books.[3] Citations of her work figured regularly in educational references and anthologies on teaching.[4] Occasionally her writing reached beyond pedagogy to embrace a larger context of childhood learning.

Near the end of her first year in Japan, she authored a short 84-page book that described in a simplified version her method of building democratic education around topics of social studies.

Complete with her picture and name printed on the cover, the book circulated among Japanese teachers. In it, she included chapters on democratic goals, titling the book, *Theory and Practice of Democracy Education*, a title in line with the purpose of the Allied Occupation to establish democracy in Japan. The book spoke to both educational and political audiences. Freedom, she wrote, comes from a framework of general welfare. Justice is to actively "do the right thing" or "behave fairly" as defined by the laws and rules of a community. Freedom arises from knowing the laws that govern a society. If ones freedom violates the rights of others, it becomes necessary to restrain that freedom.[5]

She believed that teachers could and should teach social lessons on such topics as democracy at an early age. The time to cultivate a healthy social environment is childhood, she said. Children must learn to respect the rights of others early on, to apologize for misbehavior, to share with others, and to help others. She believed strongly that learning these lessons came from children interacting with each other and not just from the lessons of textbooks. She said, "It is better to make good habits by doing good things."[6] Children are intrinsically able to experience deep satisfaction of what they do right when given the opportunity to learn about social concerns because they carry them out within the boundaries of their own lives.[7]

In her book, Pauline urged the Japanese to teach democracy from their own cultural roots. "It is important," she wrote, "for a school to be able to manage school life according to its own nationality."[8] It is important to judge whether the school is preparing children to live and progress in a society that has the ability of self-government. In a veiled message to the Japanese, she added, this depends on whether a society has the capacity of self-governance.[9]

The child should always be at the center of education, Pauline believed, and urged the Japanese to adopt such an idea in the future. For a democracy to succeed, it must do so with the will of the people beginning with the youngest generation. The teacher in that regard "is the light of the world."

She outlined principles of teaching based on ideas she had worked to accomplish throughout her teaching career. It is the teacher's responsibility to be careful so that the assigned work is within the limits of the ability of the child, she cautioned. This infers that a teacher knows the difference in abilities among the students and makes appropriate adjustments to the assignments. Every child should enjoy an equal opportunity for success at his or her level. In a true democracy, individuals have a value of their own; individuals have the right to equal opportunities and deserve respect for who they are, she declared. This means that each individual has an obligation not only to respect others but also to respect themselves and thus gather respect from others.

As part of this idea in a democracy, she said, children learn to honor authority and live together for the benefit of the community. Freedom arises from observing the rules of a democratic society. However, instead of just benefitting from society, she wrote, you must fulfill a duty to be part of it.

In her instructions to Japanese teachers, she did not overlook her strong belief in the holistic approach to learning. Whether a child can learn to rule his own life by the principles of democracy depends on certain things; that is, is she/he healthy, happy, and in a stable environment. A healthy mental condition is necessary, she said. "Reassurance means not just knowing where the next meal can come from. It is a sense of security found in the deep satisfaction that arises from knowing that I [the child] am loved and needed in the school and the family."[10] Moreover, Kids must learn health and physical well-being as a responsibility. Children must play. It is necessary to balance study, play, and activity.

The principle of the study of social studies at each grade of the elementary school, according to Pauline, was to probe the depth of each individual mind. She set forth a teaching approach that today is standard at most levels of learning; that is, present the problem; confirm the problem with the students; have the class list possible methods of solving the problem; choose a method to use; and exchange knowledge so that from all the knowledge collected the whole class can use it. She showed that this method of planning worked even at the first grade level. She urged teachers not to overlook the benefit of allowing students to do several little things in problem solving, reminding them that a small child's attention span is no more than 20 minutes.

She cautioned teachers to be understanding. A child sometimes makes an error whether in deed or in thought. If handled correctly, she said, it could be like the blooming of a rose. Taking the time to build on a teaching moment may give a child a flowering of knowledge that otherwise would be buried through thoughtless criticism or incorrect disregard for a student's dignity.

Pauline's book presented topics ranging from a practical guide for school organization to a section on unity and society. She included chapters for problem solving, goals for social education in a democracy, and play in social studies, including the significance of the effect of acting in a play. She added supplements at the end of the book that outlined examples of potential interest to Japanese students like the Samurai and the role of kites in Japan. The book ended with obligatory sections on the Board of Education and the PTA.[11]

Pauline finished her book in December 1948 and published it the following year. Despite its potential general value to a broad audience of educators, it was only available in the Japanese language. As head of the Allied High Command Education Section on elementary education, she obviously intended it specifically for Japanese teachers because of its suggested themes related to the culture of Japan, and because of its clear emphasis on democracy in Japan, which was the objective of the Allied Occupation. Regrettably, her book had limited distribution in Japan and none outside the country. The only known surviving copy is the Japanese language version in the National Diet Library in Kyoto, Japan.

Meanwhile, in January 1949, she published "Improving the Program in English" in the prestigious *English Journal,* the journal of the National Council of Teachers of English. She had worked on the article before and during her time in Japan. In it, Pauline summarized her philosophy of teaching reading. The article had an immediate impact on reading programs across the country. Among other things, the article contained two important messages for teachers. First, adjust reading experiences to each child's needs; and secondly, make reading a part of a child's daily life. A child should be able to enjoy what he/she reads independent of the teacher's help.

The article received wide public acclaim from educators throughout the country and further propelled Pauline into the national spotlight. For example, it appeared in the *Elementary School Journal*, on a list of 34 of the most important works on reading instruction at the elementary-school level.[12] The compiler of the list was none other than University of Chicago professor William S. Gray, author and prominent literacy advocate who edited and illustrated the iconic "Dick," "Jane," and "Sally" characters (and their pets "Spot" and "Puff") of mid-century American culture that were a mainstay of elementary reading in the baby boom years.

Pauline's article carried a subtle reprimand of current reading methods in schools. She contrasted traditional approaches to regimented routines of teaching with her holistic alternative technique, which she based on the individual needs of each student, rather than children forced into formal reading programs without any attention to their readiness for reading.[13]

Her mild rebuke singled out often-used excuses generally known to exist in classrooms when it came to reading. There was a litany of pretexts for why a child was unable to read. Teachers blamed administrators, the children's former teachers, their parents, or the children themselves for a child's poor reading performance. A second-grade teacher blamed poor reading skills on the first-grade teacher who did a poor job. Teachers entrenched in intractable methodologies spoke of any attempt to adjust the school reading program to the needs of the children as "lowering the standards."[14]

Pauline argued that a child's successful progress in reading depended on much more than a concern for the mechanics of reading whereby a child may lose sight of the end purpose of learning to read. She pointed to preschoolers' curiosity about content. They love to look through books, they try to give the illusion of reading by making up content to go with pictures, they ask what printed words say, and they give rapt attention to stories read to them. She wrote, "We want our children to gain experience, make literary friends, be informed, be amused, and be spiritually moved by the content they read."[15]

In her insightful and compelling approach to reading, Pauline described the impact of environment on a child's ability to read, citing insecurity, and the lack of a feeling of security at home that kept minds preoccupied in the learning process. Citing personal experiences in Ventura County, she wrote, "We want our teachers to realize how much a child's reading ability depends on his whole life. In addition to his grade placement in reading, we want a teacher to know if a child has a normal, wholesome home life, enough of the right kind of food, books to read at home, someone to share his interests, friends at school, health, emotional stability, and good hearing and vision."[16]

The focus of Pauline's philosophy of teaching was on the children. The necessary conduit of her ideas was through teachers; hence, her workshops and demonstration classes designed to aid teachers. "We try to relieve her [the teacher] of the strain of striving to make the reading level of each youngster in her room to correspond to the label on her door," Pauline said. "We want her to set her goals in terms of progress rather than in grade levels." She added, "We want a child to be aware of his status so that he can enjoy his own progress. We try to sell the teacher the idea of reading readiness as a matter of continuous growth and development, not just a brief phase a child goes through at about the time he loses his front teeth."

Throughout the article, Pauline's interchangeable use of gender when referring to students and teachers illustrated her careful attention to the individual. An example of a student or teacher might be "she" on one page and in the next example "he" on another page.

The details of her method extended to the classroom environment. Her workshop demonstrations always included a section on how to arrange rooms to stimulate the drive to learn in the child. She advocated a classroom organized into a symphony of colors and ideas in an environment that contained elements to arouse curiosity and move children to mental and physical activity.

When a teacher needed help, Pauline would often go herself on weekends to meet with the teacher. She hauled materials to a school to create bulletin boards, set up flower arrangements, arrange a science corner, or show a teacher how to combine colors, and how to cut out letters and patters to add a dash of excitement to a room. If a teacher resented her makeover of a classroom, she would do it a little at a time.

47

Scholars, Clubs, and Folklore

As part of the working middle class, Pauline accepted her accolades in stride, never losing sight of her determination to improve elementary education on behalf of the Ventura County school system. She worked out of her new office in the Ventura County Courthouse, an imposing Doric Roman Order building five blocks from Ventura Beach and recently renovated to house the school superintendent and his staff.

Her busy schedule as a school administrator did not impede her dedication to the teaching of elementary school children. She penned several articles and books for grade school teachers. She delighted in teaching short courses and did so during numerous summers, teaching sessions at Redlands, California; University of Utah, Salt Lake City; University of California at the UCLA-Berkley campus and at Santa Barbara. She found time, too, to advance her own education, taking graduate courses during the summer at UCLA.

She wrote a series of articles in the 1950s, adding ten more publications to her already lengthy resume.[1] Educators recognized her growing list of contributions to the field when the California Congress of Parents and Teachers honored her with a lifetime membership.

In 1953, the *Journal of Childhood Education*, a highly respected publication of worldwide circulation, invited Pauline to join the editorial board of the journal representing the Pacific Coast Region. The *Journal of Childhood Education,* started in 1924, was the flagship publication of the Association of Childhood Education International, which itself dated to 1892. Part of a movement in education for the specific purpose of improvement of conditions for children living in poverty, the work of the organization among war refugees and immigrant communities was notable for singling out for attention kids facing challenging circumstances such as discrimination, war, and hunger.

The organization aligned with many of Pauline's own objectives; that is, a vision that every child in every nation should have access to a quality education. It fit her aim also for democracy in education, which aspired to educate children to become responsible and engaged citizens, ready for life in a changing world. The journal focused on issues and projects that took innovative approaches to teaching. It later adopted as a masthead *Childhood Education: Innovations*. Pauline took her place among a small group of new appointees to the editorial board, six of whom were women, including prominent educator Pauline Hilliard from the University of Florida, at Gainesville, and Katherine E. Hill, professor of education at New York University.[2]

As Pauline grew in stature among educators, she continued to give of her time and resources to the Ventura community, always eager to share the merits of her national attention with others. She kept up her busy schedule of club appearances and storytelling, except now her presentations often included stories of her travels in Japan.

The members of the Ventura County American Association of University Women elected Pauline president of the organization in 1953, elevating her from her status the previous year as member-at-large on the executive committee. One of the oldest and most prestigious organizations in the nation, the AAUW came into existence in 1881 as a voice for advancing educational and professional opportunities for women and girls, a group well suited to Pauline's interest in women's issues.

The naming of new AAUW association officers marked a special occasion in Ventura. The Pierpoint Inn had never looked spiffier, all decked out in red, purple, and blending shades of rose sweet peas. Not since Josephine Pierpoint first opened the Inn at Ventura back in 1910 had it looked so gala with its sweeping bluff-side panoramas of the Pacific Ocean and cozy craftsman-bungalow-style architecture. The 1935 Spanish revival Banquet Center and nearby English Tudor Revival cottages added to the romantic coastal charm and reminded members of the international scope and mission of the AAUW.[3]

Pauline had occasion to meet many celebrities in her job, moments she took in stride never allowing a brush with fame to alter her personable, down-to-earth demeanor. One time she hosted the artist Millard Sheets when he came to Cabrillo junior high to address a meeting of the AAUW. Sheets, a California native and newly appointed to head the Otis Art Institute, in Los Angeles, was at the peak of his fame as a prominent American artist known, among other things, for the California Style watercolor movement of the 1930s and 1940s.[4]

Among her most prized luminary contacts, however, was Dr. Margery Bailey, a retired professor of English and Dramatic Arts and Literature at Stanford University. Regarded as one of the influential people in John Steinbeck's formative years, Dr. Bailey enjoyed widespread recognition for her teaching of Shakespeare. On one occasion, Pauline wrote to invite her to be a guest at a Ventura workshop conference. A witty, clever, and perceptive letter writer, the 71-year-old Dr. Bailey wrote back, "This is a lengthy letter of the type to be found from Geriatric Resorts, where conversation is limited to exchanges of symptoms." Nevertheless, she assured Pauline, "I go nowhere to address conferences or professional sessions."[5] The letter reminded Pauline now in her sixties of the inescapable reality of the infirmities of old age.

Pauline found time, too, to indulge in her interest in folktales.

Georgia Browne was a kindred spirit when it came to folktales. She was an avid collector of stories, especially stories related to Ventura County. Whether reading stories written by early settlers, studying letters and records left by first explorers or by interviews with people who remembered Ventura County in the early days, Mrs. Browne gathered tales from wherever she found them. In the early 1940s, during a brief period as director of Radio Education for Ventura County Schools, she used the material to develop a series of interesting and authentic radio broadcasts on Ventura County history. She left employment with the Ventura schools about the time Pauline arrived in 1944. The radio scripts ended up in a file until Pauline rediscovered them in 1955.

Ever on the lookout for a good folktale and a way to excite students about reading and learning, Pauline saw in Mrs. Browne's work the potential for both, at the same time folding history lessons into the reading experience.

It was a natural fit for Pauline's theory on integrated learning. Instead of learning to read unfamiliar and often boring textbook primers, students could learn something about local history using recognizable people and places and at the same time enjoy the subject of a good folktale. What fourth grader could resist a good bear story? Who would not want to know about the mystery of the lost woman of San Nicholas Island left behind on the island for 18 years by herself?

Pauline collected 44 short stories and arranged them chronologically to follow the period of discovery and settlement of Ventura County. With Mrs. Browne's permission, she revised the radio scripts into story form and added some stories of her own that she kept conveniently in a file of mimeographed material for just such an occasion. In her down to earth writing style, she selected stories about places that students knew in Ventura County, like the legend of the mission aqueduct that carried water from the mountains to the mission gardens, sparkling mountain water pouring from the mouth of a stone horse's head into the fountain. Traces of masonry lay still visible on the hillside above the mission grounds. Students traveling along the hillside could see and relate to the patches of loosely set stones that marked the path of the old aqueduct.

There were tales in the collection about ship travel from northern California where the trains from the east deposited travelers before they boarded ships to Ventura because the stages could not traverse parts of the road along the ocean at high tides.

The tales about the Port of Hueneme were particularly germane to Ventura students who learned that the name Hueneme was for a beautiful Indian maiden who in despair over the fickle behavior of her husband threw herself into the sea and perished. Her husband, having come to his senses, in a moment of great sorrow for the lost Hueneme followed her into the ocean and perished. Students saw the two great stones visible at low tide, said according to legend to be the lost couple, and they knew that Hueneme in the Chumash Indian language meant resting place.[6]

Pauline's aspiration for equality of education for all children shone through in lightly veiled stories like the beekeeping story, which gave girls the upper hand. A young girl whose father kept bees proved she could handle bees. She searched out a drone in the hive and placed it in her mouth. Drones do not have stingers. She did this, according to the story, to impress a bullying boy who thought girls did not know anything, and the bees would sting her.

When Pauline put aside her editor's hat and became the writer, as she did on a couple of occasions in the anthology, to write stories in her own voice, her writing skills stood out. For example, the visual descriptions of "Matillja Canyon" sparkled with language that was vintage Pauline. "Numerous springs of various hues bubbled up and flowed away in different directions through a lovely grove of willows and elders. Ferns grew among the trees. There were many birds and butterflies, and occasionally, a rattlesnake."[7]

Then there was the story of George McCoy who made his living by driving the town water wagon. This tale had all the elements that drew a young reader into its history, human enterprise, colorful description, and light humor that characterized much of Pauline's writing. Written intentionally at a beginner's level, the story like all the tales in the collection assimilated the reading experience. "One of Mr. McCoy's horses was white; the other was bay. He hitched his team to a lumber wagon. The sideboards held in place four or five fifty-gallon whiskey barrels. When loading his water supply, Mr. McCoy drove his team and wagon right into the river, where the bridge is now. He drove to mid-stream where the water ran deepest. It came well up on the sides of his wagon. It was possible to lean over the side of the wagon, dip water from the river into his barrels, and fill them quickly and easily. With all five barrels filled, he drove back to town, where he siphoned the water from his barrels to those of the residents. His regular customers knew when to expect him, and he knew his customers so well that he knew just when it was necessary for their water barrels to be filled again."[8]

48

A Time of Change

In the fall of 1955, Pauline returned to Billings, Missouri, for the first time since leaving Christian County thirty-eight years before. The occasion was the Kastendieck family reunion, a chance to reacquaint with cousins and family members from five different states. Verda, Pauline's sister, came to the reunion, too, with Ruth and Deanne. It was a relatively small gathering of about 25 people. Nevertheless, it was almost everyone that remained of Pauline's family. The years had taken a toll. The first generation of Kastendiecks had passed. Only Augusta Kastendieck remained to represent the second generation. It would be the final time Pauline would see many of them.

Despite the melancholy circumstances, the event was like old times; a basket dinner at the park on a beautiful October Saturday; visiting and renewing acquaintances; and watching kids skate, swing, and scream with delight down the sliding board. A side trip to the old home place at Billings and a visit to Andrew's grave at Rose Hill brought back memories of long ago when life was at a different place for Pauline.[1] Too soon, everyone went his or her separate way.

The joy of seeing family together turned to anxiety and sadness. Verda became seriously ill. Her prognosis was not good.

Pauline was a prolific letter writer, especially to family in Fennimore, Wisconsin, in frequent exchanges of letters with Verda and Ruth. Her letter writing was usually on weekends after a busy week at work. However, now she devoted her time to a chain of letters to cheer on Verda toward a speedy recovery. On one occasion, she wrote on elegant stationery with a Japanese pine twig design, "Dear Verd, Today is a beautiful day. It rained like the dickens day before yesterday and today all is clean and sparkling. I sure should get out in the yard and do some work. Yesterday things were too wet. But today it looks as if it could be done. Last night I went to a real good show—Walt Disney's *Old Yeller*. If you can go be sure to do so and take Deanne. it is about a wonderful old dog. It is a little sad, but ends on an optimistic note."[2]

Pauline broke off her letter because she had to fare forth and collect for Red Cross, not a task she looked forward to because, in her words, she was "not a great lover of Red Cross," particularly since women usually did the collecting and the man in charge sat back and waited for the money. "There are a lot of things I would rather do," she wrote.[3]

"I went to the paint store yesterday and got my wall paper. It is even more beautiful than I thought it was. I can hardly wait to get at it...Tell Davie I got the material to make my wedding dress the other day and if I don't make a mess of making it I think I really will do him credit. It is a pale blue lace. The most gorgeous material. It cost plenty, but was half price at that, because it was in three short pieces."[4] Davie was her soon-to-be-married nephew.

"After buying all the gear for making my house look pretty, the termite man found two hundred dollars' worth of termites in the attic. That sure makes me mad. I hate to spend so much money for something I can't eat or wear. This I can't even look at."[5]

"Verd, your progress report sounded pretty good last week. Keep up the good work."

When the encouragement of carrying on life as usual did not seem enough, Pauline would tell Verda a story or joke. "I went to a luncheon yesterday and heard a good speech. The man said, in talking about the state of the world, that it was not important that Russia got Sputnik up in the air first, but the way American people acted about it was important. We made such fools of ourselves, nationally speaking. There was a story in our paper that said, Sputnik II and Van Guard I met up in the air and one said to the other, 'Lets stop and visit some time' and the other said, 'Why not? We both speak German.' More truth than poetry in that, I reckon."[6]

No amount of good humor could lighten the gravity of Verda's situation. Without being morose, Pauline acknowledged her difficult prospects. "According to the papers you are having a cold spell out there. I hope spring is not far away...I am sending a check to help pay for the telephone bills. What with a hospital bill to pay, you no doubt have enough on your hands...Sure hope things are improving for you. Love, Pauline."[7]

In another letter, Verda's deteriorating condition was evident. "It was good of you to make the effort to write to me while you were in the hospital. Your hand must have been functioning pretty well. The letter made good sense, but it wasn't too cheerful. Under the circumstances, that was to be expected.

"I sure was glad to hear that you were at home again. Maybe in a good atmosphere you will improve faster. I sure hope so. Seems to me you have born your cross long enough...Today is a beautiful day. Wish you could be here to enjoy it."[8]

Verda died on March 22, 1958. She was only 61 years of age. Her death came after an illness long diagnosed as terminal. Yet, there was no way to prepare for the loss of a loved one. The times Verda and Pauline spent together at Billings and then at Fennimore were full of treasured memories. Never was there a closer bond between two sisters.

Verda eventually chose farm life over teaching after twelve years in the classroom, two years in Christian County, Missouri, and ten years in the rural schools of Grant and Iowa counties, Wisconsin. She was an early inspiration for Pauline's career in education.

After her marriage, Verda lived first at Mt. Ida and then Mt. Hope before moving permanently to the farm near Fennimore. Like Mollie and Pauline, Verda was a lover of nature. She surrounded her home with beautiful flowers many of which were rare specimens. She taught Sunday school and served as a member of the school board. For many years, she was a faithful member of the Woman's Christian Temperance Union (WCTU), and served as an officer of the Grant County group. One of her early community memberships in which she took great pride was the Women's Society of Christian Service (WSCS). She became a charter member of the organization and continued in the society after moving to Fennimore.[9]

She shared the same concerns for gender equality that ran in the family. The WSCS organization, for instance, was a relatively new women's society that formed in 1940 throughout the Methodist church. It automatically bound into one unit the many former women's organizations of the church.

Verda dedicated her time to helping others. Her love of young people and children kept her young. Those who knew her said, "Her kindly spirit made everyone feel she was their friend, and if she knew of anyone in need, she was glad to lend a helping hand." For 18 years of her life, Verda cared for Mollie her mother in the Brandemuehl home.

Verda was gone from Pauline's life, replaced by an emptiness that nothing could fill.

Meanwhile in Ventura, things were changing, too. The wave of political pressure across the nation for more centralized and economical school districts swept into California. The topic of consolidation and reorganization crept into the politics of Ventura County.

Consolidation was an ironic and controversial issue. Ironic because educational standards in Ventura County were at their highest levels since the end of World War II, and expected to continue as facilities grew. Students were learning better, and expanded facilities allowed for smaller classes. More qualified teachers and more of them gave a stability to the system in which teaching was more of a profession than in the past when many considered it a stopgap along the road to other career goals.[10] Pauline expressed special pride in the parts of the system that she oversaw. Students could not only read but also read better than their parents could at the same age, and understand more of what they read. Ventura County youngsters steadily scored above the national median in reading achievement tests.

Pauline never voiced a public position on school unification. Nevertheless, she vented her frustration in a letter to Verda shortly before Verda's death. She asked, "Are people going crazy wild out there about the schools? It is just awful out here. You can't pick up a paper out here without reading the most crackpot statements by people who know nothing about it. Sometimes it is rather discouraging."[11]

For the most part, she allowed the success of her work with the rural school districts across Ventura County to illustrate her position. For example, in an article that appeared in the *Ventura County Star-Free Press*, she gave an upbeat report of the progress of reading. "Some of the books haven't altered much from the days of Dick and Jane," she said, "But in the first grade they're so fascinated with the process of reading, they don't care what they read."

"Few schools demanded outside reading in the early years," she continued. "It's like eating spinach; you're better off not to demand, but to make it sound good." She pointed out that a recent survey showed that even television's lazy charms failed to lure most youngsters away from books. Some were even stimulated to look up material on subjects they saw on a television program. She gave a succinct overview of her teaching method. Students received reading material of all kinds from the earliest possible moment. Skills were taught by figuring out new words through a combination of tools, including phonics; paying attention to how a word is used in a sentence; analyzing words by studying prefixes, roots, and endings, and using a dictionary. She added that any parent who thought of phonics as an extinct technique was mistaken. True to the Jeidy method, she urged individualized reading to encourage youngsters to absorb as much as he/she can as fast as she/he can.[12]

California schools were slow to change. Consolidation of schools seemed an anathema to American values. One observer wrote, "Local citizens preferred to maintain the status quo and retain some local control over the schools." Citizens looked upon the local school district and its elected board as one of the last vestiges of the American way of life, one of the last places where people had a voice in the affairs of government.[13] The schools in Ventura County were excellent, so why change that.

Unfortunately, Ventura had changed over the years from a provincial community of yesteryear into an urbanized center. Pauline's philosophy of teaching the individual needs of a child and helping each school meet its specific unique needs came under scrutiny during the consolidation craze. Ventura underwent rapid transformation from a closely-knit community where everyone knew everyone else to become a suburban area where a person became a stranger to his next-door neighbor. A rapidly growing, bustling city replaced the fond memory of the Ventura of an earlier day.

Meanwhile, the pace of her research and publication slowed over the next decade. Nevertheless, Pauline remained active in professional organizations and education advocacy groups that frequently listed her on their rosters.[14] She maintained a lifelong active role in community organizations beginning with the time in Oregon when she helped start the first annual Christmas celebration at Rickreall. Her passion for public service was primarily for organizations that advocated for women and education. At different times in her life, she served as president of the Soroptimists, the American Association of University Women, and Delta Kappa Gamma. At the same time, among her professional associations, the Association of Childhood Education was her favorite. She also held prominent positions in the Elementary Administration Association, the California Retired Teachers Association, the Early Childhood Education Association, and the California Association of Supervision and Curriculum Development, serving the Southern Section two years as treasurer. She served eight years on the Federal Housing Authority Board in Ventura and was an active member of the YWCA board for many years.[15] She reprised her military association with US Army forces in Japan by serving as an officer of the United Service Organizations (USO).[16]

Pauline's passion for social studies and their use as a holistic teaching method never faltered. Nevertheless, social studies became less and less important to a new wave of educators as a means of studying democracy. Progressive education began to collapse in the 1950s amid a disjuncture between the proponents of consolidation and the collective vision of progressive educators like Pauline and Helen Heffernan.[17] One writer observed, "The struggle between conservatives and liberals; the continuing power of race and racism; the impact of the demographic and economic changes; and the ways different groups mobilized around calls for democracy and claims of patriotism attempted to reshape educational policy."[18]

School consolidation finally came down to money and resources. Local school districts had the final say, and California was one of the last states to reorganize. Nevertheless, politics eventually prevailed based on such feeble arguments as "better modes of transportation and improved highways made distance less of a negative factor for kids riding long bus routes." As a final incentive, the California legislature offered a bonus for every student attending a unified school district, in effect buying consolidation in California.[19]

Pauline did not stay around to see the result of Ventura County school consolidation, which became final in 1966. Many believe that public school consolidation, which closed thousands of local rural schools, dealt a blow to American education from which the country never fully recovered. Before it was over, the political goal of securing a more efficient use of the educational tax dollar resulted in the reduction of school districts nationwide from 94,926 to less than 16,000.[20] The United States has since ranked consistently well down the list as one of the best-educated nations.

49

Twilight

Pauline turned 65 in 1963, and on June 30 retired after 40 years as an educator. Looking back over her 18 years of work with the elementary schools in Ventura County, she counted many accomplishments. One of the most interesting phenomenon to her was the growth of the county. She recalled, "When I came, there were 350 elementary schools. Now there are more than 2,000."[1] Her assessment came before consolidation of the Ventura County schools. In less than three years after Pauline retired, consolidation slashed the number of schools in Ventura County by more than half.

It had been a long and satisfying career for Pauline, starting with her graduation from Springfield Normal School in Missouri, and then as teacher and county school supervisor in Wisconsin.[2] Her work as school supervisor in Oregon rounded out her first 17 years as an educator before coming to Northern California. After three years as school supervisor for Butte County, she came to Ventura. With the exception of two years in Japan when she took a leave of absence to help the American Occupation, she spent the majority of her career at Ventura.

Reminiscing about her work, she took special pride in the unique teachers' workshop she created. "It was the first one in California set up as a demonstration school," she recalled. It had been 20 years since her first workshop broke the bounds of the usual teachers seminar confined to lectures and discussions. Her workshop model included demonstrations for teachers to observe how to teach.[3]

Educators from across the state and nation honored her upon her retirement. More than 500 persons in the education field showed up at a reception tea to say goodbye "to the much admired Mrs. Jeidy."[4] The *Ventura County Star-Free Press* voiced what many felt. "In time, new generations may forget the name of Pauline Jeidy, but her mark in the history records of elementary education in Ventura County will long be remembered."[5]

Pauline spent the earlier part of her last day on the job talking with new teachers. She came away feeling she had made the right decision to retire. "The talks were so rewarding," she said, this was a good place to quit. It left a good taste."[6] When pressed to comment on why she was retiring, she said it was a matter of choice. "I want to retire," she said, her eyes sparkling, "while I still have time to enjoy myself."[7]

Regrettably, there was more to it than that. Events in California education rapidly escalated toward reorganization. Voters elected a staunch conservative and proponent of consolidation to become the Superintendent of Public Instruction in California in 1962. Consequently, Dr. Helen Heffernan's network of supporters fell into disarray, and her programs disbanded.[8]

Nevertheless, so much had happened in Pauline's life that it was time to slow down and pause to reflect on the amazing changes she had witnessed. She ticked off various inventions that came during her lifetime: radio, television, airplanes, talking pictures, automobiles, and phonographs. "I've lived during a good era," she remarked. "I've seen so many firsts."[9]

She looked forward to retirement, to indulge her interests in American folktale stories, to read a lot, and to travel. She had plans for an upcoming trip around the world to India and Ceylon, and a return visit to Japan to see the parts of it she missed before, and to look up old friends.

She cut short an interview about her upcoming retirement to hustle off to Poinsettia School on Victoria Avenue to oversee the Ventura County Spelling Bee, an activity much closer to her heart than job titles and political shenanigans.[10]

Pauline was not a rich person. She still lived in the same modest house on Evans Street. She never broke the glass ceiling to become County Superintendent, an office many believed she should have occupied. However, County Superintendent was an elective office, and Pauline was not a politician. She contented herself with remaining as second in command. Her salary as Assistant Superintendent never rose much above $12,500,[11] still a good salary at the time for an academic professional of her qualifications and standing. Money was never part of her formula for success. After her retirement, she lived comfortably on Social Security and monthly retirement payments from the California State Teachers Retirement System.[12]

Pauline continued to give generously of her time but generally avoided publicity on her own behalf. When a school official once pressed her for a picture of herself, she replied, "I have no picture except a very old one, which would not be a true representation of my appearance at present. The idea of having one made repels me, so I hope you will not insist."[13]

When Verda died, Pauline became the surrogate to Verda's grandchildren. Her visits to Fennimore were exciting times. The children crowded around, competing to sit beside her and enjoy her subtle humor and quiet chuckle. When she traveled, wonderful gifts arrived from wherever she was in the world. She was not effusive or demanding of her young protégés but always encouraged them and helped them believe in themselves. She found enough money to pay for her grandniece's college education and was her biggest cheerleader, filling a much needed role in her life.[14]

There were times when her thoughts went back to Missouri. She learned of the passing of Miss Neyer, her fourth-grade teacher in Billings. The years that had passed and the distance that separated them never dimmed Pauline's love and respect for Miss Neyer. The loss of her childhood teacher conjured up all the memories of growing up, the good times and the bad times, and surprised her that the memories of school remained so vivid in her mind. Miss Neyer was of the Catholic faith, which she practiced diligently until the end of her life. She instilled a caring discipline in her students that in its brief influence helped to shape many a life in the Billings community.[15]

Although distance separated them, Pauline kept up contact with friends and family that remained. She never abandoned a feeling that she was part of the Billings community. She joined members of the Kastendieck family to make a donation for the upkeep of Rose Hill Cemetery, the resting place of her father and most of the Kastendieck deceased.[16]

She kept up a correspondence with family members, often reminiscing about events of her childhood. When she was in her late 70s, she was thrilled to learn that her father's baptism certificate survived in the hands of her grandniece. She used the occasion to call up memories of him, in particular his love of music. She remembered the good days in Billings when Andrew filled the house with his singing and the rhythmic clacking of a set of rib bones.[17] She missed the times when he read aloud to her and the children, as he often did.[18]

"I wish you could have known your great grandfather. He was gay and witty, knew lots of songs and loved to sing. He never had a lesson, but he could play drums. He always had some rib bones trying to shake along with his singing. I can see him yet when he would come in out of the cold, put his feet on the oven door and sing and clatter his bones. He loved to read and read aloud a lot to your grandmother and me."

Pauline kept track of her Kastendieck relatives and liked to pass on family information to those who showed an interest. The closeness of her knowledge about the family is in a letter she wrote to her grandniece. "We have a cousin Ray who is an architect in Gary, Indiana. The Texas boys say Ray is very well known. They read about him in books and hear him mentioned in lectures."[19]

Her love of cats never diminished. Tommy the cat, namesake of her beloved Billings pet of the same name, had the run of the Ventura neighborhood, sometimes coming home the worse for wear, sleeping off his prowling ways on the best furniture of whoever would let him in their house, and often to the consternation of his hosts.[20]

Whenever a church function came up, Pauline took the lead, shouldering most of the work to relieve the older members of her group. She took delight in doing it and never complained. It was common to host luncheons for 60 or more. One time after such an event, she was to show slides of her travels to India after the luncheon. The old projector refused to work, and she could only tell them what she intended to show them but without pictures. In the meantime, someone left the meeting and loaded all her slides into another projector. The aide came back to the meeting with the slides about the time Pauline was running down. The group adjourned to the church chapel where Pauline repeated her talk, this time with pictures. She thought the whole thing seemed a little muddled, but everyone else pronounced it a huge success.

Pauline wrote her last article in 1967 fittingly for the *California Journal for Instructional Improvement.*[21]

She traveled to Berkley in February 1973 for a conference of the Retired Teachers Association—albeit reluctantly because she was not fond of such events—where she learned the ins and outs of running the RTA. Ironically, the following July at the age of 75, she took over the post of president of the association.

She prepared her will in 1973 to put her personal affairs in order. In a letter to Ruth, her niece, she wrote, "By now I assume you have read The Will. It won't be much for you. Less than $10,000 each. Settling an estate is terribly expensive in California. I want you and Davie to go through the house (after I am through with it) and take what you want before selling."[22]

50

Going Home

Pauline signed a living will on May 8, 1979. The living will took the form of a standard directive to physicians that she did not desire to have her life artificially prolonged should doctors diagnose her with an incurable terminal condition. She wished to die naturally. At the time, the document indicated that no such diagnosis of a terminal condition existed.

She struggled with the ailments that accompany advancing years. Her health declined. She had heart problems, and at the last had cancer. She became unable to live alone and to take care of herself. She sold her house and afterward lived in various care facilities, and was in and out of the hospital.[1] A biopsy on June 20, 1985, revealed that cancer had spread and was inoperable.

Her only surviving family came to be with her in her final days. David, her nephew, traveled from the family home in Fennimore, Wisconsin, and Ruth, her niece, came from her home in Arizona.[2] There was no other immediate family left. Pauline outlived her Kastendieck cousins, none of whom lived to see her passing. She was the last of her generation of the Kastendieck family.

Mrs. Pauline K. Jeidy died July 29, 1985, at the age of 87.[3] Doctors ruled her death to be of natural causes.[4] She died at the California Convalescent Hospital, a relatively small nursing home that had a reputation for its above average care.[5] Surrounded by large trees in a park like setting, she died less than two miles from her home of 41 years on Evans Street.[6]

The city of Ventura paid its last respects at a memorial service for her on the afternoon of August 1, at the Charles Carroll Funeral Home, in Ventura.[7] Most of her friends and acquaintances were gone or too infirm to attend. Nevertheless, a large attendance at the services showed that those who did not know her personally knew about her, who she was, and what she meant to the history of Ventura County.

The attorney for her estate sent letters to her close friends and colleagues in Japan informing them of her passing. Pauline especially valued the friendship of Oosima-Isao, Principal of Nipon Rowa Gakko, in Tokyo.[8] Letters also went to Miss Tsune Hirano, Yokohama, Japan, and Mrs. Sueno Sakaura, Matue-City Simane Prefecture, who had just a few months earlier inquired about Pauline's health, recalling fond memories of their time together in Japan.[9]

David carried her ashes home to Fennimore for burial in the peaceful solitude of Prairie Cemetery next to Mollie and Verda. In the presence of a small gathering, Pastor Russell May conducted graveside services on the afternoon of August 27.

She rests beside her mother and sister close to home. Her local obituary made note that she was a widow since 1930, a small error because Casey Jeidy was her husband for but a year when he died in 1925. For 60 years, she remained faithfully Mrs. Pauline Jeidy. Her plain gray, granite gravestone honored her final wish, engraved with her name Pauline Jeidy, and below that in bold letters the name Kastendieck, followed by the simple words, “She lived life to the fullest.”

VERDA KASTENDIECK BRANDEMUEHL. **Despite the great geographic distance that separated them, Pauline and Verda remained close as sisters throughout their lives. This was one of the last pictures taken of her on the Brandemuehl farm near Fennimore, Wisconsin.**

KASTENDIECK COUSINS. **L to R George, Frank, Great Aunt Gussie, Mildred, Minnie, Katherine, Hazel, Pauline**

OLD FRIENDS. **Pauline traveled extensively after her retirement. One of her great pleasures was a return trip to Japan to renew acquaintances with friends made during her assignment to the CIE Allied Occupation force. These unidentified residents of Tokyo display the same warmth for her that she felt for them.**

VENTURA ADDRESS. **Pauline lived at 2009 Evans Avenue during the 41 years she worked and lived in Ventura, except for 27 months spent with the Allied Occupation forces in Japan. Her house stood conveniently near Ventura High School, and about a mile and a half from her office in the old courthouse building.**

AT HOME. **Pauline spent her retirement years traveling and enjoying life at home in Ventura, California.**

Notes

Chapter 1. Introduction

1. Andrews, *Virginia, the Old Dominion,* 357.

2. Dabney, *Virginia, the New Dominion,* 165.

3 1910 US Census, Missouri, Christian, Polk Twp., Series T624 Roll 776 p. 139, Kanendick [*sic*] Andrew 46; 1900 US Census, Missouri, Christian, Polk Twp. (south part), district 21, p. 3B, household 61. Andrew Kastenctiecke [*sic*].

4. *Christian County*, pp. 11, 84.

5. Hutter, "History of Billings, Mo." *The Billings [Missouri] Times*, 15 Oct 1914.

6. Mossberg, "High Honor Given Venturan: Mrs. Pauline Jeidy to Aid MacArthur," *Ventura (California) County Star-Free Press*, 6 Dec 1947.

Chapter 2. Immigrant Roots

1. 1912 Christian County Plat Map of Townships 27 & 28 N. Range 24W. NW ¼ of NW ¼ Section 21 Township 21 N. (Pond Township) Range 24 W. Library Center, Springfield, Mo.

2. Kastendieck, *Biography of John D. Kastendieck*, p. 1. Marriage and death certificates confirm the ancestral seat of the Kastendieck family at Morsum.

3. David Gay Genealogy, 2014. Johann Kastendieck 16 Jul 1789-12 Oct 1816.

4. Missouri Death Certificate No. 35748, dated 1923, Missouri Secretary of State. The John Dietrich Kastendieck, Sr. death certificate names Johann as his father. This document gives Johann's birthplace and that of his wife Trina as Mannheim, Germany. Both, however, were born in Morsum. The writer also misspelled the name Gömann as Gorman on the death certificate.

5. David Gay Genealogy, 2014; Tombstone Inscription, Green-Wood Cemetery, Brooklyn, N.Y.

6. Kastendieck, *Biography of John D. Kastendieck*; 1855 New York Census, New York, Kings, Ward 8 Brooklyn City.

7. Stern, Mellins, and Fishman, *New York 1880.*

8. *Brooklyn Daily Eagle*, 27 Jul 1870, 4.

9. "Red Hook Point," *Brooklyn Daily Eagle*, 2 Dec 1872, 4.

10. *Real Estate Record and Builders' Guide* Vol. 16 No. 381 (July 3 1875)-No. 406 (Dec. 25 1875), [Brooklyn, N.Y.]: C.W. Sweet, 1868-1884. See Vol. 16, No. 393, p. 631.

11. *Brooklyn Daily Eagle,* 4 Feb 1876, 2.

12. *Brooklyn Daily Eagle,* 24 May 1876, 4.

13. John Herman and Bridget Kastendieck Bible, Collection of Jayme Burchett; Baptism Certificate of Andrew Kastendieck, 13 December 1863, Brooklyn, New York. Dee Willauer Collection, Dodgeville, Wisconsin, great granddaughter of Andrew Kastendieck.

14. Christian County Recorder, Christian County, Missouri, Marriages, 1859-1940, Christian County Library. Kastendieck, Andrew, Dewey, Mollie, 11/28/1894, License ML000Z0034; Obituary of Mary A. Kastendieck. *The Fennimore Times,* 20 May 1942. The obituary of Molly Kastendieck states that she married 27 Nov and not 28 Nov. The spelling of Molly Dewey's name appears in the records as both Molly and Mollie, more frequently as the latter.

Chapter 3. The Legacy of Austin Dewey

1. 1850 US Census, Indiana: Adams and Allen Counties, Series M432 Roll 135, National Archives and Records Administration. Austin Dewey, age 14, living in the household of Austin Ransom; Family Search. Samantha Richmond b. 12 Dec 1839, m. 16 Dec 1860, Fennimore, Grant County, Wisconsin.

2. Civil War Pension Record, National Archives; 1860 U S Census, Wisconsin, Grant County Series M 653, National Archives. Austin R. Dewey in the home of S.C. Ransom, Fennimore, Wisconsin.

3. Military Service Records, Series M559 Roll 7, National Archives. Austin R. Dewey.

4. Quiner, *Military History of Wisconsin,* p. 682; Holford, *History of Grant County, Wisconsin,* pp. 339-344. Austin R. Dewey, Company K, Fennimore. The regiment enrolled volunteers in June and July 1862, and rendezvoused at Camp Randall, Wisconsin. It left Wisconsin August 20 for Benton Barracks, St. Louis, Missouri.

5. Civil War Pension Record, National Archives.

6. 1870 US Census, Missouri, Greene County, Center Twp., Series M593 Roll 777, p. 274, National Archives. Austin Dewey; Greene County Archives Bulletin #36, An Index to the Springfield Land Office Sales Book 1833-1892; Index to Greene County Stray Records 1833–1913,1877-1913, pp. 9, 373. No record exists of land purchases in Greene County in the period covering the time Austin and Samantha lived there, thus, confirming they rented their farm. A deposition in Austin's Civil War pension record verifies this rental arrangement. The Greene County Stray Records Index records his presence

in 1877. Missouri statutes provided specific guidelines for individuals finding and harboring lost cattle, horses, mules and other livestock. Before a person could take possession of the stray, he was required to post a notice of intent for at least thirty days.

7. Civil War Pension Record; Obituary of Mrs. Mary Kastendieck, *The Fennimore Times*, 20 May 1942,

8. According to his daughter, Nellie, Austin Dewey had two wounds that never healed, one on his side and another on his leg below the knee,

9. Civil War Pension Record, National Archives, p. 83.

10. Civil War Pension Record, National Archives, pp. 31-30, 84.

Chapter 4. Civil War Orphans

1. Pension Record, National Archives, p. 80. The Pension record of Austin Dewey contains more than 200 pages filed in connection with three Civil War pension claims: soldier's claim #70,145, 30 May 1865 accepted and allowed under certificate 73,754; widow's claim #243,134 28, Mar 1879 lapsed and closed; minors' claim #380,479 15, Sep 1888 rejected.

2. Pension Record, National Archives, pp. 31-39.

3. 1880 US Census, Missouri, Greene County, Series T9 Roll 687-688, National Archives. Locations of the Dewey children are from the 1880 US Census. James, 19, Henry R. Jones, Roll 687, Brookline Twp. p. 124. Nellie, 13, James Bray, Roll 688, Center Twp. p. 179. Willard, 10, A.F. Brown, Roll 687, Brookline Twp. p. 124B. Lilly (Lillie), 9, J.W. Frame, Roll 688, Ash Grove, p. 157A. Mary Ann [Duey], 7, Ransum [sic] D. Blades, Roll 687, Pond Twp. p. 147. Austin, 5, Jeremiah Kiblinger, Roll 688, Ash Grove, p. 159A.

4. *Reminiscent History of the Ozark Region*. Chicago: Goodspeed Brothers, 1894.

5. I.T. Blades, Statement of Service, Record and Pension Office, War Department, Washington, D.C.

6. Johnson, *Battles and Leaders of the Civil War*, Vol. 1, New York: Century, 1887, p. 334.

7. Turley, *Blades Lott, 1634-1991*, (Limited Print Book), Wichita, Kan.: Author, 2007, p. 32-33.

8. Find A Grave Memorial# 9195609. Gillie S. Blades.

Chapter 5. Mollie's Lost Estate

1. Pension Record, National Archives, pp. 31-39.

2. Pension Record, National Archives, pp. 5-10

3. Pension Record, National Archives.

4. 1900 US Census, Nebraska, Douglas, Omaha city Ward 3, Series, T623, p. 4B, National Archives; Find A Grave 69103110.

5. Dee Willauer Family Information, c. 1970.

6. Find A Grave 101092705.

7. Pension Record, National Archives; World War I Draft Registration Report, 12 Sep 1915, National Archives.

8. Find A Grave 138754957.

9. 1880 US Census, Missouri, Greene County, Pond Twp., Series T9 Roll 687, 147D, National Archives. Molly Ann Duey [*sic*].

Chapter 6. Family Circle

1. 1900 US Census, Missouri, Christian, Polk Twp., Series T623 Roll 848, p. 133. Kastendick [*sic*] Andrew.

2. Christian County Plat Map, 1912. Sections 16, 20, and 21 of Township 27N, Range 24W.

3. Christian County, Missouri, Personal Property Tax Index, 1879-1900, Missouri State Archives.

4. 1880 US Census, Missouri, Christian, Polk, Series T9 Roll 681, p. 7; Kastendirk [*sic*], Andrew.

5. Find A Grave Memorial# 9195607. Ranson Dudley Blades.

6. Information about the Ranson Dudley Blades family comes from the U. S. Census and Find-A-Grave cemetery records.

7. 1880 US Census, Missouri, Christian, Polk, Series T9 Roll 681, p. 7; Kastendirk [*sic*], Andrew.

8. 1900 US Census, Missouri, Christian, Polk Twp., Series T623 Roll 848, p. 3B, National Archives. Andrew Kastenctiecke [*sic*].

9. Christian County Plat Map, 1912. Sections 16, 20, and 21 of Township 27N, Range 24W.

Chapter 7. Country Girl

1. Pauline Kastendieck letter to folks in Wisconsin. Undated about 1938 from Forbesville, Butte County, Calif. Pauline compared her school in Butte County to "the old Hale district where we went in Missouri."

2. Pauline Kastendieck's grade card; Miss Neyer teacher in charge, signed by Andrew Kastendieck, 1907, Willauer Collection.

3. Inscription on the back of a postcard addressed to Mrs. Andrew Kastendieck; Billings, Mo. R.F.D. No. 1, Willauer Collection.

4. Jeidy, Pauline, Essay #4, University of Iowa, c. 1930.

5. Pauline Jeidy, "I have a grudge against science," Unpublished paper. Prepared for class at the State University of Iowa. n.d.

6. Jeidy, Pauline, Essay #6, University of Iowa, c. 1930.

7. A good incubator was among the items listed for sale by Verda Kastendieck in 1918.

8. Statement of Billings Creamery, May 1, 1907 to May 1, 1908, David Gay Collection. John Hutter reported in the *Billings Times* in 1914 that the Billings Creamery cooperative increased proceeds due to patrons from $5,000 in 1899 to $30,000 in 1914.

9. 1910 US Census, Missouri, Christian, Polk, Series T624 Roll 776, p. 3A. George D. Kastendieck.

Chapter 8. Andrew's Sword

1. Harper, *White Man's Heaven: The Lynching and Expulsion of Blacks in the Southern Ozarks, 1894–1909,* Fayetteville, Ar.: University of Arkansas Press, 2010.

2. Andrew Kastendieck Select Knights of America sword. Private Collection.

3. David Rauch, *125 Years of Ministry*, manuscript, n. d.

4. *San Francisco Call*, Vol. 85, No. 158, 7 May 1899; George Washington Masonic National Memorial Association, Alexandria, Va. The Select Knights of America originated as part of the Ancient Order of United Workman in 1868 following the Civil War, a time of great economic stress and uncertainty for many families. The organization died out by the decade of the 1940s.

5. *Billings Times,* 4 Nov 1909; 10 Aug 1911.

Chapter 9. Remember Well and Bear in Mind

1. Photograph of Pauline Kastendieck's Sunday School Class, inscribed on reverse, abt. 1910, Willauer Collection.

2. John Hutter. "History of Billings, Mo.," *The Billings Times,* Vol. 33, No. 39, Billings, Missouri; 15 Oct 1914.

3. In a letter from Pauline Jeidy to Deanne (Dee) Lombard Willauer, she described Andrew Kastendieck's love of music; dated 27 Sep 1975. 2 pp. on 1, handwritten on blue paper front and back, Willauer Collection.

4. 1910 US Census, Missouri, Christian, Polk Twp., Series T624 Roll 776, p. 139. Kandendick [*sic*] Andrew.

5.. 1910 US Census, Missouri, Christian, Polk, Series T624 Roll 776, p. 5B, National Archives. John H. Kastendieck.

6. Jeidy, "I have a grudge against science." Unpublished paper. Prepared for class at the State University of Iowa, n.d.

7. Andrew Kastendieck Death Certificate 16520 filed 3 May 1912, Bureau of Vital Statistics, Missouri State Board of Health.

8. Funeral Announcement of Andrew Kastendieck, found in the John Herman and Bridget Kastendieck Family Bible, Private Collection.

Chapter 10. Carrying On

1. Death Certificate of Andrew Kastendieck 16520, Missouri Secretary of State Archives.

2. Rose Hill Cemetery visit, 2010.

3. Statement of Billings Creamery; May 1, 1907 to May 1, 1908, David Gay Collection.

4. Hutter, John, "History of Billings, Mo." *The Billings [Missouri] Times*, 15 Oct 1914.

5. Hutter, John, "History of Billings, Mo." *The Billings [Missouri] Times*, 15 Oct 1914.

6. Verda and Pauline Kastendieck photograph taken about 1915 in Missouri, Robert E. Hinchey Studio, Aurora, Missouri, Willauer Collection.

7. *Billings Times*, 2 Sep 1915; 24 Feb 1916 p 3; 20 Apr 1916.

8. Photograph of Billings High School Graduating Class of 1914, Willauer Collection.

9. *Billings Times*, 4 Jun 1914, p. 5.

10. 1920 US Census, Missouri, Christian County.

11. Obituary of Celestine Leitensdorfer 27 Dec 1896-22 Jul 1964; *Christian County Republican*, 30 Jul 1964.

12. Springfield Normal School became Southwest Missouri State Teacher's College in 1919. After several name changes, it is today Missouri State University.

13. *Billings Times*, 17 Nov 1915, p. 8.

14. *Billings Times*, 29 Jun 1916, p 3; 20 Jul 1916 p 3.

15. Background on the teaching career of Pauline Kastendieck comes from a Ventura County School memorandum prepared February 4, 1963, in response to a request January 15, 1963, for information from the Association of California Educators that was considering her for honorary membership in the organization. The memorandum came from the Ventura

superintendent's office, probably written by Pauline who was serving then as assistant superintendent in the final year before her retirement.

Chapter 11. Out of Billings

1. Pauline Jeidy to Dee Willauer, Sept. 1975.

2. *Billings Times,* 18 May 1916.

3. *Billings Times*, 13 Sep 1917 p. 3; 27 Sep 1917.

4. Obituary of Mary A. Kastendieck, *The Fennimore Times*, 20 May 1942.

5. Dee Willauer notes, n.d.

6. *Billings Times,* 6 Sep 1917, p. 3.

7. Mary A. Kastendieck Obituary, *The Fennimore Times*, 20 May 1942.

8. *Billings Times,* 7 Mar 1918.

9. Public Sale Flyer, 20 Apr 1918, Willauer Collection; *Billings Times*, 18 Apr 1918, p. 4.

10. *Billings Times*, 25 Apr 1918, p. 3.

11. As of the year 2020, Andrew Kastendieck's Select Knights of America sword was in the possession of Rene (Brandemuehl) Wehler, great granddaughter of Andrew.

Chapter 12. Prairie Land

1. Cauffman, et al, *Fennimore—Then and Now*, 4.

2. Cauffman, et al, *Fennimore—Then and Now*, 4, 142.

3. 1830 US Census, Iowa, Michigan Territory, Series M19 Roll 69, p. 235, National Archives. John G. Fennimore, white adult couple each under 30 years; one daughter under age 5.

4. Cauffman, et al, *Fennimore—Then and Now*, 6.

5. Cauffman, et al, *Fennimore—Then and Now*, 8; Holford, *History of Grant County, Wisconsin*, 56, 125. The community of Fennimore suffered several deaths in the cholera epidemic of 1850.

6. Cauffman, et al, *Fennimore—Then and Now*, 12.

7. Cauffman, et al, *Fennimore—Then and Now*, 11, 13.

8. *A History of the Origin of the Place Names*, 70. This source attributs the Fennimore name to M. Fennimore and not John Fennimore. Nevertheless, historians link the name of John Fennimore to both the city and township of Fennimore.

9. Cauffman, et al, *Fennimore—Then and Now*, 12, 13.

Chapter 13. The Millinery Shop

1. Cauffman, et al, *Fennimore—Then and Now,* 13.

2. Cauffman, et al, *Fennimore—Then and Now,* 14, 142-144.

3. Cauffman, et al., *Fennimore—Then and Now,* 204-211, 280.

4. Mary A. Kastendieck Obituary. *The Fennimore Times,* 20 May 1942.

5. Missouri State Archives, Soldiers' Records: War of 1812-World War I, Office of the Missouri Secretary of State.

6. United States World War I Draft Registration Cards, 1917-1918.

7. Letter from Pauline to Deanne (Dee) Lombard Willauer describing Andrew Kastendieck's love of music; dated 27 Sep 1975. 2 pp. on 1, handwritten on blue paper front and back, Willauer Collection.

8. Cauffman, et al., *Fennimore—Then and Now,* 49.

9. Cauffman, et al., *Fennimore—Then and Now,* 19.

1. Cauffman, et al., *Fennimore—Then and Now,* 123-124.

2. Cauffman, et al., *Fennimore—Then and Now,* 142-144.

3. Cauffman, et al., *Fennimore—Then and Now,* 131-135.

4. Cauffman, et al., *Fennimore—Then and Now,* 67-68, 276.

5. Cauffman, et al., *Fennimore—Then and Now,* 278.

6. Cauffman, et al., *Fennimore—Then and Now,* 280.

7. Cauffman, et al., *Fennimore—Then and Now,* 74, 273.

8. Cauffman, et al., *Fennimore—Then and Now,* 60, 276.

9. Cauffman, et al., *Fennimore—Then and Now,* 181.

10. Cauffman, et al., *Fennimore—Then and Now,* 218-219.

11. Cauffman, et al,, *Fennimore—Then and Now,* 122, 155-157.

Chapter 14. Fennimore

12. 1920 US Census, Wisconsin, Grant 2-Wd., Fennimore, Series T625 Roll 1987, p. 237. Molly Kastendieck. Fennimore changed its street names in 1949 when the city began postal delivery. The old-named east-west streets became numbered streets, including Spring Street.

13. Pauline Kastendieck's Teaching Certificate. Second-grade teaching certificate, Iowa County, Wis., given at Dodgeville, Wis., 1 Sep 1922, Willauer Collection.

Chapter 15. Cokerville

1. Photograph. Inscribed on reverse "Pauline's school at Cokerville, Livingston, Wis." Willauer Collection.

2. Knebel and Fine, *In the Shadows of the Mines,* 1980.

3. Crawford, *Memoirs of Iowa County, Wisconsin* Vol. 1, 1913.

4. Gregory, *Southwestern Wisconsin,* 1932; Reynolds, *An Airplane Was My Burro,* 2006; Archives of Southwest Wisconsin Room, University of Wisconsin-Plattville.

5. Correspondence from Cheryl D. Lemanski, Archives Assistant, Southwest Wisconsin Room, University of Wisconsin-Plattville, 13 Jan 2011.

6. Agnew, and Heyl, "Zinc deposits of the Mifflin-Cokerville Area of the Wisconsin Lead-Zinc District," Series 44-24, Washington, D.C.: U.S. Geological Survey, 1944.

7. Reynolds, *An Airplane Was My Burro,* 2006.

8. Perkins, "This is what I know of New Diggings and Cokerville, Wisconsin, 1911-1926." Substantial information about Cokerville comes from a 1963 account written by Donna Perkins, a former resident of Cokerville and student at Pauline Jeidy's school.

9. Jeidy, Pauline, Essay #4, University of Iowa, c. 1930.

10. Dolphin, *James, George, Adam: A Dolphin Family Descendant Register*, 1994, 158.

11. Perkins, "This is what I know of New Diggings and Cokerville, Wisconsin, 1911-1926."

12. Perkins, "This is what I know of New Diggings and Cokerville, Wisconsin, 1911-1926."

13. Correspondence from Cheryl D. Lemanski, Archives Assistant, Southwest Wisconsin Room, University of Wisconsin-Plattville, 13 Jan 2011.

Chapter 16. Oscar and Casey

1. Pauline Kastendieck Grant County Teaching Certificate. second-grade teaching certificate, Grant County, Wis., given at Lancaster, Wisconsin, 22 Aug 1923, Willauer Collection.

2. United States World War I Draft Registration Cards, 1917-1918.

3. Find A Grave 139942631 & 139942642.

4. 1910 US Census, Wisconsin, Grant, Lancaster Twp., Series T623 Roll 1790, ED 38, National Archives.

5. 1920 US Census, Wisconsin, Grant, Mount Ida, Series T625 Roll 1988, ED 115, National Archives.

6. Lizzie Kastendieck to Mollie, at Fennimore, Wis., July 1, 1923. Elizabeth (Lizzie) Kastendieck was the wife of George Dietrich Kastendieck, Mollie's brother-in-law.

7. The Jeidy name is spelled variously as Jeidy, Jeide, Judy, Jeiday. The correct pronunciation is the Dutch, Yi-dee. Her name appeared in a book in

Japanese characters spelled phonetically as Yaidi and Yai Day. Mispronunciation became an expected part of Pauline's experience. The popular pronouncing of Jeidy was Judy.

8. Photograph of Jeidy family; about 1940, Willauer Collection.

9. 1920 US Census, Wisconsin, Grant, Little Grant, Series T625 Roll 1988, p. 74. Judy [*sic*], Charles, 40. See also 1910 US Census Wisconsin, Grant, Little Grant, Series T624 Roll 1711, p. 108. Judy [*sic*], Charles, 29.

10. Melvin Jeidy Obituary. *The Fennimore Times*, 20 May 1925.

11. Verda Kastendieck and Oscar Brandemuehl Wedding Announcement, 1923, Willauer Collection.

12. Death Certificate, Melvin Lavern Jeidy, Grant County, Wisconsin; Vol. 19, p. 164.

13. *Billings Times,* 21 May 1925 p 5.

14. Death Certificate, Melvin Lavern Jeidy, Grant County, Wisconsin; Vol. 19, p. 164.

15. Casey Jeidy Tombstone. Little Grant Union Cemetery, Grant County, Wisconsin.

16. Obituary of Melvin Lavern "Casey" Jeidy. *The Fennimore Times*, May 20, 1925, Fennimore Library.

Chapter 17. Finding Hope

1. 1930 US Census, Wisconsin, Grant, Mount Hope, Series T626 Roll 2574, National Archives. Oscar Brandenwhl [*sic*], Mount Hope.

2. Unidentified correspondence to Mollie Kastendieck, undated c. 1925.

3. Civil War Pension Record, National Archives, p. 43.

4. Cauffman, et al, *Fennimore—Then and Now,* 280.

5. Group Christmas portrait of the Jeidy family, Willauer Collection.

6. 1930 US Census, Wisconsin, Crawford, Prairie du Chien, Series T626 Roll 2566, ED 14, p. 5A, National Archives. The census taker enumerated the 1930 census in Prairie du Chien on April 5-7, 1930. Pauline was age 32, working as a supervising teacher in the public schools. The entry for "age at time of marriage" appeared erased.

7. Pauline Jeidy, Gays Mills Post Office, Crawford County Official School Directory, 1926, 105 districts 139 teachers.

8. *La Crosse Tribune,* 12 Oct 1927, p 6; 14 Jan 1928, p. 2.

9. *La Crosse Tribune,* 16 Oct 1927 p. 4.

10. Kathleen Kalina, Prairie du Chien Library, to K. Burchett, 21 Jan 2020. South Church Street became South Beaumont Road in the early 1900s.

11. Pauline Jeidy, Essay #5, University of Iowa, c. 1930. Quotations about Crawford County are from a paper Pauline wrote while a student at the University of Iowa. The experiences described come from the five years she worked as a supervising teacher for the Crawford County schools.

12. *La Crosse Tribune*, 21 May 1928, p. 10.

13. *La Crosse Tribune*, 17 May 1931, p. 14.

14. 1940 US Census, Wisconsin, Grant, Mount Hope Village, Series T627 Roll 4481, ED 32, National Archives. Oscar Brandemuehl, Mount Hope.

15. 1930 US Census, Wisconsin, Grant, Mount Hope, T626 Roll 2574, ED 32, National Archives.

16. Mount Ida Township, from Grant County, Wisconsin, published by Farm Plat Book Publishing, 1956.

Chapter 18. Reflections on Nature

1. Jeidy, Pauline, Essay #5, University of Iowa, c. 1930.

2. Jeidy, Pauline, Essay #5, University of Iowa, c. 1930.

Chapter 19. The Great Depression

1. Pauline Kastendieck Jeidy Obituary. *The Fennimore [WI] Times*, 21 Aug 1985. A version of her obituary that appeared in the *Ventura Star Free Press* cited this quote in connection with her first job in Springfield, Mo. The quote is a variant of one that originally appeared in a 1963 memorandum detailing her work experience. The quote was in connection with her supervisory duties in Crawford County, Wisconsin.

2. Jeidy, Pauline, Essay #5, University of Iowa, c. 1930. This lengthy quote was part of a paper Pauline wrote as an undergraduate student at State University of Iowa.

3. Reynolds, Robert R., *An Airplane Was My Burro: The Memoirs of a Venturesome Geologist,* iUniverse, 2006, n.p; Agnew, Allen F., and Heyl, Allen J., Jr. "Zinc deposits of the Mifflin-Cokerville area of the Wisconsin lead-zinc district," Series 44-24, Washington, D.C.: US Geological Survey, 1944. Despite the downturn in mining, production continued on a modest scale during World War II. Ore still shipped out of the area at the end of 1943, and geologists indicated as late as 1952 that further prospecting for zinc ore was justified at the old Cokerville mines. The Cokerville-Livingston School joined several other one-room schools in 1959 to form the consolidated Iowa-Grant School District.

4. Letter from Lot to Mrs. Mollie Kastendieck Mt. Hope, Wis. from Billings Dec 19, 1932.

5. Letter from Lot to Mrs. Mollie Kastendieck Mt. Hope, Wis. from Billings Dec 19, 1932.

6. State University of Iowa originated in 1847 coincidental with the admission of Iowa to the Union. Created as the Flagship University of Iowa, the name University of Iowa began usage by authority of the Board of Regents in October 1964.

Chapter 20. Back to School

1. Jeidy, Pauline, Essay #1, University of Iowa, c. 1930.
2. Jeidy, Pauline, Essay #1, University of Iowa, c. 1930.
3. Jeidy, Pauline, Essay #1, University of Iowa, c. 1930.
4. Jeidy, Pauline, Essay #2, University of Iowa, c. 1930.
5. Jeidy, Pauline, Essay #1, University of Iowa, c. 1930.
6. Jeidy, Pauline, Essay #1, University of Iowa, c. 1930.
7. Jeidy, Pauline, Essay #3, University of Iowa, c. 1930.

Chapter 21. Cats

1. Jeidy, Pauline, Essay #6, University of Iowa, c. 1930. The stories of Pauline's cats come from a paper she wrote while studying for her undergraduate degree at the State University of Iowa. Quotations appear in context as written in the paper.
2. Jeidy, Pauline, Essay #6, University of Iowa, c. 1930.
3. Jeidy, Pauline, Essay #6, University of Iowa, c. 1930.
4. Jeidy, Pauline, Essay #6, University of Iowa, c. 1930.
5. Jeidy, Pauline, Essay #6, University of Iowa, c. 1930.

Chapter 22. Word Theory

1. Bachelor of Science Degree, State University of Iowa, 31 Jan 1933, Pauline K. Jeidy B.S. Degree, The State University of Iowa, The College of Liberal Arts, Bachelor of Science in School Supervision Degree, Iowa City, Iowa; 31 Jan 1933, Willauer Collection.
2. *Capital Times (Madison, Wisconsin),* 17 Jun 1933 p. 5.
3. *Wisconsin State Journal* (Madison), 28 Jan 1935.
4. Jeidy, *A Critical Study of the Ability of Sixth Grade Children*, 14.
5. Jeidy, *A Critical Study of the Ability of Sixth Grade Children*, 62.
6. Master of Arts Degree, State University of Iowa, 20 Aug 1036, Pauline

Jeidy MA Degree, State University of Iowa Master of Arts Degree, Iowa City, Iowa, Willauer Collection.

7. The University of Iowa. Dissertations and Theses. Available Index online: InfoHawk. See also Sarah Scott, comp. *Theses and Dissertations Presented in the Graduate College of the State University of Iowa, 1900-1950,* Iowa City: University of Iowa, 1952. Jeidy, Pauline, "A Study of the Ability of Sixth-Grade Children to Comprehend Biographically Descriptive Words and Phrases in Historical Content." Master's, 1936. Iowa. 305 pp. manuscript. Cataloged in *Statistics of Land-Grant Colleges and Universities,* Issues 4-11, United States, Office of Education, Govt. Print. Off., 1937; see also: Jeidy, Pauline K. [Kastendieck], *A Critical Study of the Ability of Sixth Grade Children to Comprehend Biographically Descriptive Terms In Historical Content,* 1936, Thesis-Manuscript . Special Collections University Archives T1936.J47.

Chapter 23. West Coast Journey

1. 1940 US Census, Oregon, Polk, Election Precinct 28, Series T627 Roll 3378, p. 61A, National Archives. Pauline K. Jeidy. County of residence in 1935 was Richland County.

2. Ammon, Ralph E., "Wisconsin Fairs," *Fairman's Handbook,* Wisconsin Department of Agriculture and Markets *Bulletin* No. 173, (May 1936), pp. 12-13. Pauline Jeidy, Richland Center.

3. Remembered as Monmouth College; its official name was Monmouth University. From the time of its beginning in 1856, the school underwent numerous name changes. The Oregon legislature again changed the name to Oregon College of Education in 1939 while Pauline was an instructor there. Today it is Western Oregon University.

4. United States, Bureau of Labor Statistics, (1927-1990), *Handbook of Labor Statistics,* Washington: U.S. G.P.O., pp. 311-312.

5. *Statesman Journal (Salem, Oregon),* 13 Sep 1936, p. 2.

6. *Statesman Journal (Salem, Oregon),* 10 Jan 1937, p. 3; 17 Sep 1937, p. 7.

7. *Capital Journal (Salem, Oregon),* 19 Sep 1936, p. 2.

8. *Capital Journal (Salem, Oregon),* 9 Nov 1937.

9. *Statesman Journal (Salem, Oregon),* 6 Feb 1938; 30 Mar 1938, p. 10; 11 May 1938, p. 3; 18 Sep 1938, p. 14; 11 Oct 1938; 29 Nov 1938, p. 3.

10. *Polk County Itemizer-Observer;_Statesman Journal (Salem, Oregon),* 9 Nov 1937.

11. *Capital Journal (Salem, Oregon),* 28 Dec 1938; 19 Dec 1939, p. 2.

12. *Capital Journal (Salem, Oregon),* 21 Nov 1939, p. 2; Pauline Kastendieck Jeidy Obituary. *The Fennimore [WI] Times*, 21 Aug 1985. Her obituary noted that she worked in Oregon.

13. *Capital Journal (Salem, Oregon)*, 15 Aug 1940.

14. University of Iowa *Hawkeye* yearbook, 1933 Kappa Phi, active member 1933, Junior Class, p. 450

Chapter 24. Being Pauline

1. *Capital Journal (Salem, Oregon)*, 26 Feb 1940, p. 12.

2. *Capital Journal (Salem, Oregon),* 16 Mar 1940, p. 12.

3. *Capital Journal (Salem, Oregon)*, 28 Mar 1940; 6 May 1940, p. 3.

4. *Statesman Journal (Salem, Oregon),* 2 Jun 1940, p. 3.

5. *Capital Journal (Salem, Oregon)*, 2 Nov 1940, p. 2.1940.

6. *Capital Journal (Salem, Oregon),* 9 Oct 1940.

7. *Statesman Journal (Salem, Oregon)*, 24 Dec 1940.

8. *Statesman Journal (Salem, Oregon).* 17 May 1939; *Capital Journal (Salem, Oregon),* 11 Mar 1939, p. 11.

9. *Capital Journal (Salem, Oregon)*, 7 Dec 1939, p. 2.

10. Delta Kappa Gamma Society Individual Membership Certificate, May 23, 1941.

11. *Capital Journal (Salem, Oregon)*, 14 Jun 1941, p. 2; *Statesman Journal (Salem, Oregon)*, 14 Jun 1941, p. 9.

12. Photograph of Pauline Jeidy in the 1940s inscribed on reverse "Aunt Pauline 1940s," Willauer Collection.

13. Letter from Pauline in Los Angeles to A. Kastendieck, Fennimore, Wis., postmarked Los Angeles, Aug 4, 1941.

14. *Statesman Journal (Salem, Oregon),* 14 Jun 1941, p. 9.

15. *Capital Journal (Salem, Oregon)*, 29 May 1941.

16. *Statesman Journal (Salem, Oregon)*, 15 Aug 1941, p. 15. Information about Pauline's education career comes also from a letter dated 24 Apr 1063 to Mrs. Grace Piper, Administrative Assistant, University of California-Santa Barbara, in which Pauline lists her education and work experience. She notes at the beginning, "Information about my Educational career will not make exciting copy, but here it is."

17. *Capital Journal (Salem, Oregon)*, 31 May 1941, p. 9.

18. *Capital Journal (Salem, Oregon)*, 29 May 1941.

19. Letter from Pauline in Los Angeles to A. Kastendieck, Fennimore, Wis., postmarked Los Angeles, Aug 4, 1941.

20. *Statesman Journal (Salem, Oregon)*, 15 Aug 1941, p. 15.

Chapter 25. Mountain Letter

1. *Ventura County Star-Free Press*, 18 Jan 1964, p. 19.

2. Jeidy, Pauline K. General Supervisor, Public Schools, Oroville, Calif. *Yearbook*, Vol. 20, American Association of School Administrators, 1942.

3. *Sacramento Bee (Sacramento, California)*, 9 Jan 1944, p. 12.

4. *Feather River Bulletin (Quincy, California)*, 18 Sep 1941, p. 2.

5. *Appeal-Democrat (Marysville, California)*, 25 Sep 1941, p. 8.

6. *Capital Journal (Salem, Oregon),* 2 Jan 1942, p. 2; *Statesman Journal (Salem, Oregon)*, 4 Jan 1942, p. 14.

7. *Sacramento Bee (Sacramento, California),* 7 Dec 1942, p. 8.

8. *Appeal-Democrat (Marysville, California)*, 10 Feb 1843, p. 2.

9. *Appeal-Democrat (Marysville, California)*, 7 May 1943, p. 4.

10. Kroeber, Theodora, and Kroeber, Karl, *Ishi in Two Worlds: a Biography of the Last Wild Indian in North America,* Berkeley: University of California Press, 2002.

11. Undated letter from Pauline to folks in Wisconsin describing her trip to Forbestown, Lake Madrone, and Bald Rock; 5 pp. front & back, transcribed by Dee Willauer, Willauer Collection. Pauline probably wrote her letter about 1942. Forbestown was in Butte County, Calif.

1. "Thumbnail History of Public Education in California," California Department of Education, August 1961.

2. Undated letter from Pauline to folks in Wisconsin describing her trip to Forbestown, Lake Madrone, and Bald Rock; 5 pp. front & back, transcribed by Dee Willauer, Willauer Collection.

Chapter 26. Past Is Prologue

3. Weiler, *Democracy and Schooling in California,* 100.

4. Find A Grave 15915275.

5. Obituary of Mrs. Mary Kastendieck, *Fennimore Times*, 27 May 1942.

6. Obituary of Mary A. Kastendieck. *The Fennimore Times*, 20 May 1942.

7. Obituary of Mollie Kastendieck. *Fennimore Times*, Fennimore, Wisconsin; 27 May 1942.

Chapter 27. Remembering Mollie

1. Funeral Announcement of Mrs. M. Kastendieck. *The Fennimore (Wisconsin) Times*, 20 May 1942.

2. Cauffman, et al, *Fennimore—Then and Now,* 183-184.

3. Obituary of Mrs. Mary Kastendieck. *Fennimore (Wisconsin) Times*, 27 May 1942.

4. Letter from Mildred Fulbright to Verda, 16 Jul 1942.

5. Letter from Katherine Kastendieck Andrews to Verda, 30 May 1942, from Milton, Iowa.

6. Letter from George Kastendieck to Verda typewritten on Green County Stationery, 7 Jun 1942.

7. Letter from Bertie to Verda, 17 May 1942.

8. Letter from Harold Allison to Verda, 17 May 1942, from Black River Falls Wisconsin, Methodist Episcopal Church pastor.

9. Letter from Katherine Kastendieck to Verda, 30 May 1942 to Verda, from Milton, Iowa.

10. Letter from Lulu Adams to Pauline and Verda, 17 May 1942, from Mt. Hope, Wis.

11. Letter from Pearl to Verda, Chicago, Ill. 16 May 1942.

12. Letter from Pauline to Deanne (Dee) Lombard Willauer describing Andrew Kastendieck's love of music; dated 27 Sep 1975. 2 pp. on 1, handwritten on blue paper front and back, Willauer Collection.

Chapter 28. Kindred Spirits

1. *Appeal-Democrat (Marysville, California)*, 31 Aug 1943, p. 6.

2. Weiler, *Democracy and Schooling in California,* xi.

3. Weiler, *Democracy and Schooling in California,* 204.

4. Weiler, *Democracy and Schooling in California*, xii.

5. Weiler, *Democracy and Schooling in California*, xi, xv.

6. Jeidy, "Reactions of Children of Different Age Levels in the War," 12-21. Summary of a study done at the University of California at Los Angeles at the suggestion of Helen Heffernan, Chief of the Division of Elementary Education, California State Department of Education, and under the direction of Dr. Lloyd N. Morrisett, Professor of Education.

7. Weiler, *Democracy and Schooling in California,* 97.

8. *Sacramento Bee (Sacramento, California)*, 9 Jan 1944, p. 12; *Appeal-Democrat (Marysville, California)*, 19 Apr 1944, p. 2.

9. *Appeal-Democrat (Marysville, California)*, 15 May 1944, p. 6.

10. *Sacramento Bee (Sacramento, California)*, 9 Jan 1944, p. 10.

11. *Appeal-Democrat (Marysville, California)*, 31 Aug 1943, p. 6.

12. *Sacramento Bee (Sacramento, California)*, 9 Jan 1944, p. 12.

13. *Sacramento Bee (Sacramento, California)*, 24 Jun 1944, p. 14.

14. *Ventura County Star-Free Press*, 28 Jun 1944, p. 5.

Chapter 29. Mission San Buenaventura

1. Presentation, Mrs. Pauline Jeidy, General Supervisor, Butte County, *CTA Journal*, Vol. 40, California Teachers Association, 1944. The title of her presentation was "The Reading Program in the Elementary School."

2. *Ventura County Star-Free Pres*, 4 Nov 1944, p. 4.

3. *Ventura County Star-Free Press*, 13 Oct 1944, p. 6.

4. Gidney, et al., *History of Santa Barbara, San Luis Obispo and Ventura Counties, California*, 1:279-280.

5. Fernandez, "Storyteller Keeps Chumash Ways Alive in Word, Deed," *Los Angeles Times*, 1997.

6. More than 40 sites in Ventura County are on the National Register of Historic Places.

7. Jeidy, *Ventura County History Stories*, 157.

8. Jeidy, *Ventura County History Stories*, 147.

9. Gidney, et al., *History of Santa Barbara, San Luis Obispo and Ventura Counties, California*, 1:306-307.

Chapter 30. A Man's World

1. Storke, *A Memorial and Biographical History of the Counties of Santa Barbara, San Luis Obispo and Ventura, California*, 183-260.

2. Henry, *National Society for the Study of Education, The Forty-Fifth Yearbook*, 126.

3. U.S. Department of Commerce, Bureau of the Census, Historical Statistics of the United States, Colonial Times to 1970; and Current Population Reports, Series P-23, Ancestry and Language in the United States: November 1979.

4. Directory of Supervisors & Directors of Instruction in California Elementary Schools; Ventura County Office of County Superintendent of Schools. California State Department of Education, Sacramento, California. February, 1947; Directory of Public Schools. Ventura County (Calif.), 1947, Jeidy, Mrs. Pauline, Education Building, Ventura. *Year book*, Vol. 19; California Elementary School Administrators Association, 1947; Listed. *Education Index*, Vol. 7, H.W. Wilson, 1947; Mrs. Pauline Jeidy, Ventura County Schools, Ventura. California School Sirectory; California Society for the Study of Secondary Education; California Association of Secondary

School Administrators; Association of California School Administrators, 1947.

5. *Ventura County Star-Free Press*, 27 Oct 1944, p. 7.

6. Nelson, *National Society for the Study of Education Forty-Fifth Yearbook*, p. xxvi. Jeidy, Pauline, Director, Elementary Education, Ventura, Calif.

7. Winkler and Jolly, "National Society for the Study of Education." 602.

8. Henry, *National Society for the Study of Education, The Forty-Fifth Yearbook*, 7, 19, 154, 157, 225.

Chapter 31. Fable in Ethics

1. Jeidy, Pauline. "Fable in Ethics," *California Journal of Elementary Education* 14 (August 1945): 40-48.

Chapter 32. Quintessential Storyteller

1. Ventura County Schools memorandum, 4 Feb 1963.

2. *Ventura County Star-Free Press*, 20 Jan 1945, p. 5.

3. *Ventura County Star-Free Press*, 24 Jan 1946, p. 6.

4. *Ventura County Star-Free Press*, 12 Mar 1945, p. 5; 26 Apr 1945; 30 Apr 1945.

5. *Ventura County Star-Free Press*, 12 Apr 1945, p. 5.

6. *Ventura County Star-Free Press*, 16 Apr 1945, p. 4.

7. *Ventura County Star-Free Press*, 18 Jan 1945 p. 6.

8. *Ventura County Star-Free Press*, 3 May 1945; 10 May 1945; 28 Jun 1945, p. 4; 27 Jul 1945, p. 49; Aug 1945, p. 8; 16 Aug 1945, p. 5.

9. *Ventura County Star-Free Press*, 11 Aug 1945, p. 3; 23 Aug 1945.

10. *Ventura County Star-Free Press*, 30 Aug 1945, p. 4.

11. *Ventura County Star-Free Press*, 3 Aug 1945, p. 4.

12. *Ventura County Star-Free Press*, 25 Apr 1945, p. 5; 19 Sep 1945, p. 4; 22 Oct 1945, p. 5.

13. *Ventura County Star-Free Press*, 3 Oct 1945, p. 4.

14. *Ventura County Star-Free Press*, 15 Dec 1945, p. 5.

Chapter 33. The Jeidy Method

1. Adams, *Educating America's Children*, 161.

2. Jeidy, *Ventura County Course of Study in Reading*, 66.

3. *Ventura County Star-Free Press*, 14 May 1946, p. 3.

4. *Ventura County Star-Free Press*, 5 Aug 1946, p. 2.

5. Weiler, *Democracy and Schooling in California*, 202.

6. *Ventura County Star-Free Press*, 3 Sep 1946, p. 6.

7. *Ventura County Star-Free Press*, 7 Jan 1946, p. 5; 13 May 1946, p. 4.

8. *Ventura County Star-Free Press*, 18 May 1946, p. 6; 16 May 1946, p. 6; 20 Jun 1946, p. 6; 27 Jan 1946, p. 8; 18 Jul 1946, p. 6.

9. *Ventura County Star-Free Press*, 11 Sep 1946, p. 3.

10. *Ventura County Star-Press*, 14 Nov 1946, p. 2.

11. *Ventura County Star-Free Press*, 14 Dec 1946, p. 5; 19 Mar 1946, p. 6.

12. *Ventura County Star-Free Press*, 16 Jan 1947, p. 6.

13. *Ventura County Star-Free Press*, 3 Jun 1947, p. 7.

14. *Ventura County Star-Free Press*, 20 Jun 1947, p. 6; 12 Sep 1947, p. 9.

15. *Ventura County Star-Free Press*, 6 Mar 1947, p. 6.

Chapter 34. The Year That Was

1. *University of California Register*, 1946-1947; *Courses and Announcements for 1947-1948*, Vol. 2, Berkeley: University of California Press, 1947.

2. Jeidy, Pauline, 1946, "Ventura County Course of Study in Reading," (Ventura: County Superintendent of Schools Office), In *Reading Behavior, Achievements and Attitudes of First Grade Boys* by Daniel Emil Johnson, School of Education, Stanford University, 1959; Pauline Jeidy, Director of Elementary Education, Ventura County, California, "Supervision of Reading"; also in the same publication, Pauline Jeidy, Director of Curriculum, Ventura County, "First Grade Mexican-American Children in Ventura County." *California Journal of Elementary Education*, Vols. 15-16, California, State Dept. of Education, California Elementary School Principals' Association, State Department of Education, 1946.

3. Jeidy, "First Grade Mexican American Children in Ventura County," 200-208.

4. Mendez v. Westminster School Dist., U.S. District Court for the Southern District of California-64 F. Supp. 544 (S.D. Cal. 1946), February 18, 1946.

5. Pauline's article appeared in many publications including *Selected Collections of the Chicano Studies Library*, Issues 1-7, University of California, Berkeley; *Chicano Studies Library*, 1974; reproduced in *Education and Income of Mexican-Americans in the Southwest* by Walter Fogel, Division of Research, Graduate School of Business Administration, University of California, 1965; reproduced in *The Mexican-American People: the Nation's Second Largest Minority* by Leo Grebler, Joan W. Moore, Ralph C. Guzmán,

and Jeffrey Lionel Berlant, New York Free Press, 1970; cited *Adapting the Curriculum of an Elementary School to Serve the Language Needs of Spanish Speaking Children* by Robert Ves Way, R and E Research Associates, 1974; cited *Integrated Education* Vols. 5-6, *Teachers for Integrated Schools*, 1967; cited *Chicano Education in the Era of Segregation* by Gilbert G. Gonzalez, Balch Institute Press, 1990; cited *American Educational History Journal*. Vol. 32, No. 1, Mark McKenzie, Editor, Information Age, 2005.

6. Jeidy, "First Grade Mexican American Children in Ventura County," 200-208.

7. Jeidy, "First Grade Mexican American Children in Ventura County," 200.

8. Jeidy, "First Grade Mexican American Children in Ventura County," 202.

9. The California state legislature officially ended all segregation in its schools in 1947. Nevertheless, a few communities continued to practice separate but equal education.

10. *Ventura County Star-Free Press*, 12 May 1947; 16 Sep 1947, p. 4.

11. *Ventura County Star-Free Press*, 17 Oct 1947, p. 7

12. *Ventura County Star-Free Press*, 18 Sep 1947, p. 5.

13. The Foreign Service offer came from the civil information and educational section, civil affairs division, Gen. MacArthur's headquarters.

Chapter 35. Assignment Japan

1. *Ventura County Star-Free Press*, 13 Dec 1947, p. 10.

2. *Ventura County Star-Free Press*, 31 Dec 1947, p. 5.

3. *Ventura County Star-Free Press*, 6 Dec 1947, p. 2.

4. *Ventura County Star-Free Press*, 16 Dec 1947, p. 6.

5. *Ventura County Star-Free Press*, 6 Dec 1947, p. 2.

6. *Ventura County Star-Free Press*, 6 Dec 1947, p. 2; 24 Jan 1949, p. 2.

7. *Ventura County Star-Free Press*, 6 Dec 1947, p. 2.

8. Takemae, *Inside GHQ*, 141-142 n93; 180-186. The list of prominent educators in the Occupation Education Department in addition to Dr. Helen Heffernan included Dr. Lulu Holmes, Dr. Verna A. Carley and Dr. Billie Hollingshead.

9. *Ventura County Star-Free Press,* 8 Jan 1948, p. 13.

10. Takemae, *Inside GHQ*, xxxix; Craven and Cate, *The Pacific*, 617. American estimates of casualties tended to be lower than Japanese estimates. The Japanese historian Takemae, for example, put the number of B-29

bombers at 2,500 and not the 334 listed by the US military. However, both agreed that no other air attack of the war in Japan or Europe was so destructive of life and property as the March 10, 1945, firebombing of Tokyo.

11. Takemae, *Inside GHQ*, xxxix.
12. *Ventura County Star-Free Press*, 8 Jan 1948, p. 13.
13. *Ventura County Star-Free Press*, 6 Dec 1947, p. 2.
14. *Ventura County Star-Free Press*, 6 Dec 1947, p. 2.
15. *Ventura County Star-Free Press*, 6 Dec 1947, p. 2.
16. *Ventura County Star-Free Press*, 24 Jan 1949, p. 2.
17. Jeidy, Pauline, Letter #7 to Soroptimist Club, February 1948.

Chapter 36. On Board the *Thistle*

1. Jeidy, Pauline, Letter #7 to Soroptimist Club, February 1948.
2. Jeidy, Pauline, Letter #7 to Soroptimist Club, February 1948.

Chapter 37. MacArthur and GHQ

1. Takemae, *Inside GHQ*, xxviii, 48.
2. Takemae, *Inside GHQ*, xxix.
3. Jeidy, Pauline, Letter #7 to Soroptimist Club, February 1948.
4. Jeidy, Pauline, Letter #7 to Soroptimist Club, February 1948.
5. Takemae, *Inside GHQ*, xxi
6. Takemae, *Inside GHQ*, 191.
7. Takemae, *Inside GHQ*, xxviii.
8. Takemae, *Inside GHQ*, 6.
9. President Truman dismissed Gen. MacArthur from the Army in 1951.
10. Takemae, *Inside GHQ*, 7
11. Jeidy, Pauline, Letter #7 to Soroptimist Club, February 1948.
12. Takemae, *Inside GHQ*, 74.
13. Takemae, *Inside GHQ*, 187 n75; Baltz, *The Role of American Educators*, 57-9, 60-1, 63.
14. Takemae, *Inside GHQ*, 369.
15. Takemae, *Inside GHQ*, 422.

Chapter 38. Cherry Blossoms, Tea, and PTA

1. *Ventura County Star-Free Press*, 20 May 1948, p. 7.
2. Jeidy, Pauline, Letter #9, March 1948,
3. Jeidy, Pauline, Letter #9, March 1948,
4. Jeidy, Pauline, Letter #10, April 1948.

5. Jeidy, Pauline, Letter #10, April 1948.
6. Jeidy, Pauline, Letter #10, April 1948.

Chapter 39. Art and the Occupation

1. Takemae, *Inside GHQ*, 187.
2. Takemae, *Inside GHQ*, xx, xxi.
3. Jeidy, *Theory and Practice of Democracy Education*, 29-35
4. Jeidy, *Theory and Practice of Democracy Education*, 14-23.
5. *Ventura County Star-Free Press*, 20 May 1948, p. 7
6. *Ventura County Star-Free Press*, 20 May 1948, pp. 2, 7.
7. Jeidy, Pauline, Letter #10, April 1948.
8. *The Town Musicians of Bremen* was a popular fairy tale recorded by the Brothers Grimm. It tells the story of four aging domestic animals, who after a lifetime of hard work are neglected and mistreated by their former masters. Eventually, they decide to run away and become town musicians in the city of Bremen.
9. Jeidy, Pauline, Letter #10, April 1948.
10. Jeidy, Pauline, Letter #10, April 1948.
11. Jeidy, Pauline: Conference Reports, Education Division. GHQ/SCAP, Civil Information and Education Section, Education Division; Administrative Branch. Correspondence, Reports and Publications, 1945-51. Box number: 5359; Folder number 1; also available as Record Group 331, National Archives, Washington, D.C.
12. Jeidy, Pauline, Tokyo, Letter #12 to Ruth, November 1948.
13. Jeidy, Pauline, Tokyo, Letter #12 to Ruth, November 1948.

Chapter 40. Boy's Day

1. Jeidy, Pauline, Letter #11, May 1948.
2. Jeidy, Pauline, Letter #11, May 1948.
3. Jeidy, Pauline, Letter #11, May 1948.
4. Shortages of gasoline during World War II caused many civilians to convert vehicles in Japan and Europe to operate on gases generated from coal or wood. Condensed gases in the form of liquid hydrocarbons fed the carburetor with sufficient volatility to operate the gasoline engine.
5. Jeidy, Pauline, Letter #11, May 1948.
6. Jeidy, Pauline, Letter #11, May 1948.
7. Jeidy, Pauline, Tokyo, Japan, Letter #13 to Ruth 14 Dec 1948.
8. Jeidy, Pauline, Tokyo, Letter #13 to Ruth.

Chapter 41. The Mombusho

1. Takemae, *Inside GHQ*, xx.
2. Takemae, *Inside GHQ*, xl.
3. Jeidy, Pauline, Letter #8, June 1948.
4. Jeidy, Pauline, Letter #8, June 1948.
5. A torii is a traditional Japanese gate that symbolically marks the transition from the banal to the sacred.
6. Jeidy, Pauline, Letter #8, June 1948.
7. Onoe Kikugorō was a Japanese Kabuki actor.
8. Jeidy, Pauline, Letter #8, June 1948.

Chapter 42. Christmas

1. Takemae, *Inside GHQ*, xxi.
2. Takemae, *Inside GHQ*, xxxii.
3. Takemae, *Inside GHQ*, xl, 185-186.
4. Takemae, *Inside GHQ*, 367.
5. Jeidy, Pauline, Tokyo, Japan, Letter #13 to Ruth, 14 Dec 1948.
6. Jeidy, Pauline, Tokyo, Letter #13 to Ruth, 14 Dec 1948.
7. Jeidy, Pauline, Tokyo, Letter #14 to Verd, December 1948.
8. Jeidy, Pauline, Tokyo, Letter #14 to Verd, December 1948.
9. Jeidy, Pauline, Tokyo, Letter #14 to Verd December 1948.

Chapter 43. Nagasaki

1. Takemae, *Inside GHQ*, 44.
2. Takemae, *Inside GHQ*, xxvi.
3. Washington University, Department of Physics Newsletter, Fall 2010, p. 13.
4. *Albuquerque Journal* (Albuquerque, New Mexico), 25 Aug 1946, p. 13; *Princeton Alumni Weekly*, 46 (May 3, 1945): 7.
5. Jeidy, Pauline, Tokyo, Japan, Letter #15 to Ruth, January 1949.
6. Jeidy, Pauline, Tokyo, Letter #15 to Ruth, January 1949.
7. Jeidy, Pauline, Tokyo, Letter #15 to Ruth, January 1949.

Chapter 44. Textbooks and Train Trips

1. *Ventura County Star-Free Press*, 20 May 1948, p. 7.
2. *Ventura County Star-Free Press*, 18 Jan 1964, p 19.
3. Takemae, *Inside GHQ*, 81, 191.

4. *Ventura County Star-Free Press*, 1 Jul 1949, p. 2.

5. *Ventura County Star-Free Press*, 1 Jul 1949, p. 2.

6. Jeidy, Pauline, Tokyo, Letter #6 to Family, January 1949. Connie was Connie McCullough. Members of the CIE staff usually traveled to schools and conducted meetings in teams.

7. Jeidy, Pauline, Tokyo, Letter #6 to Family, January 1949.

8. Konnichiwa is Japanese for hello or good afternoon.

9. Jeidy, Pauline, Tokyo, Letter #6 to Family, January 1949.

Chapter 45. Going Home

1. Jeidy, Pauline, Tokyo, Letter #17 to Verda and Ruth, spring 1949.

2. Jeidy, Pauline, Tokyo, Letter #17 to Verda and Ruth, spring 1949.

3. Jeidy, Pauline, Tokyo, Letter #17 to Verda and Ruth, spring 1949.

4. *Ventura County Star-Free Press*, 23 Sep 1949, p. 1-2.

5. Pauline Jeidy Album, Willauer Collection.

6. Passenger Manifest. British Overseas Airways Corporation. 16 Apr 1950.

7. Passenger Manifest. British Overseas Airways Corporation. 16 Apr 1950.

Chapter 46. Advice to Teachers

1. Letter notes, County of Los Angeles Superintendent of Schools, 15 Jan 1963.

2. Jeidy, Pauline, "First Grade Mexican American Children in Ventura County." *California Journal of Elementary Education*, 15-16: 200-208, Feb. & May, 1947, in *Selected Collections of the Chicano Studies Library*, Issues 1-7, University of California, Berkeley, Chicano Studies Library, 1974; reproduced in *Education and income of Mexican-Americans in the Southwest* by Walter Fogel. Division of Research, Graduate School of Business Administration, University of California, 1965; reproduced in *The Mexican-American People: the Nation's Second Largest Minority* by Leo Grebler, Joan W. Moore, Ralph C. Guzmán, and Jeffrey Lionel Berlant. Free Press, 1970; cited *Adapting the Curriculum of an Elementary School to Serve the Language Needs of Spanish Speaking Children* by Robert Ves Way, R and E Research Associates, 1974; cited *Integrated Education* Vols. 5-6, *Teachers for Integrated Schools*, 1967; cited *Chicano Education in the Era of Segregation* by Gilbert G. Gonzalez, Balch Institute, 1990; cited *American Educational History Journal*. Vol. 32, No. 1, Mark McKenzie, Editor, Information Age, 2005.

3. Jeidy, Pauline. "Improving the Program in Reading," *Elementary English*, Vol. 26 (January, 1949), 27-31, 34. Describes the steps taken in Ventura County, California, to improve the reading programs in elementary schools, in *The Elementary School Journal*, Vol. 50, Dept. of Education, University of Chicago, Graduate School of Education: University of Chicago Press, 1950; cited *Teaching Children to Read* by Fay Greene Adams, Ronald Press, 1949.

4. *Bibliografía de Aztlán: an Annotated Chicano Bibliography* by Ernie Barrios, Centro de Estudios Chicanos Publications, San Diego State College, 1971.

5. Jeidy, *Theory and Practice of Democracy Education*, 14-18.

6. Jeidy, *Theory and Practice of Democracy Education*, 18-23.

7. Jeidy, *Theory and Practice of Democracy Education*, 24-28.

8. Jeidy, *Theory and Practice of Democracy Education*, 7.

9. Jeidy, *Theory and Practice of Democracy Education*, 24-28.

10. Jeidy, *Theory and Practice of Democracy Education*, 24-28.

11. Jeidy, *Theory and Practice of Democracy Education*, 5, 14-18.

12. Jeidy, Pauline, "Improving the Program in Reading," *Elementary English*, 26 (January 1949): 27-31, 34. This article describes the steps taken in California to improve the reading programs in elementary schools, cited in "Selected References on Elementary-School Education," *The Elementary School Journal*, 50 (Oct. 1949):101, University of Chicago Press, 1950.

13. Jeidy, "Improving the Program in Reading," 27.

14. Jeidy, "Improving the Program in Reading," 28.

15. Jeidy, "Improving the Program in Reading," 29.

16. Jeidy, "Improving the Program in Reading," 29.

Chapter 47. Scholars, Clubs, and Folklore

1. Pauline Jeidy, "Improving the Program in Reading," *Elementary English* (January 1949): 26, 27-31, in *Teaching Individuals to Read* by Homer L. J. Carter, Dorothy J. McGinnis, Heath, 1962, cited *Grade Teacher*, Vol. 68. CCM Professional Magazines, 1950; cited *Elementary English*, Vol. 29, National Council of Teachers of English, 1952; Pauline Jeidy, University of Utah. *Language Arts Workshop: Elementary Education* 232 pp, (Conference Publication) Salt Lake City, Utah: University of Utah, 1954; Jeidy, Mrs. Pauline. *Directory of Public Schools, Ventura County (Calif.),* Office of Superintendent of Schools, 1955; Pauline Jeidy, Ventura, California. We wish to say "thank you" to those members whose final contribution was helping

plan the 1955-56 issues; *Childhood Education*, Vol. 32; Association for Childhood Education International; International Kindergarten Union; Association for Childhood Education (US); Association for Childhood Education International, 1955; Resolutions Committee Chairman, Mrs. Pauline Jeidy, Assistant Superintendent of Schools, Ventura County, 1955; Pauline Jeidy, Assistant Superintendent, Ventura County, *Teachers Guide to Education in Early Childhood,* California, Bureau of Elementary Education,California State Dept. of Education, 1956; Pauline Jeidy, Assistant Superintendent, [Ventura] Court House. *ASCD Handbook.* Association for Supervision and Curriculum Development, 1956; Jeidy, Pauline. *150 [sic] Ventura County History Stories,* Ventura County Board of Education: 1957; mimeographed with photographic illustrations, 278 pp., written for the elementary school children of Ventura County, cited in *California Jewish History: a Descriptive Bibliography: Over Five Hundred Fifty Works for the Period Gold Rush to Post-World War I.* Norton B. Stern, A.H. Clark, 1967; contributor. *Teachers Guide to Education in Later Childhood.* California, Bureau of Elementary Education, California State Dept. of Education, 1957; *Building Curriculum in Social Studies for the Public Schools of California: a Progress Report,* California, State Central Committee on Social Studies, California State Dept. of Education, 1957.

2 ."Over the Editor's Desk," *Journal of Childhood Education*, Vol. 30 no. 1, 1953, p. 56.

3. Mrs. Jeidy Installed as AAUW President. Article in *The Ventura County (CA) Star-Free Press*; Tuesday, June 16, 1953, Willauer Collection.

4. Pauline Kastendieck Jeidy and Millard Sheets. Photograph published in *The Ventura (CA) County Starr-Free Press,* undated, Willauer Collection.

5. Persky, Phillip (Ed.), "Letters of Margery Bailey." *San Jose Studies* 17 (Winter 1991): 8-102. One of Stanford's most celebrated teachers, Dr. Bailey died in 1963, the year after she wrote her letter to Pauline.

6. Jeidy, *Ventura County History Stories*, 165.

7. Jeidy, *Ventura County History Stories*, 119.

8. Jeidy, *Ventura County History Stories*, 37. In 1957, Pauline published the collection under the title *Ventura County History Stories,* an imprint of the Ventura County Board of Education intended for use by fourth grade children in their study of early California. Many of the stories subsequently became the basis of other contemporary histories of Ventura County, cited often as a source of their research.

Chapter 48. A Time of Change

1. *Billings Times*, 8 Oct 1955.

2. Pauline Jeidy to Mrs. Verda Brandemuehl; RFD 3, Fennimore, Wisconsin; 11 Feb 1958.

3. Pauline Jeidy to Mrs. Verda Brandemuehl; RFD. 3, Fennimore, Wisconsin, 23 Feb 1958.

4. Pauline Jeidy to Mrs. Verda Brandemuehl; RFD. 3, Fennimore, Wisconsin, 23 Feb 1958. Davie who Pauline mentioned in this letter was David Brandemuehl, her nephew who was soon to be married.

5. Pauline Jeidy to Mrs. Verda Brandemuehl; RFD. 3, Fennimore, Wisconsin, 23 Feb 1958.

6. Pauline Jeidy to Mrs. Verda Brandemuehl; RFD 3, Fennimore, Wisconsin; 11 Feb 1958.

7. Pauline Jeidy to Mrs. Verda Brandemuehl; RFD 3, Fennimore, Wisconsin; 11 Feb 1958.

8. Pauline Jeidy to Mrs. Verda Brandemuehl, RFD 3, Fennimore, Wisconsin, 2 Mar 1958.

9. *Fennimore Times*, 27 Mar 1958.

10. *Ventura County Star-Free Press*, 23 Jan 1959, p. 6.

11. Pauline Jeidy to Mrs. Verda Brandemuehl; RFD. 3, Fennimore, Wisconsin, 11 Feb 1958.

12. *Ventura County Star-Free Press* 12 Jan 1963.

13. Rooney, *A History of the Ventura Unified School District*, i:

14. Pauline Jeidy (Ventura County). *AAUW Journal*, Vols. 56-57, American Association of University Women, 1962; Mrs. Pauline Jeidy, Assistant Superintendent of Schools, Ventura County. *Bulletin of the California State Department of Education,* California, State Dept. of Education, 1963; *Annual Meeting,* Association for Supervision and Curriculum Development, 1964.

15. Pauline Kastendieck Jeidy Obituary. Published in the *Ventura County [CA] Star Free Press,* 30 Jul 1985; 23 May 1964, p. 7.

16. *Ventura County Star-Free Press,* 11 Jan 1960, p. 4.

17. Weiler, *Democracy and Schooling in California*, xv.

18. Weiler, *Democracy and Schooling in California*, xii.

19. Rooney, *A History of the Ventura Unified School District*, i.

20. Rooney, *A History of the Ventura Unified School District*, i.

Chapter 49. Twilight

1. *Ventura County Star-Free Press*, 18 Jan 1964, p. 19.

2. *Ventura County Star-Free Press*, 23 May 1964, p. 7.

3. *Ventura County Star-Free Press*, 18 Jan 1964, p. 19.

4. *Ventura County Star-Free Press*, 23 May 1964, p. 7.

5. *Ventura County Star-Free Press*, 23 May 1964, p. 7.

6. *Ventura County Star-Free Press*, 23 May 1964, p. 7.

7. *Ventura County Star-Free Press*, 18 Jan 1964, p. 19.

8. Weiler, *Democracy and Schooling in California*, viii. Dr. Heffernan retired in 1965. She died in 1987 at the age of 91.

9. *Ventura County Star-Free Press*, 18 Jan 1964, p. 19.

10. *Ventura County Star-Free Press*, 31 Mar 1965, p. 3.

11. Ventura County School Service Contract, May 1, 1961. Pauline's salary went from $9, 996 in 1958 to $12,500 in 1961.

12. Margaret Keller letter to the California State Teachers Retirement System, Sacramento, California, 1 Aug 1985.

13. Letter to Grace Piper, University of California-Santa Barbara, April 24, 1963.

14. Dee Willauer to Ken Burchett 20 Mar 2020.

15. *Christian County Republican*, 28 Jul 1966 p. 1. Miss Louise Neyer died at the age of 80 in a rest home in St. Louis. She never married. Her family of nieces and nephews carried her remains back to Billings for her final rest in St. Joseph Cemetery

16. Family Bible of James Keatts. Found in the Bible a receipt from Rose Hill Cemetery Association; Perpetual Maintenance Trust Fund for Lot 36, Block 2, 23 May 1968, $100 paid by Frank A. Kastendieck, Geo. H. Kastendieck, Katherine Andrews, Hazel Shafer, Pauline Jeidy and Oscar Brandemuehl [Pauline was the daughter of Andrew Kastendieck; Oscar was Andrew's son-in-law]. Holy Bible, Philadelphia: John E. Potter, 1880. Possession of Jayme Burchett

17. Letter from Pauline to Deanne (Dee) Lombard Willauer describing Andrew Kastendieck's love of music; dated 27 Sep 1975. 2 pp. on 1, handwritten on blue paper front and back, Willauer Collection.

18. Letter from Pauline to Deanne (Dee) Lombard Willauer describing Andrew Kastendieck's love of music; dated 27 Sep 1975. 2 pp. on 1, handwritten on blue paper front and back, Willauer Collection.

19. Pauline Letter about the Kastendieck Family to Deanne Willauer, probably September or October 1975, Willauer Collection. Ray was Raymond Stone Kastendieck, Pauline's cousin and prominent architect in Gary,

Indiana. One of the Texas boys mentioned in this letter was the son of Cousin George Kastendieck who was at the time studying architecture at the University of Texas.

20. Pauline Jeidy letter to her niece Ruth dated 17 Feb 1973, Willauer Collection.

21. Pauline Jeidy. "Basis for Teaching the Social Studies," in *California Journal for Instructional Improvement*, Vol. 10, California School Supervisors Association, Association for Supervision and Curriculum Development, California Chapter, 1967.

22. Pauline Jeidy letter to her niece Ruth dated 17 Feb 1973, Willauer Collection.

Chapter 50. Going Home

1. Margaret Keller letter to Oosima-Isao, Tokyo, Japan 1 Aug 1985, Willauer Collection. Margaret Keller was Pauline's personal attorney.

2. Obituary. *The Ventura County (CA) Star Free Press.* 30 Jul 1985, p. A-8.

3. Social Security Death Index. Confirms her death as July 1985 but gives a birth date of 6 March 1898, instead of 7 March; Obituary. *The Ventura County (CA) Star Free Press.* Tues., July 30, 1985, p. A-8. Pauline's obituary incorrectly stated her age at the time of her death as 96. The obituary writer gave her birth as 6 March 1898, which made her age 87 years 4 months and 22 days. Pauline's living will directive expired five years from its date of signing, which meant it expired May 8, 1984. She died fourteen months later on July 29, 1985. Nevertheless, doctors and family honored her wishes.

4. Pauline Kastendieck Jeidy Death Certificate, No. 1852, State of California, July 29, 1985. Doctors attributed Pauline's death to carcinoma of the cervix with metastasis to the colon

5. The address of the California Convalescent Hospital was 4020 Loma Vista Road, Ventura, California.

6. Pauline Kastendieck Jeidy Death Certificate, No. 1852, State of California, July 29, 1985. Pauline's remains were cremated on July 31, 1985, at Ivy Lawn Crematory at Ivy Lawn Memorial Park, in Ventura.

7. Rev. Hollis Allen and Rev. Edwin Crist of the Community Presbyterian Church officiated at Pauline's memorial service.

8. Margaret Keller letter to Oosima-Isao, Tokyo, Japan 1 Aug 1985, Willauer Collection.

9 Margaret Keller to Miss Tsune Hirano, Yokohama, Japan 1 Aug 1985;

Margaret Keller to Mrs. Suerno Sakaura, Matue-City, Japan 1 Aug 1985, Willauer Collection.

Bibliography

A History of the Origin of the Place Names Connected with the Chicago & North Western and Chicago, St. Paul, Minneapolis & Omaha Railways. Chicago: Chicago and North Western Railway Company, 1908.

Adams, Fay. *Teaching Children to Read.* New York: Ronald Press, 1949.

Agnew, Allen F., and Heyl, Allen J., Jr. "Zinc deposits of the Mifflin-Cokerville area of the Wisconsin lead-zinc district." Series 44-24. Washington, D.C.: U.S. Geological Survey, 1944.

Anderson, Kent H. *An analysis of selected abandoned settlements in Wisconsin* (Vol. 2). M.A. Thesis, University of Wisconsin—Madison, 1983.

Baltz, William M., *The Role of American Educators in the Decentralization and Reorganization of Education in Postwar Japan (1945-1952).* PhD dissertation. State University of New York-Buffalo, 1965.

Butterfield, C. W. *Butterfield's History 1881 Grant County, Wisconsin.* Mt. Vernon, Ind.: Windmill Publications, 1881.

Cauffman, Betty L., Finnegan, Gilda A., and Stauffacher, Harold. *Fennimore—Then and Now, 1830 to 1980: A History of Fennimore, Wisconsin.* Minneapolis, Minn.: Josten's, 1980.

Chin, Tsung, and Li, Wendan. *East Asian Calligraphy Education.* University Press of Maryland, 2004.

Craven, Wesley F., and Cate, James L. *The Pacific: Matterhorn to Nagasaki. The Army Air Forces in World War II.* (Vol. 5). Chicago: University of Chicago Press, 1966.

Crawford, Robert M. *Memoirs of Iowa County, Wisconsin: From the Earliest Historical Times Down to the Present*, (Vol. 1). Iowa County, Wis.: Northwestern Historical Association, 1913.

Ells, Walter C., Supreme Commander for the Allied Powers. *Post-War Developments in Japanese Education.* Tokyo: General Headquarters, SCAP, Civil Information and Education Section, Education Division, 1952.

Fernandez, Lisa. "Storyteller Keeps Chumash Ways Alive in Word, Deed". *Los Angeles Times.* (August 2, 1997).

Gannett, Henry. *The Origin of Certain Place Names in the United States.* Washington, D.C.: Government Printing Office, 1905.

Gidney, Charles M., Brooks, Benjamin, and Sheridan, Edwin M. *History of Santa Barbara, San Luis Obispo and Ventura Counties, California* (2 vols.). Chicago: Lewis, 1917, pp. 1:273-485.

Gregory, John G. *Southwestern Wisconsin: a history of old Crawford County.* Chicago, Ill. : S.J. Clarke, 1932.

Henry, Nelson B. (Ed.). *National Society for the Study of Education. The Forty-Fifth Yearbook*, Part 2: "Changing Conceptions in Educational Administration." Chicago: The University of Chicago Press, 1946.

Henry, Nelson B. (Ed.). *National Society for the Study of Education. The Forty-Sixth Yearbook*, Part 2: "Early Childhood Education." Chicago: The University of Chicago Press, 1947.

Holford, Castello N. *History of Grant County, Wisconsin: Including Its Civil, Political, Geological, Mineralogical, Archaeological and Military History, and a History of the Several Towns.* Lancaster, Wis.: Teller Print, 1900.

Jeidy, Pauline. *A critical study of the ability of sixth grade children to comprehend biographically descriptive terms in historical content.* M. A. Thesis. Iowa City, Iowa: University of Iowa, 1936.

Jeidy, Pauline. "Reactions of Children of Different Age Levels in the War and Their Implications for Teachers." *California Journal of Elementary Education.* (August 1943): 12-21.

Jeidy, Pauline. "Fable in Ethics". *California Journal of Elementary Education* 14 (August 1945): 40-48.

Jeidy, Pauline: Conference Reports, Education Division. GHQ/SCAP, Civil Information and Education Section, Education Division; Administrative Branch. Correspondence, Reports and Publications, 1945-51. Box number: 5359; Folder number 1. Also available as Record Group 331, National Archives, Washington, D.C.

Jeidy, Pauline. *The Ventura County Course of Study in Reading.* Ventura: County Superintendent of Schools Office, 1946.

Jeidy, Pauline, "First Grade Mexican American Children in Ventura County." *California Journal of Elementary Education,* 15 (Feb. & May 1947):200-208.

Jeidy, Pauline. "Improving the Program in Reading." *Elementary English* 26 (January 1949): 27-31, 34.

Jeidy, Pauline. *Theory and Practice of Democracy Education: Especially on Social Studies.* Japan-US Educational Book Study Group. Hiroshima: Silver Bell Hiroshima Books, 1949.

Jeidy, Pauline, Ed. *Language Arts Workshop: Elementary Education.* Salt Lake City, Utah: University of Utah, 1954.

Jeidy, Pauline (Ed.). *Ventura County History Stories.* Ventura: Calif.: Ventura County Board of Education, 1957.

Jeidy, Pauline. "Basis for Teaching the Social Studies." *California Journal for Instructional Improvement* May 1967): 82-87.

Knebel, Melva, and Fine, Linda. In the shadows of the mines: the village of Rewey, Wisconsin, 1880-1980 and southern part of town of Mifflin. N.p.:n.p., 1980.

Mossberg, Midge. "High Honor Given Venturan: Mrs. Pauline Jeidy to Aid MacArthur. *Ventura County (Calif.) Star-Free Press,* 6 Dec 1947, p. 22.

Nishi, Toshio. *Unconditional Democracy: Education and Politics in Occupied Japan, 1945-1952.* Hoover Institution Press (Stanford University), 1982.

Perkins, Donna C. "This is what I know of New Diggings and Cokerville, Wisconsin, 1911-1926." Archives, Wisconsin Historical Society, 1963. *Wisconsin Magazine of History* 48, (Autumn 1964): 73

Quiner, E. B. Military History of Wisconsin, Chicago, 1866, p. 682; Holford, Castello N. *History of Grant County, Wisconsin: Including Its Civil, Political, Geological, Mineralogical, Archaeological and Military History, and a History of the Several Towns.* Lancaster, Wis.: Teller Print, 1900

Reynolds, Robert R. *An Airplane Was My Burro: The Memoirs of a Venturesome Geologist.* iUniverse, 2006.

Rooney, Patrick O. *A history of the Ventura Unified School District: 1962-1986..* Ventura, Calif.: Ventura Unified School District], 1992.

Storke, Yda A. *A Memorial and Biographical History of the Counties of Santa Barbara, San Luis Obispo and Ventura, California.* Chicago: Lewis, 1891, pp. 183-260.

Takemae, Eiji. *Inside GHQ: The Allied Occupation of Japan and its Legacy.* Translated and adapted from the Japanese by Robert Ricketts and Sebastian Swann. New York: Continuum, 2002.

Weiler, Kathleen. *Democracy and Schooling in California: The Legacy of Helen Heffernan and Corinne Seeds.* New York: Palgrave Macmillan, 2011.

Winkler, Daniel, and Jolly, Jennifer L. "National Society for the Study of Education." In *Encyclopedia of Curriculum Studies*, edited by Craig Kridel. Thousand Oaks, Cal.: SAGE, 2010.

Index

CPSIA information can be obtained
at www.ICGtesting.com
Printed in the USA
LVHW081909280520
656842LV00012B/212/J